# GHANA'S INDEPENDENCE STRUGGLE:
## The Unfinished Task

# BARIMA OKYERE-DARKO

Foreword: Prof. Baffour Agyeman-Duah

ISBN:9798345480014

# DEDICATION

**'We of the Six martyrdom in pursuit of ideology of Ghanaism- the grand and dynamic idea that from our ancient and medieval Ghana ashes, we should create a modern State in the Guinea lands.'-J.B Danquah**

This Book is dedicated to the Big Six and all Patriots who believe in Ghana in spite of the difficulties. In addition, I dedicate this book to my childhood friend, Shadrack Adu-Antwi.

# CONTENTS

## ACKNOWLEDGEMENT

I want to thank God Almighty for given me the grace and ability to write this book. I must thank Mr. Eugene Aikins for assistance to me these years in my noble calling.

Professor Baffour Agyeman-Duah did a yeoman's job of reading through the entire manuscript and reviewing contents, paying particular attention to editorial and grammatical details. I am very grateful to him for accepting to write the Foreword of the book.

Mr. Kwesi Okyere-Darko, former registrar of Valley View University accepted and did the editing of this book. I am grateful to him for spending ample time to make suggestions especially his advice for me to make the writing simple.

I thank Mr. Shadrach Adu-Antwi, my childhood friend. Shadrach and I had intimate friendship that helped to shape my knowledge to write this book. I am also grateful to him for reviewing and proofreading the manuscript. His approval to this book is a big boost to my morale.

I thank Rita, a presenter at Ghana Broadcasting Corporation for making time to read through the manuscript. I also appreciate the services of Rev. Dr. Owusu-Bonsu for also reading through the manuscript. I must also acknowledge, Ambassador Kofi Acquah-Harrison (PhD), former Secretary of Local Government and Rural Development under the PNDC for his knowledge and support.

Last but not least, I want to thank Kelvin who designed the page layout and did the cover design of this book. And to all friends and lovers whose names may not be here, I say God richly bless you.

GHANA'S INDEPENDENCE STRUGGLE: THE UNFINISHED TASK

## FOREWORD

After nearly a century of British colonization, the Gold Coast struggled to unchain itself to become the independent nation of Ghana in 1957. Three years later, in 1960, the new nation cut all sovereign ties with Britain to gain the status of a Republic. Taking their destiny fully into their own hands, Ghanaians have, since then, endeavoured to build a peaceful, united, just and prosperous nation.

Needless to say, the new nation did not emerge overnight. Earlier in 1844, the people of the coastal belt had been colonized in a dubious treaty between the Fantis and Britain. Expansion of the colony beyond the coast occurred some nine decades later, when the British overcame the resistance by groups in the hinterlands, notably, the Asante Kingdom.

The kingdom succumbed, following five wars, including the famous "Sagranti War" of 1874. It was not until the Yaa Asantewaa War of 1901 that the British were able to declare Asante as a "crown colony." Simultaneously, the Northern Provinces were constituted as the Protectorate of the Northern Territories. In 1943 Asante was formally incorporated into the Gold Coast, to be followed by the Northern Territories to make up the current map of Ghana.

For many Ghanaians, especially the younger generation, however, details of the British colonization, the struggle for independence, and the efforts to consolidate the new nation remain elusive. Equally hazy are the circumstances of birthing the nation, the roles of the various groups and individuals, and engagements with the colonial government. The lack of clarity, or rather knowledge, has obscured and hampered the vision and objectives of the founding fathers for advancing the nation.

Thus, nation-building has proven to be a major challenge in Ghana. Despite the euphoric celebration and prospects in 1957, the nation was soon gripped by political uncertainties, occasioned by five military interruptions of democratic rule. Stability was regained when constitutional rule was restored in 1993 with the advent of the Fourth Republic. But democratic dividends have been illusive, just as the national economy has continuously wobbled.

True to the warning of Ghana's first president, Kwame Nkrumah, against the possibility of a relapse into a neo-colonial state, the country's tottering economy remains stubbornly tied to western capital. The persistent recourse to the IMF and donors for economic bailouts has not only deepened the country's dependency syndrome, it has led to a stunted or "arrested" development. Increasingly, the strident declaration of Nkrumah on the eve of independence, that "the Blackman is capable of managing his own affairs" is ringing hollow.

Not surprisingly, the enthusiasm with which constitutional rule was restored in 1993, following eleven years of military dictatorship, has waned. Seemingly, we embraced western democratic practice without much regard for local realities and sensibilities (traditional, cultural and political). Governance and meaningful progress, therefore, have been stymied by political divisiveness, polarization, extremism and ethnocentrism.

Against this backdrop, *Ghana's Independence Struggle: The Unfinished Task,* presents incisive historical narratives and analysis. It unties some key knots and throws greater light on some of the intricacies of the struggle, including some perspectives and visions of the founding fathers. As the author, Barima Piesie Okyere-Darko surmises, Ghanaians appear to take the attainment of independence and the status of a republic as the endgame. Rather, these historic achievements should only mark the beginning of the endless journey to nation-building.

Seven decades after independence, as Okyere-Darko laments, the country "still wallows in the wilderness, crying for deliverance in its governance, education, infrastructure….." The seeming failures raise questions about keeping faith with the founding fathers. The author's reference to the "glory and power" of Ancient Ghana reminds us of the origins of the country's name and source of inspiration for the two key intellectuals of the time, Kwame Nkrumah and J.B. Danquah, for their quest.

The reference implicitly calls for a return to those core values that made our forefathers great: patriotism and nationalism. Noting the depressing challenges of our time, the author makes the case for revisiting the past. The absence of these values in our modern democratic settings has contributed hugely to the waywardness in leadership, governance and development.

In essence, therefore, we should see the independence of Ghana as an unfinished project. It is work in progress. The "unfinished task" includes regaining the virtues of our founding fathers during their struggle for independence. Imbued with patriotism and nationalism, our leaders should be able to put the country, which was wildly celebrated on independence eve, on the path of nationhood.

Readers would readily appreciate the clarion call of the book to restore Ghana to "glory and power." Those desirous of understanding the making of Ghana and its development predicaments, and are anxious for remedies will find it very useful. The young generation, particularly, will read with much profit, as I did.

Baffour Agyeman-Duah (Prof)

CEO, The John A. Kufuor Foundation

Accra, Ghana

GHANA'S INDEPENDENCE STRUGGLE: THE UNFINISHED TASK

## ABRREVIATIONS

| | |
|---|---|
| UGCC | United Gold Coast Convention |
| NCBWA | National Congress of British West Africa |
| WASU | West Africa Student Union |
| ASAD | Union for Students of African Descent |
| YC | Youth Conference |
| JPC | Joint Provincial Council |
| AWAM | Association of West African Merchants |
| CPP | Convention People's Party |
| CYO | Committee of Youth Organisation |
| GRA | Ghana Representative Assembly |
| TUC | Trade Union Congress |
| UN | United Nations |
| GNP | Ghana National Party |
| GAP | Ghana Action Party |
| NPP | Northern People's Party |
| GCP | Ghana Congress Party |
| MAP | Moslem Association Party |
| AYO | Anlo Youth Organisation |
| NLM | National Liberation Movement |
| CPC | Cocoa Purchasing Council |
| CMB | Cocoa Marketing Board |
| TC | Togoland Congress |

UAC  United African Company

CFAO  Corporation for Africa & Overseas

UTC  Union Trade Company

PDA  Preventive Detective Act

TUC  Trade Union Congress

NADECO  National Development Corporation

CAST  Consolidated African Selective Trust

VALCO  Volta Aluminium Company

GHANA'S INDEPENDENCE STRUGGLE: THE UNFINISHED TASK

## PREFACE

I have been a student and lover of Ghana's history right from my infancy. I was privileged to read well researched books written by great authors like W.E.F Ward, Prof. Adu Boahen and other well recognised historians at my tender age. This passion has helped to shape me to become very patriotic for my country and race. It is this passion that fired me to write the book entitled the *'The Dream of a New Ghana: Reality or Myth'* which was approved by the National Curriculum Centre of the Ghana Education Service. This book, *Ghana's Independence Struggle: the Unfinished Task* is a sequel to *The Dream of a New Ghana: Reality or Myth?* I sincerely believe that there is an unfinished task for today's generation to solve and the best way to achieve results is for us to take a critical look into our independence struggle. As Walter Rodney in his book *How Europe Underdeveloped Africa* wrote that to understand how the present came to be, we must delve into the past. I have done that and I believe readers will find it essential in solving the current challenges of Ghana.

During the research for this book, I was conscious to rely on very reliable information to make my submissions. I sincerely believe that for anyone to write a very detailed and fair report on Ghana's independence, one cannot overlook the writings of the torchbearers of the independence struggle such as Dr J.B Danquah, Dr. Kwame Nkrumah and the British governor Arden Clarke. This book does that and it makes it a unique one. It provides detailed account on what these gallant people contributed to the struggle of Ghana's independence. It also gives accounts of other first eye witnesses to the independence struggle such as Mr K.B Ayensu, the first Clerk of Parliament, Fio Meyers, Ghana's ambassador to China and others.

Isaac Newton said, 'if I have risen far, it is because I stood on the shoulders of giants'. Like Isaac Newton, I acknowledge the giant authors of the history of Ghana and the writers of Ghana's independence struggle such as Prof. Adu Boahen, W.E.F Ward, Prof. David Kimble, Prof. Francis Agbodeka, Prof. JH Ofosu Appiah, K.B Ayensu and S.N Darkwa former Clerks of Ghana's Parliament, H.K Acheampong, J.G Amamoo, Prof. K.A Busia, C.C Reindorf, Seth

Gadzekpo, Dr. Obed Asamoah, David Rooney, J.G Amamoo and many great authors in the said area on whose writings I relied on.

I owe much gratitude to newspaper publications from the Daily Graphic and other such publications. I had to constantly visit the George Padmore library for more research materials and I say a big thank you to their staff especially to Philip, Eric and Sarah.

This book seeks to instil in the readers the hope of the great men and women who contributed to the founding of this nation, Ghana. It reveals to readers what exactly needs to be done to solve the current challenges of Ghana and Africa as well. And the solutions offered are easily adaptable by any individual or group of people who sincerely want change.

## INTRODUCTION

Many great scholars have contributed immensely on Ghana's political history and its independence struggle narration. Yet I have come to observe that there are so many distortions when it comes to Ghana's political history narration in the media and the public domain. I decided to give more attention to reading on the political history and realised that many of the good books had omission of certain relevant topics and such topics, in my opinion, are not well addressed. It is such omission of events and narrations that I want to highlight to readers to make the narration a more balanced one. For instance, the Watson Commission made a number of important recommendations that could make Ghana's independence a meaningful one. Among the recommendations was the building of the hydroelectricity on the River Volta to process Ghana's aluminium to boost the economy of Ghana. The hydroelectricity has been built but its main purpose has been abandoned. Again many of the narration on the history of Ghana or Ghana's independence struggle fail to appreciate that the leaders of the independence movement had a common dream for this nation. Many writings emphasise on the rivalry that existed between the two main political traditions: the Danquah-Busia and Nkrumah more than the dream they all cherished together. But in this book, the author emphasises on that common dream they shared that inspired them to contribute to the struggle for independence. It is the intent of this book to inspire readers to unite and pursue this dream of the leaders of Ghana's independence struggle.

As many readers are aware, in 1947, a group of nationalists met to conceive a dream to achieve political independence for the Gold Coast and form a new nation that would be called Ghana. Among these nationalists are George Alfred Grant, RS Blay, De Graft Johnson, Dr. J.B Danquah, Dr. Kwame Nkrumah, Edward Akufo-Addo, Ako Adjei, William Ofori-Atta, K. Brakatu Ateko, Obetsebi Lamptey and many other people. They chose the name Ghana to replace Gold Coast. The reason for the name Ghana was to draw inspiration from that ancient kingdom Ghana to build a new golden kingdom, a first class nation which would be devoid of colonial or western influence. This is what was referred to as Ghanaism. Barely ten years after their struggle was the new nation born on 6 March 1957.

On the eve of independence, at midnight, Dr. Kwame Nkrumah who had emerged as the leader of the independence movement declared, **"At long last, the battle has ended and thus Ghana your beloved country is**

**free forever"**. This news brought inexpressible joy to all Ghanaians and blacks elsewhere seeking their freedom. Many were the dignitaries who joined to grace this premium occasion in the history of a Sub Saharan African nation. The most prominent and unimaginable among them were the official delegates from Russia and the USA, the world's greatest rivals, meeting for a common purpose, to witness an African freedom, on the soil of Ghana. They all pledged their support to this little independent nation.

Many were the hopes of the Ghanaians and the world at large. However, nine years after independence, Nkrumah, the hero, had become a villain and ousted out of power. By contrast, many Ghanaians celebrated the overthrow of this national hero almost as much as they did during the independence. When Ghanaians thought his overthrow would return Ghana to the paradise they had expected from their independence, things turned in a nose dive direction. It is over 65 years now and many people, especially the youth, are wondering when and how and by whom Ghanaians' hope will crystallise into a reality.

On lamenting on the cause of the problem of Ghana, there have been many schools of thought. There are those who believe that had Nkrumah been allowed to continue to rule Ghana, he would have taken the nation to the promise land. On the contrary, another group of activists also think that it was Nkrumah's mismanagement and abuse of power that brought so many hardships on Ghana. Other activists think it was the military interferences that jeopardised Ghana's development and advancement. Interestingly, there is an emerging opinion lately that asserts that the 1992 Constitution and its two beneficiaries NPP and NDC are the cause of Ghana's problems. This group wants a constitutional review and a third force party to bench both the NPP and NDC.

Sincerely all these schools of thought have a point. However, none has discovered the root cause of Ghana's problem and the pivotal solution for Ghana. That is why I wrote this book. It is a book to reveal to Ghanaians what really is the main problem and solution for Ghana. As an engineer, the best approach to solve any problem or case is to perform the root cause analysis. In that light, I thought it wise to share with readers how colonisation emerged in Chapter 1. I sincerely believe it will help readers to discern the causes of Ghana's pending problems.

Long before the Europeans arrived on our shores, the early tribes of Ghana lived as families which emerged into states. In the course of the expansion of these states through wars, the Europeans first arrived in

Shama on our shores. These Europeans began to build forts and traded with the indigenous people. Among the Europeans who arrived were the Portuguese, Dutch, English, Danes and others. It appears the British merchants gained control or influence which discouraged the other Europeans to migrate out of this land which was first called the Gold Coast by the Portuguese. The British who remained signed a treaty in 1831 with the Ashanti and the Fante chiefs which promoted peace and trade. This motivated the British to put into law their relationship with the Gold Coast which became known as the Bond of 1844. The Gold Coast became a British colony, controlled and ruled by the British. (Readers should know that initially Gold Coast excluded the Northern Territories, Ashanti and the British Togoland). The Gold Coast was made up of the Central, Western, and Eastern provinces which today are Central, Western, Western North, Greater Accra and Eastern Regions respectively.

Simply colonisation thrived because the Europeans had better skills that made them look superior. It thrived because the Whiteman had sophisticated military weapons. It thrived because of the division and tribal differences that existed among the Africans. In effect colonisation bequeathed onto us foreign culture and law that are nicely termed as civilisation. And in reward of what they did, the British established trade policies that empowered them to exploit the resources and wealth of the indigenous Africans away. Sadly, these legacies of colonisation still persist in Ghana making our independence a questionable one.

There arose a number of nationalist movements like the Aborigines Right Protection Society in the Gold Coast to resist the dominion of the British. After the Aborigines, there arose another political movement known as the United Gold Coast Convention (UGCC) to challenge the Bond of 1844 and ask for political independence for the colonies. That is the focus of Chapter 2. It discusses the activities of this movement. As if fate was on the side of the UGCC, not long after its formation, it rose to popularity because of certain remarkable events in connection with the swollen shoot, the boycott of Nii Kwabena Bonne and the protest of the ex-servicemen which culminated into the popular 1948 riot. Chapter 3 discusses into detail of the 1948 riot and its positive impact on Ghana's independence. The success earned six leaders of the Convention a title, 'The Big Six'.

Not long after their collective heroism, there arose a split. Nkrumah formed his party: the Convention People's Party (CPP) within the UGCC and left with his followers. So chapter 4 discusses the rift between the UGCC and the CPP. In spite of the split, the impact of their collective success produced the Coussey Constitution that called for the first national elections in the country in 1951.

Chapter 5 narrates in vivid terms the impact of the 1951 elections on the attainment of Ghana's independence. Just when all parliamentary requirements had been fulfilled for the Gold Coast to attain her full independence, a new party emerged, the National Liberation Movement (NLM). Chapter 6 shares with the reader how NLM contributed to Ghana's independence struggles with their strong desire to stop corruption and the unitary constitution for a federal constitution. Eventually the date 6 March 1957 was fixed on a compromised constitution. Chapter 7 narrates the beauty of Ghana's independence and the successes of Nkrumah at the helm of affairs.

Three years after independence, Ghana obtained her republic status. Chapter 8 discusses the Republic which was the final phase of independence and how Ghana performed under constitutional governance and the economic challenges the government faced. Strangely within six years after obtaining her republic status, the government demonstrated abuse of power and poor strategic management of state resources and assets which plunged the nation into crisis making Nkrumah, the hero of independence struggle a villain. The first republic was overthrown. The sad story is that successive governments have not learned any better lessons to ease the problems of the Ghanaian citizens. The sad part is all governments put deaf ears to the recommendations of the Watson Commission for Ghana's independence to be a meaningful one.

Chapter 9 therefore discusses where the nation must begin from to solve her chronic challenges. It reveals that the nation needs and must draft a national vision or dream and a national philosophy that will serve as the model of development for every institution of Ghana. It elucidates the need for Ghana to officially adopt and develop its laws and policies on the common aspiration of the forebears of independence. It explains how the economy of Ghana can regain strength through an urgency of paradigm shift, good governance and political unity.

It inspires Ghanaians to claim ownership of the national economy and explains the strategy to resort to in order to build a strong economy for the nation. This cannot succeed in an environment of constitutional dictatorship which has been the mark of leadership and governance in the executive, judicial, legislature and all institutions in the nation. The chapter urges Ghanaians to stand for good governance and the respect for human rights and the rule of law to make Ghanaians really free and protected citizens of the world.

I sincerely believe in a new Ghana, a first class Ghana and I trust the points discussed in the book can lead to the attainment of such a dream. In writing this, there is something I tried doing by heeding to the legacy of J.F. Kennedy, that the writer's biggest challenge is remaining truthful to himself or herself. I have tried my best to remain truthful to my conscience in presenting these facts. I hope readers will find the book worth reading.

CHAPTER 1

# HOW COLONISATION EMERGED

Ghana was called the Gold Coast before 6 March 1957. It was a British colony for a little over hundred years. During the colonisation, it consisted of four jurisdictions consisting of the Gold Coast proper which was often referred to as the Colony, Ashanti, the Northern Territories and the British Togoland now the Volta Region.  Prior to colonization, the indigenous people lived in groups of families who emerged into tribes and states. The popular states that emerged were the Guan who are believed to be the first people to migrate to modern Ghana and lived as families in several parts of Ghana. The other states are Ga-Adangbes, Ewe, Fante, Nzema, Bono, Ahanta, Akuapem, Kwahu, Gonja, Mamprusi, Sisala, Nanumbas, Frafra, Kokombas, Dagomba and many other ethnic groups.  These kingdoms were governed by priests, clan heads, chiefs and kings. Most of these states or kingdoms were independent states and others were vassal states.

In 1471, the Portuguese were the first Europeans to arrive at the shores of the Gold Coast and erected a wooden cross at Shama. Eleven years later in 1842, they founded their settlement at A Mina.[1] Some writers refer to the same place as "El Mina" meaning The Mine. This name is foreign and was given by the Portuguese but historians reveal that the original local name of the place is Edina. A Mina or El Mina is

1

now officially referred to as Elmina and the fort built by the Portuguese is now popularly referred to as the Elmina Castle. The essence of this fort was to provide shelter and security to them to accomplish their main task which was trade. The main commodities the Europeans sought for were timber, ivory, gold, diamond and other minerals. On the other hand, the indigenous Africans traded for schnapps, umbrellas, mirrors and other similar goods. The genesis of their trade was batter. Due to the enormous quantity and rich quality of the gold in the land, the Portuguese called the land Gold Coast, a name which all the other Europeans adopted.

In the course of time many more Europeans arrived on the shores of the Gold Coast. Among these were the British, the Danes, the Dutch and few others. Activities between these Europeans and the Africans increased as the Europeans added the buying of slaves which was already an ongoing trade among the Africans. This motivated the building of a number of forts and castles on the coastal shores. Among such forts are the "Cabo Corso" castle which in English is the Cape Coast castle built in 1555, the Christiansborg castle built in 1661 by Denmark-Norway which later became the seat of the colonial government.

During these periods, there were several wars among the indigenous states for acquisition of land, slaves, and minerals such as gold. Whereas a number of the indigenous people had already emerged into states, it was during and after the arrival of the Europeans that some of the local people emerged into states. For instance, the Bono had already emerged into a strong kingdom by 1295 before the arrival of the Europeans. That cannot be said about Asante; though they existed in individual towns, it was not until the 1690s that they formed the union of Asante which became a dominant kingdom before it was defeated by the British in 1874 who compelled Asante to free her vassal states.

In 1653, the Swedish Africa Company was established purposely for trade in timber and gold but later was diverted for Atlantic slave trade. As time advanced, the dominance of the British superseded that of many of the Europeans. For instance, the establishment of the Company of Royal Adventures of England Trading into Africa and the

Royal Africa Company in the 1660s by the British dominated the trading during that time. In effect many of these Europeans left the Gold Coast.

In 1821, as the success of the British merchants became evident, the British Parliament advised the British Government to take over administration of the areas under the control of the British merchants in the Gold Coast. As a result, the government dispatched Sir Charles McCarthy who served as the governor for the Sierra Leone and the Gold Coast.

The Asante had conquered most of the states in the south and north of Ghana. The size of the empire had become almost the size of today's Ghana if not bigger than that. But with the emergence of the British influence, most of these coastal tribes sought protection of the British. In 1817 for instance, the Asantehene said all Fantes were his slaves by conquest, and by act of homage they were supposed to send presents and tribute to him. This statement did not go down well with the British Governor of the Committee of Merchants, Hope Smith, who ordered William Hutchison, a British resident in Kumasi, to the Asantehene saying:

> **'You will expressly state to the king and in the most decided terms that the Cape Coast people are not his slaves nor have they ever been acknowledged as such; neither can they nor any of the natives residing under the British protection be included in that most degrading title. I have in a former letter mentioned that any interference on the part of the king in matters concerning the people residing under the protection of the Forts simply cannot be allowed.'[2]**

The British opposed the dominance of Asante at the coast largely because they wanted peace and order to settle for proper trade, evangelism, and for the British Law and Customary to prevail. In the 1800s, the British abolished the slave trade yet the trafficking was secretly done. The British wanted to pacify this by establishing schools and Christianity. The Asante and the local chiefs were eager to trade more in slaves since this earned enough money. Sir Charles McCarthy the then governor of British Gold Coast settlement and Sierra Leone described the Asantehene as 'a Barbarian chief'. Impulsively, Sir Charles McCarthy led the British to attack the Asante in 1824 (in the battle of *Nsamankow*) but the Asante proved to the British that they had miscalculated and underrated them. Asante defeated the British and Sir Charles McCarthy died in the course of the battle. It is believed he was severely wounded and helpless, and killed himself to avoid capture.[3]

Two years later, the British revenged on the Asante and defeated them in 1826. Historians reveal that the British could not have defeated the Asante alone but recruited an African army from Nigeria, Sierra Leone and the Ghanaian ethnic states. Many of these local states wanted their independence from the Asante and so the defeat of Asante freed many of their vassal states in the southern Ghana. This brought a lot of peace and order in the said areas. As a matter of fact, it was as a result of the dominance of Asante that many of the local states yoked themselves under the British protection and it was this desire from the coastal people that augmented the influence of the British.

Considering the numerous and costly wars with the Ashantis, the British Government decided to renege on their desire to control the territories in the Gold Coast in 1928. As a result, the government withdrew from the forts but retained them as nominal dependencies of Sierra Leone. The government transferred its responsibilities to a committee of Merchants in London while the local administration was entrusted to a council of Merchants at Cape Coast. This gave opportunities to a number of British traders to be appointed as Justices of Peace, for the trial of petty cases which arose within the walls of the forts but beyond them they had no authority or jurisdiction.[4kimble] These merchants protested against the government not to abandon the Gold Coast. Their protest had support from the Fantes who did not want to be left to face the Asantes in war any more.

In the midst of this despair, a ray of hope beamed. The appointment of Captain George Maclean in 1830 as the governor of the Gold Coast changed the turn of events. In 1831 he was able to sign a Treaty with Asanteman in respect of her Southern States. In this treaty, Asante agreed to free her vassal states in the south of Pra such as

Akyem, Fante, Denkyira, Wassa and others. They also sent 660 ounces of gold to the Cape Coast with two royals Owusu Ansah and Owusu Kwantabisa as security; these securities should be returned after six years. The Fantes were to free all their roads to the Asante for trade. They were to desist from insulting their former masters. Maclean kept the gold and returned it after the agreed time of six years. The two royals were eventually taken to Britain to study and return to Asante upon the request by the Asantehene. The Treaty mutually bonded the three parties, the Asantes, the British and the Fante allies by precise rules. There was a tacit understanding that the Allies would be afforded British protection in event of any further aggression on the part Ashanti. The Treaty was signed by the Governor, two Ashanti delegates, six Fante chiefs, representatives from Assin, Denkyira, Tufel and other chiefs from Apollonia. Maclean also saw that peace and order reigned among the chiefs of the southern states. He ensured that the Asantehene was duly respected. He abolished panyarring human beings. After the six years, Maclean returned the gold and the two royals of Ashanti. Maclean's legacy was so successful that it earned a lot of admiration from the chiefs and their people until he died in 1847.[5]

Maclean's legacy can be judged as the beginning of British colonisation in the Gold Coast. However, in spite of Maclean's success, there was no legal backing to the authority the governor exercised. In 1841, the British Government sent Dr. R.R Madden as an investigating Commissioner to assess the governance of Maclean. This was because Maclean's wife had died within his first two years in the Gold Coast and his critics suspected that he might have killed her. They used this as grounds to undermine the efforts of Maclean in the Gold Coast. Madden acknowledged that the justice of Maclean was accepted by all parties; however, he criticised Maclean because he felt that British Law was not sufficiently observed. The Crown reclaimed control of the Settlements in 1843, and in the same year passed the Foreign Jurisdiction Act by Parliament 'to remove Doubts as to the Exercise of Powers and Jurisdiction by Her Majesty within divers countries and Places out of Her Majesty's Dominion and to render the same more effectual. Maclean was later appointed as Judicial Assessor.[6]

On 6, March 1844, Governor Commander H.W Hill on behalf of

the British Government entered into a legal agreement with some chiefs of the Gold Coast which changed the course of events of Gold Coast and its neighbouring territories for over a century. This agreement became popularly known as the Bond of 1844. Here reads the Bond.

1. Whereas power and jurisdiction have been exercised for and on behalf of Her Majesty the Queen of Great Britain and Ireland, within diverse countries and places adjacent to her Majesty's forts and settlements on the Gold Coast, we the chiefs of countries and places so referred to, adjacent to the said fort and settlements do hereby acknowledge that power and jurisdiction and declare that the first objects of law and the protection of individuals and property.

2. Human sacrifice and other barbarous customs such as Panyarring, are abomination and contrary to law.

3. Murders, robberies and other crimes and offence will be tried and inquired of before the Queen's Judicial officers and the chief of the district moulding the customs of the country to the general principle of British law. Done at Cape Coast Castle before his Excellency the Lieutenant Governor on this 6th day of March, in the year of our Lord, 1844.

This declaration was signed by the kings of Denkyira, Abora, Assin Atandasu, Assin Apemanum, Donadie (Dominase), Anomabu and Cape Coast Between March and December 1844 the kings of Twifu, Ekumfi Adwumako, Gomoa, Asikuma, Nsaba, Wassa Amenfi, Wassa Fiasi, Dixcove and James Town also signed the declaration.

Many intellectuals have made fair criticism of this bond being the legal support of British rule in Ghana. Among them are Prof. Adu Boahen and Dr. J.B Danquah. Danquah asserted that **'The Bond, as it stands did not create the Gold Coast a British protectorate or colony. The circumstances that led to that were to develop later'.** He further expressed that, **'the bond was a mere declaration, a unilateral act', under which the Fantes chiefs granted their rights to the British Sovereign.'**[7]  Besides as can be seen, the signatories to the Bond did not consist of many of the chiefs in the Gold Coast, Ashanti, Togoland and Northern Territories.

The British strengthened their rule by establishing a separate nominated Legislative and Executive Councils for Gold Goast in 1850. Three years later, they set up the first Supreme Court in 1853 to be presided over by a Chief Justice. In 1856, they established the Gold Coast Corps and by 1857, the Legislative Council had expanded to consist of the governor, chief justice, colonial secretary and the officer commanding the Gold Coast Corps. All being white people in composition.

The British in April 1852 implemented a Poll Tax Ordinance with the consent of chiefs. The essence of this tax was to finance the cost of administration, improve the living standard of the people and promote education. It only included people who resided in the jurisdiction under British protection. This ordinance was welcomed with a little success, yet it did not meet its full expectation. After subsequent years, the people refused to pay the taxes. One paramount reason is that the leaders could not deliver on their promises. In effect, the local people began to question the legitimacy of the tax and decided to boycott it. In 1861 barely ten years of enactment, there were a nationwide riot and strikes to annul the tax and it was proscribed that year.

The annulment of the Poll Tax weakened the economic health of the colonial administration.  Around this period in the 1860s, Asante began to penetrate south Ghana again which destabilised the peace that was enjoyed before. In addition to that there arose resistance from some of the indigenous chiefs. Prominent among these kings was King John Aggrey of Cape Coast whose father King Joseph Aggrey was a signatory to the Bond of 1844. He refused the claim by the British that inhabitants of Cape Coast and neighbouring territories were British subjects. As a result, he mobilised a number of educated Africans like Bannerman to oppose the whole basis and extent of the British power and jurisdiction in Ghana. A month after his enstoolment, he wrote a letter to the governor stating that, 'Cape Coast in the eye of the law is not British territory'. He continued by saying that his court existed before Cape Coast itself was established and that the land on which British Castle was erected was rented to the British by his ancestors.[8]

As a result of these uncertainties, the British parliament appointed a

Select Committee in 1865 to investigate the matter and issue their recommendation. King Aggrey took advantage of the situation and delegated two people Joseph Martin and D.L Carr to England on his behalf to put his case before the Select Committee in 1865. They reported that the British authorities grossly disrespected king Aggrey and the local authorities. Aggrey's men did not appreciate the fact that the Judicial Assessor exercised authority over the chiefs and so asked the British government to dissolve that office. The Select committee recommended that the British Government should stop all further invasions of other territories and withdraw gradually from her colonies in the West Africa with the exception of Sierra Leone. This led to the obliterating of the Executive Council and the Supreme Court. Sadly, many of the Fante chiefs pledged their support for the British Government. They begged the British not to leave, they said, 'to leave us now would be like the parent forsaking his offspring before being able to care for itself.'[9]

Upon hearing the Select Committee's recommendation, Aggrey and his educated followers became more radical in their deviance. In a letter Aggrey asked the governor to define 'the relationship between the King's court and the British Magistrate's court between the King and the Governor and between the King and his brother Kings on the Gold Coast'. He questioned why he was denied a share of the customs and revenues the government received. He emphasized that he would establish his own military corps for self-defence. On the other hand, the Governor saw Aggrey's audacity as seditious and described the king as insolent, ignorant and stubborn and as such had to be put down. To stir up matters, the governor freed several people Aggrey had imprisoned in December 1866. Aggrey in a letter cautioned the then governor, Conran, and this is what he wrote to him:

> The time has now come for me to record a solemn protest against the perpetual annoyances and insults that you persistently and perseveringly continue to practice on me in my capacity as legally constituted King of Cape Coast. I presume your object is to incite me and my people to enact more of those fearful things that took place in Jamaica that I have heard of ... However much you wish to have me and

> my people under martial laws, you will never have that pleasure ... ....the Earl of Carnarvon has laid it down in his speech on the 2nd August last, that we are all entitled to redress at his hands as the Colonial Minister. To that quarter I shall appeal for the last time, and then if some tangible satisfaction is not accorded to me and those whose interest I am bound to protect, it will be time enough for me to adopt those measures which will ensure to me and my people something unlike the slavery that you are endeavouring to place us in.[10]

This letter of Aggrey infuriated the ego of Conran. He arrested Aggrey and sent him into exile to Sierra Leone that same December 1866. He was sent back three years after in March 1869 as a private citizen. Sadly, he died that year. Thus long before the nationalist movement of the UGCC, King Aggrey was the first to collaborate with the African intellectuals to oppose the colonial rule of the British.

The treatment that was meted out to Aggrey did not deter some Fante and Ga Chiefs. In November 1866, Kow Amonu, the King of Anomabu, refused to pay the fine imposed on him by the Governor's magistrates until he was compelled to do so by Conran. In Accra, three kings Cudjoe, Dowuonah and Tackie respectively from James Town, Christiansborg and Dutch Accra similarly challenged the authority of the British.

Around this period, a number of states, largely Fante chiefs, came together to form a unity of states called the Fante Confederation. Their purpose was to take their own destiny into their hands. Their main concern of forming the federation was due to the invasion of Asante on the south while the British hesitated to react; they felt betrayed. Even though the British reacted later, Asante dominated the war from the 1860s until in 1874 when Britain was able to defeat the Ashanti. Also around this period, there was agreement of exchange of forts between the Dutch and the British. The Fante chiefs were offended that they were not privy to this agreement. They were threatened by the agreement since the Dutch were friends with the Asantes. They opposed the exchange of the forts. The next reason for the formation of the

Federation was the influence of the educated Africans, who spread the news that, the Select Committee of Britain had advised the Government to surrender their colonies and leave for Sierra Leone. This would mean that the Fante would have no other option than to take their destinies into their hands.

In January 1868, a number of chiefs from Mankessim, Assin, Denkyira, Twifu and Wassa met to pass a resolution to support and protect themselves regardless of British interest or patronage or opposition to the Anglo-Dutch exchange, to assist Komenda and finally form a government that would be governed by themselves without having a head, or king under the British. The educated elites who catalysed the formation of the federation were Martin, Carr, Charles Bannerman, James Amissah, Thomas Hughes (West Indian), James Hutton Brew, F.C. Grant and J.A Horton from Sierra Leone who practised medicine in Ghana. They persuaded the Chiefs that the time was ripe for them to loosen the shackles of colonialism in order to govern themselves. The Confederation was able to draft its constitution even though it was changed three times. They were able to found Fante National Supreme Court and R. Ghartey was appointed as the Chief Magistrate.

However, barely five years after its formation, the federation collapsed. The paramount reason for forming the Confederation was the Anglo-Dutch fort exchange which the Fante chiefs opposed. In 1872, the Dutch left the Gold Coast making their resistance of no use. The second reason was a protracted conflict that existed between the two Fante leaders: Edu of Mankesim and Otu of Abora. The third reason was that the size of their army was not enough. The fourth reason was financial. The Confederation could not raise enough revenue to manage it. And the last reason was that the British officials succeeded in paying bribes to manipulate the natives to destroy the image of the leaders of the Fante Confederation. So in 1873, the Fante Confederation collapsed.

The invasion of Asante in the eastern province moved James Bannerman, William Lutterodt and other people like W. Addo, L. Hesse, J.E Ritcher and G.F. Cleland to form Accra Native Confederation in August 1869. It was the intention of these men to establish a government when they realized their chiefs had betrayed them by sharing among themselves some money given by the British when that money could have been used to prepare against the Asante invasion. However, this group could not survive after its inauguration largely because it lacked support and strategy. Notwithstanding their lack of strength and strategy to succeed with their objective against the British, King Aggrey, the chiefs and intellectuals set a good footprint for a future organized resistance against the British rule in the Gold Coast.

By 1874 the British under the leadership of Sir Garnet Wolseley were able to overturn the dominance of the Asante and finally defeated the Asante (in the **Sagrenti war**) by going to Kumasi to burn the city. The British compelled Asante into a treaty at Fomena that year. Subject states like Dagomba, Nanumbas, Gonja and N'Chumburu were granted independence from Ashanti.[10] With these victories over the Fante Confederation, the Accra Native Confederation, Ashanti and the departure of the Dutch, the British began to benefit more from trade, earn more revenue and were able to maximize their missionary work.

This victory caused the British to enforce the Foreign Jurisdiction Act of 1843 instead of resorting to the Select Committee's recommendation of withdrawing from the Gold Cost. They converted their forts and settlements in southern Ghana into a Crown Colony and the states south of the Pra into a Protectorate in July 1874. They abolished all the local slavery business and emancipated slaves in the Protectorates which did not go down well with some chiefs and local authorities since slavery generated enough revenue for them.

Despite the decisive defeat inflicted on Asante in 1874 the British refused to make it a protectorate. Their policy towards Asante as defined by Kimberley, the then Colonial Secretary, was rather 'to steadily encourage the independence of the countries bordering on Ashanti, and cultivate good relations with them. Any recovery by Ashanti of its former predominance will be sure to bring us serious trouble'.[11]

Soon after the British reclaimed their powers over the colony and protectorates, they restored the Executive Council and the Legislative

Council in August 1874. Two years later, the Supreme Court was established. When the Ghanaian elites realised there was no Ghanaian representation at the Legislative Council, they began to mount pressure on the colonial government for African inclusion. Leading in such protests were the founder of Gold Coast Times, Prince Brew, Edmund Bannerman, King Tackie and T.F Bruce. They organised meetings in Cape Coast and Accra. When this did not yield any positive results, they sent delegates to England to press on their demands. It was such demands that pushed the British to appoint Burnett, a European, and George Cleland an African merchant and a divisional chief from James Town as unofficial members twelve years after. The following year Cleland died and John Sarbah father of John Mensah Sarbah replaced him. After Sarbah also died in 1892, Brand Ford Griffith, the Governor, was reluctant to replace him on the reason that he could not find any African. This rather provoked the Ghanaians to push harder which got J.H Cheetham and John Vanderpuiye to be nominated to the Council. In 1898, Hutton Mills replaced Cheetham, to become the first African barrister to be appointed a member of the Legislative Council. He was replaced in 1900 by John Mensah Sarbah.

The Supreme Court Ordinance abolished the civil court and criminal justice and also annulled the office and court of the judicial assessor. This Ordinance empowered the District Commissioners to exercise the work of Supreme Court judges in their districts. Around this same period, between 1874 and 1879, the British extended their rule along the coast to Anlo and to Aflao to the far East and Agosome, inland of Volta region.

In 1877 the Government changed its seat of government from Cape Coast to Accra. Their main reason was that Accra was cleaner and healthier and strategically positioned, closer to Lagos since they were one colony. In 1883, the Native Jurisdiction Ordinance Act was passed which empowered the Governor-in-Council to dismiss or suspend any chief who abused his power. It authorized chiefs to set up tribunals and make laws subject to the approval of the Governor. In 1889, the British passed an ordinance which was amended in 1894. They established Town Councils to levy house rates. This was to help them raise their revenues and also to control various timber and mining concessions.

This led to the Land Bill which sought to commit all public or unoccupied land to the British Crown.

These bills of taking new taxes and annexing the land of the indigenous people did not sit down well with many Ghanaians. It gave birth to several protests all over the colony. Among this was the protest of about 70 chiefs who rose to demand increase in representation at the Legislative Council from four to eight and three of these must be part of the executive. There arose the slogan 'no representation no tax'. Another concerned citizen group challenged the direct taxation. About 170 people signed it under the secretaryship of John Mensah Sarbah. They added that they needed municipal councils. Women in Accra also staged a protest against the house tax and sent their petition of grievances to the colonial secretary in May 1897 and later to the governor. To keep the fire of resistance, a town committee was set up. E. Bannerman served as President, Addo as secretary and T. Hutton Mills as spokesman. The protest persisted in towns like Odumase, Winneba, Cape Coast, Akropon and Anomabu.

Strategically to quell the Asante, the British on 17 January 1896, led by Sir Francis Scott and R.S. Baden Powell captured Prempe I, the Asantehene, when he refused British protection. He was also wrongly accused of refusing to pay required tribute to the British from 1874. He was taken to Seychelles Island through Sierra Leone with his relatives and some subjects. Asante rose in protest for release of their king. Due to the rising campaign against them and the rising of Asante for their king, the Colonial government could not implement these bills.

The following year in 1897, the protest against the land bill persisted with the formation of a more formal group called the Aborigines Right Protection Society. Its president was John Sey with J.P Brown as vice President. Other prominent members were Kobina Sekyi, Joseph Casely-Hayford, J.H. Cheetham and P.A Wooner Renner. This organisation had support from many sections in the colony, protectorates, churches, newspapers such as the Gold Coast Methodist Times and even residents in London. They contended that there was no waste or public land which could justifiably be annexed by the government and again should this bill succeed it was going to reduce the legitimate occupants as mere squatters and abrogate them of their ancestral rights. In pursuance to their protest, they demanded drastic constitutional changes and the opposition to the direct tax. In 1898-99 they sent a delegation to London to appeal against the Land Bill which eventually succeeded in preventing the passage of the bill into Law.

For the fear of further Asante uprising and that of French and Germans dominating the north of Asante, the British sent George Ekem Furgeson in 1892 to make treaties with the states north of Asante. By the end of that year, he had finalized treaties with Dagomba, Bole, Bimbila and Daboya. He continued in the subsequent years and secured Bono, Mamprusi, Mossi and Chakosi.

In 1900, the British Governor, Frederick Mitchell Hodgson, demanded the surrender of the Golden Stool as an admission by the Ashanti of their submission to the British. This was refuted by Yaa Asantewaa, the Queen of Ejisu. She mobilised soldiers to fight and protect the Golden Stool. The Asante soldiers were able to lay an ambush over the governor and his soldiers in the Kumasi fort. After what appeared as initial victory over the Hodgson who was taken hostage, the British were able to mobilise more external troops to intervene. The calling of the reinforcement troops helped the governor to escape. Eventually the British defeated the Asantes and arrested Yaa Asantewaa. With regard to the Golden Stool, the British could not lay their hand hold on it. Yaa Asantewaa and 14 other Asantes were taken to Seychelles to join Prempe I. Governor Hogdson shortly after his escape from the siege left for England and was replaced with Sir Mathew Nathan. Nathan visited Kumasi in March 1901. After a thoughtful deliberation between Nathan and Chamberlain, the Secretary of States, the Colonial Office accepted their decision to annex Ashanti by an Imperial Order in Council on 26 September 1901 which specifically declared that it had been 'conquered by His Majesty's forces'. The Order delegated full power and jurisdiction to the governor of the Gold Coast[12]. This excluded Ashanti from the Legislative Council of the Colony. The northern territories were made a protectorate that same period in 1901. By 1901 the boundaries of Ghana with the exception of the British Togoland (now Volta Region) had been demarcated.

The capture of Ashanti by the British in 1901 influenced the arrival of missionaries in the area. Pioneers among these missionaries were the Wesleyans and the Basel. However good intention these missionaries had, their teachings brought new ways of life and the new beliefs which threatened the framework of Ashanti institutions and values. This is because, the new Christian converts began to isolate and disobey their chiefs and elders on matters pertaining to religious grounds which included providing sheep for sacrifice at the hearing of a case, carrying a stool or sword on ceremonial occasions. When a Christian was asked why their disobedience, they would reply, 'I now go to Church, I am not under the chief' or 'The priest (Father or Sofo) says we must not do them' or it is against the law of the church. To them by becoming Christians, they had put themselves under a new authority.[13] The District Commissioner and governor backed the Christians to disobey their traditional leaders on religious grounds. The Government took the view that while Christians were naturally freed from fetish observances, they were to perform the ordinary obligations and services imposed on them by native custom in which fetish ceremonies were not involved.[14] This disloyalty gradually broke African nationalism which is having its negative effects in the development of modern African nations. Africans appear to be disloyal to fellow Africans whereas when given the chance, they pay full obeisance to white leaders in various fields.

This is what Chinua Achebe summed as, 'the white man says our customs are bad; and our own brothers who have taken up his religion also say that our customs are bad. How do you think we can fight when our own brothers have turned against us? The white man is very clever. He came quietly and peaceably with his religion. We were amused at his foolishness and allowed him to stay. Now he has won our brothers, and our clan can no longer act like one. He has put a knife on the things that held us together and we have fallen apart.'[15]

Achebe is right. Had the British not gained support from the indigenous Ghanaians and Africans elsewhere, they would not have been able to defeat the Asantes. But the hatred and fear the native tribes had against Asante aroused them to support the British. And in Asante and elsewhere, the adaptation to the new faith triggered disloyalty in the natives against their leaders. This and other factors weakened or killed the spirit of nationalism in us. With the passage of the Native Jurisdiction Ordinance in 1924, the powers and duties of chiefs in Ashanti were defined by the British as it had been established in the Colony.[16] This drastically reduced the honour and authority the chiefs had before. Natives became recalcitrant to their chiefs but sheepishly paid obeisance to the white man.

Prior to the First World War I, the British Togoland was part of French Togoland under the rule of Germany. When Germany was defeated in the World War I, it lost its territories in Africa. As a result, The League of Nations divided Togoland territory into two and gave them to the French and the British in 1918. The territories of the Germans excluded Anlo, Tongu, Aflao, Agosome, Peki and other areas which were originally British Protectorates. Later, the British merged Anlo, Tongu, Aflao, Agosome, Peki and other territories with the inherited Togoland to form British Togoland as a colony. With this control of territories in judicial, administrative and political governance, the British began to exploit the people for economic gains and helped their missionaries to evangelise to the Ghanaians.

The missionaries did not only convert many people to Christianity, they established schools and trained a number of African intellectuals. Among the schools they established are Mfantsipim (1876), Adisadel (1910), St. Augustine (1930), Presbyterian Boys (1938), Wesley Girls' High School, Holy Child High School (1946) and many such schools all over the Gold Coast. They trained many of the scholars who formed the nationalist movement in Ghana like Kwegyir Aggrey, J.B Danquah, Kwame Nkrumah, K.A Busia, Edward Akufo-Addo and many great statesmen of Ghana. The fact remains that the missionary schools are the best and as such the back bone of first and second cycles of education in Ghana. In addition to this, they pushed for the abolition of inhuman practices such as slavery and human sacrifice. They promoted agriculture and trade. As a matter of fact, Tetteh Quarshie, who is credited with the introduction of cocoa into Gold Coast, was an apprentice of a missionary called Henrich Bohner. It was the Presbyterians who helped in the nursing of Tetteh Quarshie's cocoa. The missionaries were the first to start the scientific study of local languages and preserve the African literature through proverbs, folktales, local songs and lyrics which could have been in extinction by now.  They raised the standard of living by introducing healthier and better housing, furniture and drinking wells.  They introduced new food crops like cocoa, oranges, mangoes and many others in the Gold Coast. They built many hospitals in the country. They provided many skills such as mechanics and other skills-trained jobs.

By the good foundation of the Missionaries, the European merchants and governments were able to build the economy of the Gold Coast around some of these agriculture products such as kola nuts, palm oil, cocoa, mangoes, oranges and the rest. The production of cocoa began to record high increase in harvest. It became the leading export of Ghana before the First World War. In the year 1919, the Gold Coast exported 100,000. This increased to 120,000 tons the subsequent year in 1920. In 1927, cocoa contributed an amount of £11,727,566 million of the total export value of £14,350,355. In 1932, cocoa export had surged to 256,000 tons.[17] The Gold Coast rose to become the leading producer of Cocoa in the world.

Mining became another field to build the economy. In 1911, the Gold Coast exported an average of 280,000oz at £1 million which constituted 30% of the colony's exports. The Gold Coast began to export manganese. Its production rose from 39595 tons in 1910 to 419224 tons in 1929. By 1951 Ghana produced 806,000 tons of manganese which was valued at £7 million that made the Gold Coast the second largest producer of manganese in the world. In 1933, the nation discovered diamond at Akwatia, Oda, Kade and first produced 750000 carats. In 1941, the nation discovered bauxite at Mpraeso and later in other parts of the nation. Research shows that Ghana had bauxite reserve of 229 million tons making it one of the world's largest reserves. By 1954 minerals brought in £21·5 million out of the total exports from Ghana of £113·25 million.[18] This figure clearly reveals how the colonial governance empowered foreign merchants to milk the Gold Coast. The sad story is that this meagre proportion has not changed for better since the self-governance.

With this economic boom, the challenge the merchants faced was transport. There were no proper roads to transport these goods. The main means of transport were human beings who carried the goods. Not only was the head porterage expensive, it was disgustingly slow for business and transporting heavy machines then was unimaginably very burdensome. The government decided to embark on transport projects. In 1890, a number of roads were built which include Saltpond-Oda road, Accra to Kyebi, a wooden bridge between Cape Coast and Elmina. Later in 1895 Governor Nathan admonished that these roads should be improved to meet the standards of motor-cars and tractor engines. As a result, roads like the Saltpond-Oda were refurbished to 12 foot road, the Accra to Kyebi was designed to 18 foot road, Accra-Ayimensa-Dodowa roads were improved to a 16-foot road. These road constructions were extended to

Bono and Ahafo regions, the Northern territories. Example of such roads constructed were Kumasi-Yeji, Yeji-Krakye, Yeji-Salaga, Wa-Gambaga roads.The Colonial government realized that the vehicle roads were not enough for transport. They decided to include railways to the means of transport in the Gold Coast and Ashanti. They built the Sekondi to Tarkwa railway in 1901, Tarkwa-Obuasi in 1902 and Kumasi railway in 1903.[19]

These infrastructure developments took a leap under the leadership of Sir Gordon Gugisberg who is eulogized for his contribution in the surveying and infrastructure development for the modernisation of Ghana. It was under his watch the railway mileage increased from 269 to 375 miles. One of the railways constructed was the Kade to Huni Valley. It was under his governance that the premier hospital, the Korle-Bu Hospital was built, that the Achimota College was built, and that the Takoradi harbour was built. His infrastructural, education, and health policies paved way for the modernisation of Ghana. It was under his governorship that Prempe 1 was returned from exile through the petition of the public. The next area Ghanaians owe gratitude to Guggisberg was in the 1925 constitution. He increased the number of representatives in the Legislative Council from eleven officials to fifteen officials and nine unofficial to fourteen unofficial members.

These developments in health, education, economy and infrastructure did not occur without discrimination. The white man had come to emboss himself as superior creation of God largely due to certain skills he possessed which the African did not have. They wrongly condemned almost every culture and practice of the Africans virtually holding the African in a low esteem. Many people had to change their local names for foreign names. Kweku Dadzie(Steel) became Frank Steel. Ekow Hammah (Rope) became George Hammond. Kofi Kuntu (Blanket) became Frank Blankson.[20] This degradation brought some resilience in some religious leaders to promote religion through their African culture which gave birth to the Christian faith called the 'Sumsum sore' (Spiritual churches) like the African Faith Tabernacle and Twelve Apostles Faith. There were hospitals blacks could not attend but were reserved for only white people. An example of such hospitals was the Ridge Hospital. Ephraim Amu, a tutor at Achimota College, was humiliated for dressing in a typical African dress. William Ofori Atta one of the Big Six and another teacher on Achimota campus were asked to quit from their allotted bungalows for some white people which they refused. Chiefs did not only lose their roles but also their respect. For instance King Aggrey of Cape Coast was reduced as a private citizen before he died. Prempe I was allowed to return to Asante as a private citizen. Later when he was installed, he was reduced as Kumasihene but not Asantehene.

On trade, many of the local traders were denied licences to a number of businesses. These licenses were reserved for foreigners alone who were British, Lebanese and Syrians. Local traders sometimes were obliged to buy goods they did not want before they got their preferred goods. On education, the few elites realised that the Ghanaians were deprived of programmes like engineering, medicine and other Science programmes that would help Ghanaians to develop. Most of the learning courses were limited to reading and arithmetic. On the economy, the Colonial government restricted the Gold Coast to raw material production without building industries to add value to the raw materials. For instance, in 1954, Ghana earned £21 million out of the £110 million the country exported on minerals. On the other hand, the people of the Gold Coast were left to feed on the imported finished products of the foreign entrepreneurs.

This imbalance in governance, racial inequality and economic exploitation and trade discrimination aroused persistent nationalist protests from the few intellectuals and daring Ghanaian citizens with little or no formal education. The inspiration of these activists was partly from the issues already narrated and also from the black revolution that was emerging around the globe during the period. One of the propagators of such revolution was Marcus Garvey. He used slogans such as 'renaissance of the black race', 'Ethiopia awake' and 'Africa for Africans'. He also demanded independence for Africa and prophesied that **'her redemption is coming like a storm, it will be there'**. His journal ***Negro World***, was eagerly read not only in America but throughout West Africa. He organised a number of black conventions in New York City between 1920 and 1925 which were attended by delegates from parts of the globe including Africa. Among the nationalists he influenced were Nkrumah and Azikiwe. The two became the first presidents of their respective countries. Another patriot who also influenced these nationalists was Dr. Kwegyir Aggrey. His popular story 'Thou art Eagle' gained continental influence on many great nationalists like Nkrumah, Danquah and Nnamdi Azikiwe.

The first of these nationalist movements that rose after the Aborigines was the West African Conference formed in 1917 which metamorphosed into National Congress of British West Africa (NCBWA) in March 1920. Their objective was to invite the West African colonies to demand 'self-determination and no taxation without representation'. It first met in Accra with delegation from Ghana, Nigeria, the Gambia and Sierra Leone. Its president was J. Hutton Mills with J.E Casely Hayford as vice president. It had joint Secretaries in the persons of Dr. F.Y. Nanka-Bruce and L.E.V. McCarthy; Joint Treasurers, A.B. Quartey-Papafio and H. Yan Hein. They described the Crown Colony Government as 'archaic and anachronistic' which needed change. Among their demands were,

1. Self-government to be implemented to enable peoples of African descent to participate in the government of their own country.

2. Elective franchise should be granted. They were against the chiefs nominating their kind of representatives to the

legislative assembly.

3. The system of nomination to the Legislative Council should
be abolished because it was undemocratic.

They condemned the usage of colonies monies to pay Imperial War Debt. They demanded the repeal of the Palm Kernel Export out Ordinance. They suggested the formation of cooperatives to fund Banks.

They demanded proficient education for Africans. They wanted compulsory education by law at primary and secondary school levels. They wanted an education that would preserve in students a sense of African nationality. They wanted equity in treatment and reward for personnel at the judicial in both Britain and Africa.

This group was fiercely opposed by the governors of Nigeria and Ghana who described them as 'self-elected and self-appointed congregation whose interests are not fixed on their communities' needs but on their own political aspirations'. The fact of the matter is that the governors were wrong. The demands of the NCBWA still fit into today's African society. The truth is that NCBWA political aspirations threatened the chiefs who nominated representatives to the legislative assembly and the colonial governments who were in bed with the chiefs. Nana Sir Ofori Atta I joined forces with the colonial governments to collapse this movement.

From September 1920 to January 1921, the NCBWA despatched a deputation to London to the Colonial Secretary, Lord Milner but sadly he denied them audience. It held subsequent meetings in Freetown, Bathurst (Banjul) and Lagos in 1930. The movement collapsed after the death of J.E Casely Hayford the founder, who was the main catalyst behind the organisation.

Just when the NCBWA was losing its fervour, another nationalist group emerged in London to continue to attack the colonial system. This was the West African Students Union (WASU) founded in August 1925 with the massive support of Dr Bankole Bright and Ladipo Solanke, a Nigerian. W. Davidson Carrol of the Gambia served as president, J.B. Danquah of Ghana served as vice president. The Secretary was Ladipo Solanke of Nigeria, and Treasurer and Financial Secretary, J. Akanni

Doherty of Nigeria. The aims of WASU were to foster the spirit of national consciousness and racial pride among Africans and persons of African origin, and to prove to the whites that Africa has a history and a culture of its own.

As an amalgamation of the Union for Students of African Descent (ASAD), the Gold Coast Students' Union and the Nigerian Progress Union, their bigger aim was to create United States of Africa of West Africa which would lead to the final formation of a United Africa that would stand in the forefront of the African freedom.

Danquah returned to the Gold Coast in 1927 after his studies. Just when the NCBWA crumpled in 1930, J. B. Danquah with the active support of K.A. Korsah, A. W. Kodjo Thompson and R.S. Blay formed the Youth Conference whose objective was to unite the various clubs and societies under one umbrella for nationalist movement. The unique thing the YC brought was their acumen to unite the chiefs and the intelligentsia for a national course. They were able to prepare a 400-page memorandum entitled 'Things to Change in Gold Coast' at the request of the Joint Provincial Council (JPC). The Youth Conference contributed to the constitutional changes that brought the unity between the Gold Coast and Ashanti at the legislature under the Burns Constitution of 1946. That is to say, Asante was brought under formal administration of the British in 1946. It was not until 1951 through the leadership of Danquah and the Coussey Committee that Asante agreed to become one colony with Gold Coast.

In 1944, the Youth Conference celebrated the centenary of the Bond of 1844 with the belief that British dominion was at its expiring end and that the youth were prepared to take up the leadership of the country. It is reported that Danquah called for the 'Terms of a New Bond of 1944' and drew up a plan for a federation of the Colony, Asante, Northern Territories and British Togoland regions.[21] It is no surprise Danquah kept pressing on the union of these colonies and the renegotiations of the bond of 1844. In 1948, when the opportune time came for him to draft a scheme of a self-governing constitution for the Gold Coast at the request of the Watson Commission, he re-emphasized this union of the Colony, Asante, Northern Territories and the Togoland regions to be called Ghana.

In 1945, the Youth Conference submitted a memorandum to the Secretary of State to protest against the recommendation of one university by the Walter Elliot Commission and rather demanded a separate university college for the Gold Coast which led to the building of University College of the Gold Coast (now University of Ghana) in 1948.

Just as Nana Ofori Ata I and the Colonial government fought against Casely Hayford's radical Congress, similar radical movements were vehemently resisted. Wallace-Johnson in 1934 formed the West African Youth League with the assistance of Bankole Renner. His aims were to empower the downtrodden to fight for their constitutional rights; to fight for national self-determination of the subjugated peoples of West Africa and to overthrow the British rule in West Africa. This gained immediate support from the workers and the youth, and branches were opened in many places. Its mouthpiece was Nnamdi Azikiwe's African Morning Post. With its radical language, and attacks on the sedition bill, Water Works and Chieftaincy, the British government with the support of Nana Ofori Ata and the chiefs sought for opportunity to deport them. The opportune time arrived in May 1936 when Wallace-Johnson published an article in the African Morning Post entitled 'Has the African a God?'. This was declared to be seditious and Wallace Johnson was deported to Sierra Leone.

In Ashanti the young men had become fed up with the Ashanti Confederacy Council and the British Government. They came together to form the Asante Youth Organisation in 1947 to remove the Asante chiefs from the Legislative Council and to pursue Self Government within five years before the formation of the United Gold Coast Convention.

From these brief narrations, it is clear that the many ordinary men and women were ripe for a national political movement for political independence. It was such common passion that arrested a business man, George Grant, to create a political union with politicians, merchants, lawyers and other patriots for the independence of Ghana. It was this unquenchable fire that brought into being the UGCC, the first political movement that constitutionally fought for Ghana's independence which has changed Ghana's political history forever and has earned six of the activists, who were imprisoned by the British Government, as the BIG SIX.

CHAPTER 2

# THE FORMATION OF THE UGCC

One of the controversial topics in Ghana is the nation's political history, especially its journey to political independence. Once I sat by television and heard a gentleman saying a number of fabricated things about Danquah and the UGCC. He said that Danquah was the person who chose the executives of the UGCC and as a result of his tribal sentiment against other tribes did not choose any Ewe, Asante into the leadership of the UGCC. I was shocked at such propaganda shared on national media. His view was that Danquah was myopic in the independence struggle and that it was Nkrumah who had better strategies for independence. Such political distortions have been ongoing since the independence of Ghana. Whichever opinion, it is an undisputable fact that the UGCC is the first political movement established in the Gold Coast (now Ghana) to achieve political independence for Ghana. How did this organisation come into being?

By 1946, the main voice in the Gold Coast was the Youth Conference and Danquah served as its secretary. Danquah was also the main academic and political voice for the Colony and Ashanti. In 1934, he served as the secretary of the delegation of the Colony and Asante to Britain to send their petition. The main objective of the Youth Conference was crafting a better future for the youth on the land. The

Aborigines had grown weaker since 1912. In the Eastern province which is today's Greater Accra and Eastern region, there arose a concern of nationalism in some patriots to start a political movement in the colony. Their intent was to take over the Youth Conference. As a result, Danquah, who was one of the architects, could not officially join the new political organisation as a member because of the position he occupied with the Youth Conference. They set up a committee to plan the establishment of this political party. Among the members of the committee for the movement are Edward Akufo Addo, Enoch Mensah, Kofi Larbi, R.D Nelson, J. Quist-Therson, E. O. Lartsen and Asuana Quartey. Its first meeting was held on the 3rd of December 1946 at the King Tackie Memoriah Hall in Accra. Their chairman was Edward Akuffo Addo and his vice was Mr. K. Brakatu Ateko. The committee came up with the name National League of the Gold Coast. After this meeting, new members became interested and joined the movement. Other prominent people who became members include Obestebi Lamptey, E. A Armah, Laud Lartey and R. P Baffour.[1]

Just when the planning committee was brainstorming strategies such as a weekly newspaper, editorial board and raising capital to push the agenda, a similar vision or movement was about to take off elsewhere in the Gold Coast. There was a business mogul called George Alfred Grant, affectionately called Paa Grant from Axim, who also dreamed of a nationalist movement specifically to fight for self-governance for the Gold Coast. He was a member of the Legislative Council and the Aborigine Right Protection Society. In February 1947, Danquah attended a High Court meeting to perform his professional duty as a lawyer, something he described as 'a custom characteristic of our national life.' From there he paid a courtesy call to George Grant, a fellow legislator. Grant said to Danquah, **'Look here, Danquah, I have worked hard all my life; I have made all the money I would wish to make. And yet I feel I am not free. Look at my table, Bills, Bills, Bills...Everyday the Government passes a new law which takes away the freedom and happiness of the people. Can you not do something about it? "I am in your hand, Sir', Danquah replied. 'Very well, meet me in my house tonight at 7 pm for consultation.** Danquah honoured the invitation that evening. In a meeting with Grant were Awoonor Williams and R.S Blay both of whom were lawyers. After their discussion, the four of them took a decision that the time had come to form a real political movement dedicated to the political self-determination of the Gold Coast.[2]

They sent invitations to about fifty leading men in the entire country. Among some of the people invited were E.C Quist, Dr. J.E Armah, Solomon Odamtten, Obetsebi Lamptey, Ako Adjei and Ben A. Tamakloe who became the secretary of the Ex-servicemen who led the 1948 protest. Edward Akufo-Addo and some of his colleagues from the Gold Coast People's League were also invited. Their first meeting was held in April 1947 at Saltpond. During the meeting, Dr. Danquah motioned that the group should be called The Gold Coast People's National Party. The leaders of the National League of the Gold Coast people were to decide whether their group would serve as independent body affiliated to the new Gold Coast People's National Party or they would merge with it.

This became a very sensitive debate for the leaders of the Gold Coast People's League to decide. The factors that were considered were political, tribal and financial. Some of the members had their doubts about the success of a political movement in the Eastern province since the Aborigines Rights and Protection Society did not have support in the province. Nana Sir Ofori Atta with his influence opposed the Aborigines and stood with the government. This made the people of the province less political and so the executives were wondering if this new group, the Gold Coast People's League would have the acceptance of the people. The next issue was tribal. There was polarisation between the Ga and the Akan. This posed a threat to the unity of the future of the group. In addition, the egos of these intellectuals were high. Many were post minded and serving became an issue. Besides, getting the commitment of the executives to the affairs of the group was challenging. The last issue was financial; the organisation had not been

able to raise funds for its weekly newspapers, the editorial and other activities. It could not pay its clerk from May to June 1947. These and other factors made the choice to merge a more attractive one. Considering these challenges, Mr. Akufo Addo and Mr. K.B Ateku

PAA GRANT
The Father of Ghana's
Independence Struggle

convinced the members without subjecting the debate to vote to join the Gold Coast National Party. They asked the people to think in terms of Gold Coast and not of their particular part of the country.[3] When all were set, they agreed to adopt a new name, the United Gold Coast Convention, a name Danquah and William Ofori Atta came up with.[4] They began to hold public meetings in Accra, Sekondi, Cape Coast, Koforidua, Saltpond, Dunkwa, Axim, etc. to announce their future political aspirations. The National League then became the Accra branch of the UGCC with Akufo Addo maintaining his position as the chairman. Obestebi Lamptey, and Quist-Therson were the vice Chairmen. Mr Ako-Adjei was the elected secretary but he refused the position and recommended that a friend of his, Kwame Nkrumah would be the best fit for that position. The main reason was that they wanted a young man who would suit the Youth Conference and help to inspire the youth in the country to embrace the new vision for Self-Government.

So on 4 August, 1947, the United Gold Coast Convention was launched at Saltpond. George Grant was elected as president, J.B Danquah and D W De Graft Johnson were elected as vice presidents. The other executives were R.S Blay, William Ofori Atta, Edward Akufo Addo, Ako Adjei, Obestebi Lamptey, V.B Annan and other members. Its vision was clear-**"To ensure that by all legitimate and constitutional means the control and direction of the Government shall within the shortest possible time pass into the hands of the people and their chiefs"**· This should persuade readers away from the propaganda that the UGCC had no independence on mind and that the organization was formed by merchants to enrich themselves with the colonial masters.

George Grant, the President gave his address, and below is an excerpt of his speech:

> 'Every governor and the House of Commons in 1865 promised that the time would come when the government of the Gold Coast will be in the hands of the people. That 'time had come or will soon come', it was necessary to prepare for it.

> We have come here in the footsteps of our fathers to seek a

new way to meet new dangers that threaten our country. In a hundred years these dangers have taken a hundred different forms, but all of them have had one effect-to reduce our liberties and increase our enslavement, our subjection.

In the past our ancestors came together any time a new danger threatened. They set up a machinery such as the Fante Confederation or the Aborigines Rights Protection Society to meet the specific danger: Either to bring our chiefs together, irrespective of whether the government was British or Dutch or to protect our lands from being taken from us. Today we can no longer afford to sit and wait. We need a creative society, protests. Today we need more than a protective society. We need a creative society. The day of negative protest is over. The time has come now for Positive Action. Today we have to go into the centre of things, to where all governments policies and ordinances are planned and made. We have to go there and ask that these things should be done in a fine style, according to our own taste. In other words, and to put simply we want to look after ourselves.

I do not think that those who are not with us here are against us. Nor do I want anyone to think that we are against those who are not with us here. We have not set up this convention against any one. We are not against any Chiefs. We are not against the British. We are against slavery and subjection. We are against bad government. We are against a wrong system of government. By a wrong system of a government, I mean a government in which the people have no power to control those who are in charge of the government. We are against that. Indeed, how absurd must it be for anyone to suggest we are against our chiefs. But we are against any system which stands in the way of our freedom.

Remember, that upon what you do today may depend the happiness of millions of our countrymen and women. But above all, remember this: what we do today, we do and plan not for ourselves alone here and now, but for our country, not only for the generation of today, but for generations yet unborn'[5]

After his speech, Danquah also gave a remarkable speech which I would like to share with you.

Mr. Chairman, Ladies and Gentlemen:

We have, from all the corners of this country, come to Saltpond today for a specific purpose: for a decision. We have come to take a decision whether our country and people are any longer to tolerate a system of government under which those who are in control of government are not under the control of those who are governed.

Seven or eight, we had a Governor by the name of Sir Arnold Hodson. His policy was that it was far better for the people of the Gold Coast to remain under the official majority, under the benign and kind control of an official executive, than to be free, than to have an unofficial majority in the Legislative Council.

"That Governor, Sir Arnold Hodson, after saying this, went away to an island in the West indies, and  there he died."

"After that Governor left, another came, by the name of Sir Alan Burns. He came from the West Indies. He was a different type of person, different from Sir Arnold Hodson. He had one supreme qualification in that respect: he did not agree with Sir Arnold Hodson that we would not be better governed if we had an unofficial majority in the Legislative Council. He believed that a people governed by an official majority were not a free people. Consequently, where we presented our Memorandum for changes in the constitution to the Secretary of State in 1943, he did everything possible to secure the approval of the Secretary of State to our demand for changes.

In our Memorandum, we asked that we should have control of legislation as also of policy. We asked that there should be set up for us a committee of Government, a committee of Policy, in which the chosen representatives of the people will have charge of the blue-prints of policy.

"But, here again, this new Governor, Sir Alan Burns, had his own ideas. He did not think that a people, who controlled the unofficial majority on the Legislative Council, would be much better governed if they were given also the power to shape and to control policy.

"His idea was to keep policy in his own hands, in the hands of himself and his Executive Council. But to placate our feelings, he said this: When policy was being adumbrated the Chiefs of the Joint Provincial Council and the Chiefs of the Ashanti Confederacy Council would be consulted."

"So our position is that, at the present time, whilst our Chiefs are made to believe that they are part of the Government, it works out in practice that it is merely make belief, and that in most essential things the Government constantly and repeatedly ignores them. So our position is that, whilst we have the unofficial majority and when we meet everyone in the official side is in a hurry to close the session on a set day. In all the different policies enumerated above, not once was the advice and consent of the Legislative Council sought. In fact, in the native of things, not being a constituent assembly on policy, there never was need to consult them until after everything had been completed.

" In the specific case of the Harragin Commission's Report, the Government consulted the Financial Secretaries of the Gambia and Sierra Leone and Nigeria, and came to their own decision in what came to be called the Accra Conference before ever the elected members of the Legislative Council knew what was happening.

"This mockery of form without reality we can no longer tolerate.

"But perhaps someone would say, why not wait for a new Governor from West Indies or from the East Indies; he may come and grant us the power to control policy. He may come and change everything that Sir Alan Burns did and what Sir

Arnold Hodson did not do.

"But surely, Ladies and gentlemen, is it safe and secure for us to live under a constitution in which the system of government depends upon the whims and caprices of a man from anywhere who may be sent to us a Governor? Must we longer tolerate this system of want of continuity which forever lands us in nowhere but despair and frustration?

"We have, as I said, come to Saltpond to ponder and to deliberate upon the ways and means to bring an end to this insecurity and this frustration. **British freedom is a precious thing. But British freedom is not Gold Coast freedom. British liberty is grand to have, but you cannot have and possess British liberty in a Gold Coast atmosphere. We must have, here and now, if we are to be well governed, a new kind of freedom, a Gold Coast Liberty.**

"Perhaps I strain the point I speak of a new kind of freedom. Love of freedom from foreign control has always been in our blood. 870 years ago we struck against the attempt of the Arabs to impose a religious slavery upon us in Ghana. We left our homes in Ghana and came down here to build for ourselves a new home.

**"But there is one thing we brought with us from ancient Ghana. We brought with us our ancient freedom. Today the safety of that freedom is threatened, has been continuously threatened for a 100 years, since the Bond of 1844, and the time has come for a decision.**

"And remember this: when we were attacked by the Arabs in Ghana, there was plenty of land to escape into. There was this rain-forest area and gold and diamond bearing lands in the Gold Coast, Togoland and Ivory Coast, We came here and settled here.

Today we are cut off to the south by the sea, and to the north by the desert, and, if fearing that our ancient freedom is dangerously threatened, we decided to evacuate this land and go elsewhere, there is nowhere else for us to go. So our duty is clear. We must fight against the new domination. And we must fight with the constitutional, determined, persistent, unflinching, and unceasing until the goal of freedom is attained.

"Ladies and gentlemen, as the Chairman said, we have taken six months to draft the terms of this constitution for a United Gold Coast Convention. We call it united because we hate the idea of any saying "Who are the people?" as if the people and their Chiefs are living in a warring camps. "We are not at war with our chiefs. We are at war with our present system of government. We are at war with the system because it pretends to govern us through our Chiefs indirectly, and our Chiefs are in a very pitiable condition. It is our duty as their people to save them from that pitiable condition. They cannot by themselves act because they have been told they are part of the Government, of the colonial Power, and that they get their power from the Government.

"We must bring an end to that. We must bring an end to a system of government in which the Chiefs who govern us are made an instrument of misgovernment, even of oppression, by the Colonial power. How truly can our Chiefs say they are free to represent us before the colonial Power when they are themselves part of that Colonial Power?

Our duty is clear. It is our duty to alter the constitution in such a way that both the Chiefs and their people will have the reality of power in their hands.

That is the object of this convention, and I invite you without any reservation to accept the constitution as drafted, and, once for all, to save this country."[6]

Danquah's speech was greeted with applause, and after that, Mrs. J.B Eyeson went to the rostrum and stated: "Dr. Danquah, we had in the past given enthusiastic support to the cause of the church. Today it is the cause of the nation. Women of the country are behind you"[6a]

For many years a lot of Ghanaians have not had the privilege to read the inaugural address of the UGCC. This gave room for the propagandist to spread their myth against the UGCC that they were opportunistic merchants in bed with the colonial government. But if you reflect on the first paragraphs of the address, you will realise that the first thing they did was to question the system of governance the people of Gold Coast were subjected to. They opposed the colonial government that was not subject to the accountability of its unofficial masses.

They opposed the idea of a governor from a different nationality or race governing the people of Gold Coast. And they were determined to fight for self-governance to liberate the chiefs and the masses. And in achieving this freedom, they made it clear to build a new Gold Coast freedom. In other words, they opposed the model of government the British practised on the environment of Gold Coast. They opposed the influence of the western culture over the Ghanaian culture. They were therefore poised to re-establish their own Gold Coast democracy that is their own government on the model of African culture.

It was this hope or determination that made them reveal that they are descents of ancient Ghana Empire. And as such the freedom, the culture, the system of governance of that empire was in their blood. According to history there was a time that a certain group of Arabs invaded the kingdom to Islamise the indigenous people. Our forefathers rebelled against such oppression. This led some of them to migrate to this part of the earth. The UGCC believed the time was due to resist the colonial oppression.

Another interesting thing is that, it was on this day that the leaders also officially revealed that the people of Gold Coast or at least majority of them migrated from the ancient Ghana hence our identity change from Gold Coast to Ghana. It was this political movement that championed the name or identity of Ghana to the masses that long before independence it became a selling name for many people and many organisations. It is rather strange to hear that years later, in our time, some people could have the audacity to say that the leaders of UGCC were not responsible for our name Ghana.

The objective of the UGCC was clear; to achieve political independence or what was formally described as self-government. But how was that going to be achieved? There are a number of ways by which a colony seeks political independence. It could be by military revolution, where the colony marches an army for its freedom. That was how America got its independence from the British. But this can be very costly, in a way America was fortunate to have the French army under Napoleon Bonaparte to ally with America. The next option is to use constitutional changes. This is what the leaders of the UGCC adopted; that is why Danquah emphasised **"So our duty is clear. We must fight against the new domination. And we must fight with the weapons of today, constitutional, determined, persistent, unflinching, unceasing, until the goal of freedom is attained."** This method worked, and Ghana became politically independent, suggesting that for improvement of governance, there must always be constitutional review.

In the subsequent chapters, I will share with you how the leaders of the UGCC got their objectives right, succeeding in constitutional changes to eventually get Ghana independent. But this approach can never be successful without the support of the masses. It is the voice of the people that validate such proposals. And the leaders of the UGCC were able to secure that from the people of the colony at least when it mattered most until there was a split among them and they lost their support to their defected secretary. They deserve their rightful honour in the founding of this nation rather than to be described as selfish aristocrats or stooges of the British imperialism.

I must say the vision or the ambition of this organisation was a daring one. This is because the colonial power deeply had gripped the powers that be on the land to be on its side. Firstly, the chiefs: the colonial masters governed in a way to make the chiefs part of their system of governance. And many of the chiefs had thrown their weight behind the powers of the British. Some had been given foreign education and some even knighted. The few intellectuals who served as middle men also took their share of taxes and other services making the ordinary masses the victims of the colonial rule. Who would liberate the masses and who will support these liberators? The reason is that without the backing of the chiefs, it was impossible for any vision to thrive in the Gold Coast. For instance, the Aborigines Right Protection Society in spite of their impact could not spread and influence people of the Eastern Province because a certain powerful chief called Nana Sir Ofori Atta I decided to be in bed with the colonial government so he opposed the movement of the Aborigines. However with tact and boldness, the Danquah led movement was able to penetrate to mobilise the intellectuals, chiefs and people. This did not come without resistance, one of the prominent chiefs Nana Tsibu Darku, once asked, 'Who are these people?', disregarding the UGCC people because he was opposed to independence.

When the UGCC was inaugurated on 4 August, 1947, one major executive position was vacant. And that was the position of secretary. They expected to run the UGCC as a modern political movement that would need a full time working secretary. This secretary must be a young person to attract the youth. The leaders asked Ako Adjei to assume that position, most probably because he was young and intelligent. But Ako Adjei declined and suggested Francis Kofi Nwiah Kwame Nkrumah with whom he attended the same school: Lincoln University in the USA. Later they both met in Britain. Kwame Nkrumah was involved in student politics in the UK. He was holding a position with the West African National Secretariat in Manchester. Ako Adjei wrote to him, inviting him to accept the secretary position of the UGCC and a monthly salary of £100 and a car. He hesitated since it was about twelve years of been detached from the Gold Coast people. After Ako Adjei, Danquah also wrote to Nkrumah inviting him to accept the post of secretary of the UGCC. He requested a passage fee of £100 which was paid to him by Danquah. He agreed to come. He set forth on 14 November for Accra but made a number of transits, including visiting Liberian President Tubman in Monrovia.[6] He arrived in Accra on 16 December 1947. It had been twelve years since he left the Gold Coast for overseas.

According to him, his own mum could not recognize him which is quite normal. Prior to the time he left the Gold Coast in 1935, he had a son whose name was Francis Nkrumah with a lady called Nancy Favour. His son rose to become a medical doctor. It was not only Nkrumah's mum who was joyful to meet him, the leaders of UGCC were very pleased to have met with him. They made so many announcements prior to his coming and after he arrived. He is reported of saying that when a staff at the Takoradi harbour saw his name in his passport, he took Nkrumah aside and said "you are Kwame Nkrumah!", he went on to say they had heard so much about him and were waiting for him to help them. This is to reveal that the UGCC prepared a receptive platform for their general secretary to work. And indeed, Nkrumah brought much fervour to the independence struggle. And they were able to lay a great milestone in the founding of Ghana.

Nkrumah was first launched to the public on the 29 December 1947 at Saltpond. Before the appointment of Dr. Kwame Nkrumah as General Secretary of the convention, Danquah on behalf of the Working Committee put two questions to him: (1) Whether having read the Constitution he realised that the Convention was solely interested in the Colonial question of self-government for Chiefs and people and not in communism or communist propaganda, and (2) Whether he realised that his membership of the West African National Secretariat was not to commit the UGCC to the policy of that movement, and that the UGCC's own principal interest was to establish a Gold Coast nation, self-governing, and not a West African nation. Dr. Nkrumah gave them the requisite assurances, and spoke of his differences with Geroge Padmore on the 'nationalism' issue, and emphasised that he considered 'territorial integrity' paramount and that there could not be internationalism when there were no nations as such. The working committee having satisfied itself that Dr. Kwame Nkrumah would not preach communism and inter-West Africanism on the platform of the Convention, accordingly appointed him General Secretary.[7] They were not able to pay the £100 promised as salary but they agreed on £300 annually and gave him a car to work with and accommodation.[8]

On 20 January 1948, before the Working Committee, Nkrumah also unfolded his programmes he prepared for the convention to consider. He proposed a Shadow Cabinet which would include members to understudy various ministries of governments. The shadow cabinet would also serve as vanguard to put the executives on their toes in the quest for self-government.

His next programme was Organisational work. The Organisational work was going to be unravelled in three periods. The first period was:

To bring all organizations such as Educational, social, Political, Farmers' and Women's Organisations, Trade Unions in the country under the Convention or affiliate with the convention.

To consolidate existing branches and establish new branches in every town and village of the country;

To ensure there are branches in the Colony, Ashanti, Northern Territories and Togoland and engage the chiefs or Odikro of each town to become patrons of the branch.

Where there are branches, they should organize weekend schools. This is where they must begin their mass education on Self Governance

**Second period**

They would embark on mass demonstrations throughout the country to test their organizational strength, making use of political crises.

**Third period**

a) They would convene a Constitutional Assembly of the Gold Coast people to draw up the Constitution for Self-Government or National Independence.

b) Organize demonstration, boycott and strike as weapons to support the self-Government.

This was agreed on by the members of the Convention.

These programmes were to help make the Convention acceptable and popular. The convention was rose to become a national movement which the masses supported. But this did not happen without a price. The leaders of the Convention were arrested and that arrest soon made them national heroes.

There was also the notion that Danquah and the UGCC were not on good terms with Ashanti with the erroneous perception that the Akyems were at logger heads with the Ashantis. This was unfounded. Firstly Danquah honourably informed the Asantehene Otumfuo Sir Osei Agyeman Prempe II about the formation of the UGCC and their vision of self-governance. Below is one of the letters of Danquah to the Otumfuo.

NKRUMAH TO MEET ASANTEHENE

Ref. 060/UC/48

22 January, 1948

Otumfuo Sir Osei Agyeman Prempeh II, K.B.E.,

 Asantehene,

Manhyia, Kumasi.

Otumfuo,

You may be wondering why so much noise is being made in the political world for our self-government and you have been kept in the dark, as it were. Actually since my last personal interview with you on the Convention, matters have not advanced much except that we have appeared officially before the Joint Provincial Council and have placed our aims and objects before them, and have suggested that they should take a tip from you and leave the white man's Town Councils and Legislative Councils to himself, sending your "sons" to go and listen and report to you, and not vice versa. I am certain the Colony Chiefs quite appreciate the sensible nature of the suggestion, but they are not quite sure whether they should trust us instead of hedging for the present, but I feel certain that when the time comes in 1950 or thereabouts a good many will follow your good example.

As to our plans for self-government, I do not want to go into details here. But what I propose now is that a few members of the Working Committee of the Convention, including Mr. Grant and our general secretary, Mr Kwame Nkrumah, should make a private call on you at a date convenient to yourself and place all our plans before you.

Nana may rest assured that no vital step will be taken in this great venture for our national freedom without keeping you fully informed so that when the time comes for action it will be decisive and tremendous. The ostensible purpose of our visit may be said to give Mr. Kwame Nkrumah an opportunity of paying court to Otumfuo.

Kindly let me hear from you at your convenience and I shall make other arrangements. We have put our hands to the plough and we are not looking back.

I sincerely trust that Otumfuo is enjoying good health.

I remain,

Otumfuo,

very sincerely and obediently,

J. B. DANQUAH [9]

**"Actually since my last personal interview with you on the Convention, matters have not advanced much except that we have appeared officially before the Joint Provincial Council and have placed our aims and objects before them, and have suggested that they should take a tip from you and leave the white man's Town Councils and Legislative Councils to himself, sending your "sons" to go and listen and report to you, and not vice versa."**

The writing above clearly shows that Danquah and the UGCC were not myopic nor at loggerheads with the Ashanti thereby keeping the independence struggle only to the colony or the south. He firstly informed the Asantehene about the formation and the vision of the UGCC before they could establish the UGCC in the Ashanti. This is because Ashanti was a different colony and the Asantehene was the traditional overlord. Not only did he meet the Asantehene, the UGCC officially met with the Joint Provincial Council which had sizeable number of chiefs and introduced to them the movement and their aims and objectives.

There again, there is a malicious propaganda to undermine the work of these forebears who sacrificed their lives for this nation that, due to their tribalistic mindset, they avoided Ewes. Again these are distortions to the history of this nation. Firstly, the ex-Serviceman, Mr. Tamakloe who bears an Ewe name and led the Ex-servicemen petition in 1948 was found to be a founding member of the UGCC. I would also want us to read a letter below that showed the work the leaders of the UGCC did in Keta which is an Ewe community.

KETA CONVENTION INAUGURAL RALLY

902/UC/48

9th December 1948

J. K. A. Quarshie, Esq ,

Honorary Secretary,

The Secretary's Office,

United Gold Coast Convention (Keta Branch)

Keta

Dear Sir,

I am thankful for your letter of the 6th December. To make it possible for us to attend the rally, your branch has first to be formally inaugurated. Kindly let me know whether this has been done. In future you may have to arrange for our attendance through headquarters at Saltpond.

**I am most happy to learn of the great work done at Keta to form the branch, and Mr Ako Adjei's reports have filled us all with high hopes of your progress in this important district.** In case you fix a date for your inauguration or rally, please make it sometime next year in January so as to ensure full attendance of the principal officers. [10]

Yours sincerely,

J.B. DANQUAH.

This Keta branch reveals the leaders of UGCC were never tribalistic against the Ewes. They were happy to spread the independence movement to such area. Mr. Ako Adjei had travelled to such areas and brought good news to his fellow UGCC executives. This good work done cannot be erased by the sheer anti-Danquah or anti-UGCC propaganda. In any way, it was Danquah in 1948 who first moved for the inclusion of the British Togoland (now Volta Region) to be part of Ghana long before the plebiscite of 1956 was done.

The UGCC communicated their mission to the Joint Provincial Council, the Governor and various recognised authorities on the land. They began to hold town hall meetings. Danquah having served as the secretary to the Youth Conference and Secretary of the Gold Coast and Ashanti already had a constituency to expand their network. In addition, due to the popularity of Danquah and Ofori Atta among cocoa farmers, they began to receive massive support. They began to travel the length and breadth of the country asking the masses to join their quest of independence. And barely a few months after coming into being, the impact of the Convention was carried on the wave of a riot which was popularly dubbed as The 1948 Riot.

CHAPTER 3

# 1948 RIOT AND ITS IMPACT ON THE BIRTH OF GHANA

The year 1948 will forever remain distinct and memorable in the political history of Ghana. The Gold Coast and Ashanti welcomed a new governor in the person of Sir Greasy. He arrived at the point when there was a rising concern of economic and political issues in the Gold Coast.

The Colony and Ashanti were facing the effect of the swollen shoot on cocoa trees. The government persuaded the farmers to cut down affected trees. But with turgid attitude from the farmers, the government passed laws to legally cut down the cocoa trees. About 2.7 million of the cocoa trees were cut down in 1947 alone. This number increased in 1948. This activity did not go down well with the farmers. They registered their rigorous dissatisfaction to the chiefs, DCs, the Joint Provincial Council and to the Legislative Council. Some believed the white man wanted to take over their cocoa business by starting to grow its own cocoa trees. The frustration of the farmers made the colonial government unpopular but the UGCC very attractive in the Cocoa growing areas because UGCC wanted to topple the colonial government.

It was not only swollen shoot that was an issue in the Gold Coast, especially in the Ashanti and the cocoa growing areas, but there also arose the issue of inflation. After the Second World War in 1945, there was a global crisis of inflation. This inflation took its special effect on the Gold Coast economy. The colony and Ashanti depended on foreign imported finished foods and goods like canned fish, milk, sugar, cotton goods, paraffin etc. These goods and services were imported into the country by the British, Syrian and Lebanese merchants. They formed a group after the World War Two called Association of West African Merchants (AWAM). During that time, there arose shortage of goods and services. This astronomically doubled or increased the prices of goods and services in the colony and Ashanti. On the contrary, the wages of workers remained low. This badly affected the lives of many ordinary people. Again due to the monopoly of these foreign nationals on the imports and exports of the economy, it was difficult for indigenous Africans or Ghanaians to thrive in establishing their business. This exacerbated the ill feeling against these foreign merchants.

Nii Kwabena Bonnie
a.k.a Boycott Hene

During that time, there arose a chief who served as the Osu Alata Mantse and also the Oyokohene in Techiman. He was a successful business man and a civic right activist. His name is Nii Kwabena Bonne. He stepped in as the voice of the masses to express the anger and dissatisfaction of the Ghanaian consumer. He persuaded the chiefs and people to back him to run a nationwide boycott against the goods and services of the Europeans and Syrians. He expressed "The whites and Syrians are tricking you out of your money". He therefore aroused them to fight and die for the liberty and freedom of their country. He added, "Strangers have come to the Gold Coast not for love of its people but only to take away the riches of the country by all possible means!" His activities gained nationwide support. He threatened that unless the British and Syrian reduced their prices, he would instigate a complete boycott of imported goods. He warned the government and the AWAM that his boycott would start on 24 January

1948.

The government might have underestimated his capacity and hence kept deaf ears to the warnings or the appeals of Nii Kwabena Bonne. So the strike began on 26 January. There were natives who punished fellow citizens who broke the boycott to purchase the foreign goods. This became ugly since the opportunists made money out of this. An example of such opportunists was Krobo Edusei who set his own court and fined people who disobeyed the boycott. The boycott became successful. So deep in February, the colonial secretary, Robert Scott called for a meeting with Nii Kwabena Bonne, Council of Chiefs, committee of AWAM, and the chamber of Commerce. The AWAM agreed to reduce the prices to 50 per cent. Nii Kwabena Bonne outlined the boycott would end on 28 February.

The situation of the increment of prices of goods and the boycott had aroused the anger and frustration of many people especially those in the south. Danquah and Nkrumah were also touring the nation with their message of self-governance. Even though Nii Kwabena Bonne did not agree to the aims and objectives of the UGCC, and so did not support them, his boycott campaign became a catalyst for the success for Danquah and Nkrumah on the grounds that they had a common enemy, the white man. The youth who rallied behind Bonne supported the movement of the UGCC.

As if the colonist had well calculated, or by the act of divinity, just when the boycott was about being lifted, the ex-servicemen who fought for the British against Japan in 1945 were planning to register their protest of dissatisfaction. They had been promised rewards and so expected some fortunes after their victory. But upon returning home, nothing had come from the ends of the government to them. This period became a climax moment for them to march to the governor to present their petition.

Before sending their petition to the governor, they organised a large meeting which was chaired by Danquah. In the meeting he and Nkrumah addressed these ex-servicemen. Their initial scheduled date for the protest was 23 February but was postponed to 28 February. In his autobiography, Dr. Nkrumah revealed that he had just returned to the country since he left for overseas for about twelve years. He revealed he did not know Nii Kwabena. It was the UGCC who took him to the ex-servicemen rally. According to Nkrumah he was given the opportunity to speak. After he spoke, Danquah expressed his joy that Nkrumah and Ako Adjei, soon after their return from England and America, had joined in the struggle with him, and that he was happy in the thought that if he passed away there would be others like Nkrumah and Ako Adjei to carry on. This was misconstrued by Nkrumah in his Autobiography that Danquah told the masses that "if all the leaders of the UGCC fail them Kwame Nkrumah will never fail them". Danquah asked Nkrumah to rectify the error.

When the 28 February arrived, the European and Syrian merchants had not reduced the prices of goods as promised. The ex-servicemen took their march as arranged. The government had sent troops and police on alert. There were reports of influx of rowdy elements in the procession. As to whether that was calculated or accidental, only the leaders of the ex-servicemen knew. The procession was originally intended to march to the Secretariat offices but the ex-servicemen turned to the Christiansburg Castle, the residence of the Governor. They were opposed and shot by police superintendent Collin Imray. As a result of the shooting, Sergeant Adjetey, Corporal Attipoe and Private Odartey Lamptey died.

The marchers returned in fury and the news of the shooting sparked off an unprecedented riot that had an impact on Gold Coast and according to David Rooney the whole of Africa. The foreign firms were broken into and goods looted. The refusal of price drop with these shootings provoked the anger and led to the riots. Cars were burned. The mobbers annexed the Usher fort and released the prisoners. The police tried to calm activities but it was beyond them. The colonial government had to send security forces from Nigeria to come and help curb the situation. The riots spread to places such as Kumasi, Nsawam, Suhum, Koforidua and other parts of Ghana. More people died, about 29 in number. Over 200 people were injured and about £2 million worth of goods were destroyed.

While the shooting and looting were going on, Danquah and

Nkrumah attended a Convention meeting at Saltpond when a telephone message came from Akufo-Addo that Accra was in serious chaos. The two decided to return to Accra. The working committee of the Convention held a meeting at Akufo-Addo's house. They decided to send a cablegram to the Secretary to the Colonies in England. They decided to also send copies to UN, and other world media. Danquah was to send their request to the Secretary to the Colonies while Nkrumah would send copy to the international bodies.

**"Unless Colonial Government is changed and new government of the people and their Chiefs installed at centre immediately, outraged masses now completely out of control with strikes threatened in Police quarters, and rank and file Police indifferent to orders of officers will continue and result in worse violent and irresponsible acts by uncontrolled people.**

**"Working Committee United Gold Coast Convention declare prepared and ready to take over interim government.**

**"We ask in name of oppressed, inarticulate, misruled and misgoverned people and their Chiefs that Special Commissioner be sent out immediately to hand over Government to Interim Government of Chiefs and people and to witness immediate calling of Constituent Assembly**

**"Governor Creasy unfortunate inheritor of aftermath of Governor Alan Burns' oppressive and window-dressing administration be recalled and relieved of his onerous and impossible burden.**

**"We speak in name of inherent residual sovereignty in Chiefs and people in free partnership with British Commonwealth for our country to be saved from inept and incapable Government indifferent to sufferings of governed.**

**"Souls of Gold Coast men slaughtered in cold blood upon Castle Road cry out for vindication in cause of freedom and liberty.**

**"Firing by police and military going on this morning.**

**"Let King and Parliament act without delay in this direst hour of Gold Coast people and their Chiefs. "God save the King and Floreat United Gold Coast." [1]**

The summary of Danquah's telegram was that they wanted a recall of the governor or the removal of the governor from his post. And government should be handed over to the UGCC leaders immediately so that they would call for a constituent assembly, and a subsequent demand of full self-government. This bold assertion exposes all the propaganda that has been made against the leaders of the UGCC that the organisation was not founded for independence and that they wanted independence slowly or later.

They decided that Nkrumah should copy to the world press. These are some of the agencies Nkrumah sent the telegram. Secretary General United Nations, William Gallacher MP House of Commons London, the New African London, *Pan African New Agency, The New York Times; Editor of The Daily Worker, London;* and the *Moscow New Times*; Editor WASU Magazine London and Associated Negro Press, Chicago.

Below is the telegram Nkrumah sent.

**Secretary of State Colonies                    London**

**After permitting peaceful demonstration of unarmed ex-servicemen  police without provocation  fired on them several   killed    Many wounded. Police and political officers unable to protect   life and property. Civil authorities unable   to   Control situation appealed to certain civilians who are officers of the United Gold Coast Convention to restore order. Many shops in commercial areas looted UAC Central State burned down. People demand Self-Government immediately. Recall Governor Send Commission   supervise   formation   constituent Assembly Urgent.**

**Kwame Nkrumah**

**General Secretary**

## UGCC

### Saltpond Gold Coast[2]

The two contrasting revelations with Nkrumah's writ is that firstly it is not a vivid copy of Danquah's telegram. Secondly, he was asked to send to the world press but not the Secretary of State of the Colonies. Sending to the Secretary of State another telegram clearly suggests Nkrumah wanted to dissociate from Danquah's telegram and most clearly Nkrumah was not as daring as Danquah was. For instance, Danquah called for immediate interim government and that the UGCC were ready to take up that government for a full self-government. Danquah was specific; he declared the current government as incompetent and that ~~has~~ had led to the disturbances. Nkrumah's statement 'Civil authorities unable to Control situation appealed to certain civilians who are officers of the United Gold Coast Convention to restore order' reveals his fear and humility against the colonial government.   As to why he did that he narrated it in his autobiography that Danquah was been too wordy.

**'I felt that a simply worded telegram to the point was all that was necessary to convey what we wished to say, but Danquah thought otherwise. In the end two telegrams were dispatched, a long one drafted by Danquah and a short one drafted by myself.'[3]**

For the first time in the history of the British colonial government, the riot and the subsequent actions of the convention caused a certain fear in them. The government crumpled. The colonial government out of panic described the leaders of the convention as a clique and selfish. But this did not bother Danquah and the UGCC. He urged the Chiefs and people of Gold Coast to stand for self-government. After issuing a letter demanding self-governance to the Colonial Government, he  sent a clarion call to the people of Gold Coast entitled **"The hour of Liberation has Struck"** on 1st March, 1948. Let us read Danquah's address to the people.

Nananom and People,

In the name of United Gold Coast I address you.

After the massacre in cold blood of unarmed Ex-servicemen

on Saturday; after the wholesale and unchecked looting of merchandise and the destruction of life and property on both Saturday and Sunday; after witnessing the utter failure of governmental forces to take effective counter measures to stop the widespread deterioration of authority, the Working Committee of the United Gold Coast Convention came to the imperative and inevitable conclusion that there had been a complete break-down of Civil Government at the centre and that, in order that the deep seated economic and political causes which gave rise to such lawlessness should once and for all be removed, a change in the constitution of Government at the centre was the best constitutional solution.

Accordingly, on Sunday afternoon, the Working Committee of the United Gold Coast Convention despatched to the Secretary of State a telegram in which the facts of Saturday and Sunday were set out, and the economic and political causes, with the social consequences thereof, were analysed and docketed.

We asked in the telegram that His Excellency the Governor, Sir Gerald Creasy, unfortunate inheritor of the window-dressing administration of Sir Alan Burns, be relieved of his onerous burden. We asked for the despatch of a Special Commissioner to set up an interim Government and to supervise the bringing into being of a Constituent Assembly of Chiefs and people.

We stated that the Convention was prepared and ready to shoulder the burden of such interim Government until the Constituent Assembly of Chiefs and people should determine the form of Government under which they would live.....

In His Excellency's broadcast on Monday night we were daubed as "a clique" and accused as persons "working for their own selfish ends".

These are phrases with which we all are familiar. We do not ask for the judgement of our country and countrymen. We know what that judgment is. We do not ask for the repose of their confidence in us. We know they are not in doubt as to our intentions. Our one and only concern is liberation of our country from the old thraldom imposed by a treaty, chiefly one-sided, and altogether misapplied or unapplied.

The treaty was made exactly 104 years ago, on March 6, 1844. In effect we ask for a freely negotiated Bond of 1948, a constitution which will regulate the affairs between us and Britain in the daylight of freedom.

"It is said that the Standing Committee of the Joint Provincial Council and the Ga Native Authority have pledged their loyalty to His Majesty the King.

We, too in our telegram concluded thus: "God save the King. Floreat, United Gold Coast."

It is stated that the Joint Provincial Council, consisting of twelve Paramount Chiefs and the Ga Native Authority, praised the Government for what recently was done. We do not and cannot pretend to agree with that form of praise.

Nananom and People, it is our view that the hour of liberation has struck. Our economic strangulation has been recently accentuated for witness by all the world in the boycott of imported goods which Nii Kwabena Bonne I I I, kept going for no less than thirty-three days.

Our political ineffectiveness is daily brought to our own consciousness by the incapacity of the newly constituted Legislature to assemble even when Accra, our chief metropolis, bums; even when property is destroyed; even when life is freely taken. The Governor has promised us an enquiry. We welcome the inquiry provided it is not a Martindale.

Inheritors of Ghana's ancient Kingdom, my Message as you see, is not moved by fear. Aggrey blotted fear from our Dictionary. "Eagle fly! For thou art not a chick."

Threats in the midst of national danger are part of the danger. In this crusade, there is only one guarantee I can give you. I helped in drafting the "Memorandum of Things to Change in the Gold Coast" for the Joint Provincial Council. I helped in drafting the Memorandum upon which the present Constitution, except in one vital aspect, is largely based. I drafted it for the Provincial Council and the Ashanti Confederacy Council.

This is the mood in which we work, the mood of King Ghartey IV of Winneba, President of the Fanti Confederacy: "Be constitutional". I did not draft those Memoranda for my own selfish ends.

In this crusade the Working Committee will act constitutionally but will not fear to act.[4]

In spite of the fact that the riot made the UGCC and their leaders very popular, the Chiefs and Traditional leaders on the land refused to stand with the leaders of the Convention for independence but rather chose to show solidarity to the colonial government. Right after the riot, The Joint Provincial Council and the Ga Native Authority praised the Government for what it did. This did not go down well with Danquah, and he did not mince words in his address *The hour of Liberation has struck* by saying **"We do not and cannot pretend to agree with that form of praise."**

Danquah's call for the removal of the governor for the UGCC to assume an interim government to lead the nation into a full self-governance coupled with Nkrumah's letters to the supposed communist allies did not go down well with the governor. With the riot bringing him and the colonial government on their knees, he had gotten a reason to revenge on the leaders of the UGCC. He issued the letter of detention to Danquah and the rest of the leaders on 11 March. So the leaders of the UGCC were arrested on the 12 March and were first taken to Kumasi Prison. Below is a copy of the letter that was issued to arrest the six leaders of the Convention.

'The Removal (F. N. K. Nkrumah) Order, 1948 '. Dated 12th March, 1948, and signed by the then Governor, Sir Gerald Creasy, this read as follows:

'WHEREAS I am satisfied with respect to FRANCIS NWIA

KOFIE NKRUMAH, alias F. N. KWAME NKRUMAH, that it is expedient for securing the public safety and the maintenance of public order to make a Removal Order against him under the provisions of regulation 29 of the Emergency (General) Regulations, 1948 (inserted in such Regulations by the Emergency (General) (Amendment) (No. 2) Regulations, 1948 : Now in exercise of the powers conferred upon me by the said regulation 29 of the above Regulations, and in pursuance of such regulation, I DO HEREBY MAKE THIS ORDER, and direct that the said FRANCIS NWIA KOFIE NKRUMAH, alias F. N. KWAME NKRUMAH shall be apprehended and detained and that he shall be removed in custody, as soon as may be, to such place in the Gold Coast as I shall hereafter appoint by directions under my hand. AND I DO HEREBY FURTHER ORDER and require that the said FRANCIS NWIA KOFIE NKRUMAH, alias F. N. KWAME NKRUMAH, from the time of his removal to the place to be appointed by me, and so long as this Order continues in operation, shall at all times-

(a) remain and live in, and not leave or be absent from, the place to be so appointed by me;

(b) comply in all respects with such directions and requirements as I may issue at any time. This Order may be cited as the Removal (F. N. K. NKRUMAH) Order, 1948, and shall come into operation on 12th day of March, 1948.'

Gerald Creasy

Governor [5]

The same letter was issued to Danquah, Akufo-Addo, Paa Willie, Ako Adjei and Obetsebi Lamptey. A couple of days after their arrest, the governor issued and published his charges against the leaders of the Convention. It read:

**Brief Narrative of Events from The 17th February, 1948 to The 13th March, 1948**

The government stated,

**'There is a direct connection between the riots of the 28th-29th**

**February in Accra and the restriction imposed on the freedom of action of six members of the United Gold Coast Convention: Dr. J.B. Danquah, Dr. Kwame Nkrumah, Mr. William Ofori Atta, Mr. Akufo Addo, Mr. Ako Adjei and Mr. Obetsebi-Lamptey. The riots cannot be regarded as isolated incidents which developed because of the shooting at Christiansborg cross-roads. They have a history and they have a sequel.'** [6]

In the narrative, the government revealed that the posters that were used to mobilize the ex-servicemen were printed at the Ausco Press, which worked for the Convention which was known in Accra as "Convention Hall".

Truthfully, the government revealed that the ex-servicemen rally which occurred on the 20th February at the Palladium Cinema was chaired by Danquah. And out of the 9000 people that attended, only 1300 were ex-servicemen or members. Among the speakers of the occasion were Danquah, Nkrumah, Ako Adjei, Mr. Tamakloe and Mr. Laryea. And from the government only Tamakloe and Laryea were ex-servicemen. The rest of the speakers as we know were from the Convention. **He questioned what the convention leaders were doing in an Ex-servicemen meeting if not to incite them. He inferred that the thousands of the attendance about 7300 were Convention members or sympathisers. He accused the UGCC leaders for mobilising people to attend the ex-servicemen meeting.**

The government stated: "The proposal for a march to the Castle was soon known in Kibi. On the 26th February, a meeting of the Executive Committee of the Akim Abuakwa Farmers' Union was held at Kibi under the chairmanship of Mr. William Ofori Atta. Dr. J. B. Danquah also was present. The intention of the ex-servicemen to march to the Castle was discussed and, as a result of an interview with the Secretary of the Ex-Servicemen's Union, it was suggested that such a march might be supported by the Farmers' Union as "sufficient to weaken the Government". This, according to the government, was agreed by the ex-servicemen secretary Mr. Tamakloe.

**The Government in addition addressed Nkrumah as a communist who bore a communist who possessed a Communist Party**

**membership card (No. 57565).**

The government revealed that there was a mass meeting that was held on the 27th February by the Convention at the Palladium Cinema, Accra. In attendance of this meeting were the ex-servicemen. Mr. Akufo Addo, Mr. Obetsebi-Lamptey, Mr. William Ofori Atta and Dr. Danquah addressed the meeting. According to the government, the Ex-Servicemen present were exhorted to parade at the old Polo Ground at 1 p.m. on the following day, when they would be given further instructions.

The government referred to Danquah's demand for independence and by writing this: "On the 29th February, making its own judgement of events, the United Gold Coast Convention telegraphed the Secretary of State. They stated, among other things:

**"Civil Government Gold Coast broken down" ..."Unless Colonial Government is changed and new Government of the people and chiefs installed at the centre immediately, conduct of masses now completely out of control with strikes threatened in Police quarters and rank and file, Police indifferent to orders of officers will continue and result in worse violent and irresponsible acts by uncontrolled people. Working Committee United Gold Coast Convention declare they are prepared and ready to take interim Government".**

The Government continued, **"On the 1st of March the situation in Accra was under control but disturbances and looting were breaking out in other parts of the country such as Kibi, Suhum, Koforidua, Nsawam and Akuse. Further examination of the activities of the Working Committee of the United Gold Coast Convention showed additional links with the communist organization overseas. Investigation also showed that the ends of the Working Committee, while ostensibly for the attainment of self-government by constitutional means, were in fact revolutionary; they included plans for a more widespread and comprehensive disturbance of the peace than had been indicated or could be understood from the Convention's telegram to the Secretary of State or even from Dr. Danquah's manifesto of the 1st March**

**addressed to the chiefs which was published in the Press under the title "The Hour of Liberation Has Struck". Investigation also showed a danger of forms of terrorism, quite alien to the spirit of this country and fortunately not hitherto employed. These included assassination."**

From the government's publication, they arrested the leaders of the UGCC because they masterminded the act to weaken the government.

On their way to prison, Danquah and Ako Adjei went with their typewriters. That should inform us how confident and ready they were to fight with their pen. In prison Danquah responded to the charges of the government. On a six-page document on accusation against the BIG SIX, Danquah answered and defended the Convention on every point the Colonial Government raised. His confidence and reasoning to the Governor were amazing. On the charges against Nkrumah for being a communist, Danquah came to the rescue of Nkrumah by claiming that the Government's accusation was biased and insubstantial. This is what he had to say, **'I must confess also that I do not consider mere membership of the Communist Party to be a crime under any law in the Gold Coast or Great Britain. Two Communist members, Mr. Gallacher and Mr. Piratin, sit in the House of Commons.'**[7]

In his conclusion, this is what Danquah wrote to the colonial government.

> "For my part I stand as firmly as ever before by the United Gold Coast Convention and its policy. And I pray that their aims and objects, that the control and direction of Government shall by all legitimate and constitutional means, pass, at the earliest possible time, into the hands of the people and their Chiefs, shall have an opportunity of being realized so as to ensure that the people directly charged with the administration of Government should directly be responsible to the people with power in the people to change the personnel of Government when they feel that the Government or Cabinet of the day had failed them, or served its time. That constitutional goal I am pledged to pursue, without flinching, and **I trust Christian charity, if nothing**

**else, will give my colleagues and myself credit for not hiding our head under a bush. I am certain that when the foundation of life in this country is examined, it shall be found necessary to reconstitute it in a way that the sufferings and the privations of the people will be the first and paramount object of their Government at all times,** and the grievances of the people such as those recently expressed in the blind form of a boycott, and settled amicably in a way which even now, has not adequately assuaged their hurt, will stand a better chance of being critically examined and constructively readjusted by a parliament or legislature elected by the people direct, and responsible to the people direct. No doubt, that the paternal Colonial system of Government has served its day truly and well  but I am not happy with its modern substitute of partnership, which is a halfway house to limited liability joint stock company system, and is not a true government. Sell-government within the Commonwealth is the only solution to my mind.[8]

When Danquah got an opportunity to travel to London soon after the riot, he queried the Secretary of State, Mr. Creech Jones on their accusation of communism. The Secretary told him, his government was under manipulation to score a political point. In spite of their fight for Ghana, many writers and political analysts undermine the efforts the leaders of the Convention played at such a critical moment in Ghana's political history.

The colonial government had the Chiefs and the nominated members of the Legislative Assembly rendering their uncompromising loyalty to its side. One of the prominent chiefs, Nana Tsibu Daaku, Omanhene of Asin Atandansu ridiculed Danquah and the compatriots by asking "Who are the people?" little did he or anyone know that nature will have its own course. The arrest awoke the unflinching support of the youth and the women of the land especially the market women. The Aborigines Rights Protection Society also supported the Six. The arrest sparked agitation in students who precipitated riots in schools. One of such schools was Achimota. These students were dismissed from school. A young man called Kwasi Plange who was a teacher at St Augustine was dismissed for demonstrating against the government. In Kumasi Prison, Krobo Edusei mobilized a number of youth to break into the prison to release the six. When the government learned about that, they relocated them to Northern Protectorate at separate places.

The leaders did not only gain a nationwide support in the Gold Coast alone, but had solidarity from people overseas. For instance, people in the UK began to protest for their release. Gold Coast students in Britain sent a protest letter to the British Prime Minister and M.Ps to release the Convention leaders and set an enquiry commission to investigate the riot. The West Africans in London also protested for the same course. The West African Students in Oxford also sent protest for the release of the Convention leaders. When the colonial office could not resist the numerous protests against the detention of these Convention leaders, it finally announced in British parliament that a Commission of Enquiry had been appointed to go to the Gold Coast to make enquiry and recommendations to the Secretary of State for the colonies. The nominated chairman for this commission was Mr. Aiken Watson, K.C with Dr. Keith A. H. Murray, Rector of Lincoln College, Oxford and Mr. A. Dalgleish, a Trade Unionist as a member. Their secretary was E.G.G Hanrott from the Colonial Office. They left Britain for Gold Coast and arrived on the 6 and 7th April 1948. They swore an oath before the Acting Supreme Court Justice on the 8th April and commenced their work on the 9th April 1948.

While at Kumasi Prison they held a number of meetings concerning the independent nation yet to be born. According to Danquah it was at the Kumasi Prison that they decided the name to adopt for the independence and the name they chose was Ghana. They also discussed the colours of the national flag which is the Red, Gold and Green. They also decided whether to use Fatherland or Motherland for literature and they chose Motherland. This is not denied by Nkrumah as he puts it this way.

> "While we were in the prison we held several meetings
> among ourselves to discuss the problem that might face us if

a Commission of Enquiry were appointed to look into the causes for the recent disturbances. **We even went so far as to draw up plans for a shadow cabinet and a future constitution for the Gold Coast**, if and when the Burns Constitution was thrown overboard." [9]

These discussions were healthy. On the other side, it was at Kumasi prison that they found out that Nkrumah had a communist card in his possession which the government would use as allegation that they wanted to establish a communist nation. According to Danquah, it was there that Nkrumah confided in him that he never completed his PhD. This was likely to stir a certain mistrust against Nkrumah.

After about a month they were flown from the Northern Territories to Accra to appear before the enquiry Commission. In Accra also, they were detained in a hotel and made to appear before the commission individually.

The mission of the Watson Enquiry Commission was clear, **"to enquire into and report on the recent disturbances in the Gold Coast and their underlying causes; and to make recommendations on any matter arising from their enquiry."** The women hearing the charge of communism and not understanding its meaning, since it was their first time of hearing such a word, put on red headgear to rally behind these leaders. It was this massive support from the masses that earned the arrested leaders of the Convention a title as the **Big Six**. This honour was indirectly replying to the question of Nana Tsibu asked 'who are the people?', that these were the Big Six fathers who stood for the voiceless, who suffered for the atrocities of the masses. The ordinary masses came to the conviction that these were the leaders they could count the future of the country on hence the title the Big Six.

It is unfortunate that for propaganda and political reason, some people undermine the efforts and the toil of the six leaders. The legitimate question they fail to ask and answer is that why wasn't Nii Kwabena Bonne arrested? Why was the secretary of the ex-servicemen Tamakloe who led the protest not arrested? Why was none of the people involved in any of the riot arrested? This is because fathers suffer for the wrongs of their children. They were arrested because the government understood that these UGCC men had assumed leadership role and as such were held responsible for the wrongful acts of their people. When the youth and women realized they could believe these men to liberate them from the European rule, they rightly hailed them as their **Big Six** fathers of the land. Therefore it was not the UGCC who gave themselves that name, neither was it a single person but the masses. This title became official as it was published in the media and other official summons. In his autobiography, Nkrumah rightly admitted that the detained Convention leaders were referred to as the Big Six. He wrote, **'The 'Big Six', as we came to be known, referred to Danquah, Ofori Atta, Akufo Addo, Ako Adjei, Obetsebi Lamptey and myself '[10]**

Let me use this opportunity to share briefly with you the biography of the six men who were arrested and later came to be honoured as the Big Six.

## J.B Danquah

He was the leader of the independence movement from 1947 until 1951 when Nkrumah won a landslide victory to become the leader of Government Business and as such the leader of the independence Movement. He was largely celebrated in the Gold Coast and Ashanti from the 30s to the end of the 40s when Nkrumah dominated the political scene. He was born on 21 December 1895 to a man called Yaw Boakye Danquah at Bepong in Kwawu. He began his primary education with the Basel Mission at Kyebi. After Standard three, He continued to Basel Grammar school. He had no secondary education. He studied all by himself after basic education. He worked as a clerk in 1913. He sat for the Civil Service Examination and passed in 1914. He served as a clerk to the Supreme Court. He also worked as secretary to the Omanhene Tribunal in Kyebi. In 1916 he organized the Akyem Abuakwa Scholars Union and became its secretary. He sat for the London Matriculation exams and failed twice before passing in 1922. He went to Britain and in 1925, he passed the B.A Honours course in Philosophy. He passed the LLB in 1926 at the Inner Temple. That same year he completed his law exams and was called to the Bar. He earned his PhD in 1927. With regard to his working experience, he was the secretary of the Gold Coast and Ashanti delegation to London in 1934. He was a member of the Legislative Assembly during the year of riot. He was one of the frontiers who fought for the establishment of the University of Ghana. In 1936 he wrote a poem entitled, The Woman I love and the last stanza reads as follows:

'I love a woman,

A black woman

Golden is her personal name,

Guinea's Golden Lady,

And christened by her God-fathers

But from birth

GHANA.'


## Kwame Nkrumah


He was born in September 1909 at Nkroful, his hometown. He attended the half Assini Catholic Mission School where he ended up being a pupil teacher. He attended Government Training College in Accra by the recommendation of Rev. A.G Fraser. In 1928, this school became part of Achimota school which gave Nkrumah better opportunity. In 1935, he left for United States to further his education. He enrolled in Lincoln University in Pennsylvania and obtained B.A degree in Economics and Sociology. Later he studied Theology in the same school and graduated in 1942. In 1943, he earned M.A in philosophy and MSc in Education from the University of Pennsylvania. In US, he was a lay preacher who sometimes survived on the little honorarium he gained in preaching. He rose to be a teaching assistant and lecturer. He left US for Britain in 1945. In UK he joined Pan African movements. He served as the secretary of the West African Students Union. He arrived in Gold Coast in December 1947 to serve as the UGCC General Secretary. He became the leader of the independence movement when he won the 1951 elections.

## Emmanuel Obetsebi-Lamptey

He was born on the 26 April 1902. He was known in private life as Odarkwee. He got the name Obetsebi from a small town near Accra where he was born. He went to Accra Wesleyan School. He also attended Kumasi Government Boys' School and the Accra Royal School. After school, he was employed by A.J Ocansey as a shorthand typist. In 1923, he passed the examination to enter the Junior Civil Service. He served as Second Division Clerk in the Customs and Excise Department. He left for UK to go and study law. He had no secondary or post primary education like Danquah. With strong determination, he studied books to educate himself. He entered the law school and graduated with LLB in 1939 and called to the Bar at the Inner Temple in the same year. In 1945, He returned to the Gold Coast to practice Law. When he arrived, he participated in politics. He was elected to the Legislative Council for the Accra Municipal.

## William Ofori Atta

William Ofori Atta popularly known as Paa Willie was born in 1910 into a wealthy home. His father was the paramount chief of Akyem Abuakwa. He attended Government School at Kyebi. From there he went to Mfantsipim. After Mfantsipim, he attended Achimota School where he passed for his O and A levels respectively. He passed the London Intermediate Arts examination. He went to Queen's College, Cambridge, where he studied Economics. He also attended London School of Economics and Political Science working for an M.Sc. degree in Economics but was unable to complete due to the war. He returned to Ghana where he became a Master at Achimota College. He inspired a lot of the students on patriotic and nationalist views. He was very critical of the colonial system and was a black activist. It is believed when an army annexed the western compound of Achimota, Paa Willie and his colleague A.L Adu were asked to evacuate their bungalow for Europeans to occupy. This he defied and said did not fit into the vision of the school which was to knit the values of whites and blacks and that he would rather move to live in Kyebi than to resettle in the junior staff bungalow. He won and stayed in his bungalow. In 1943, he left Achimota to head the Abuakwa State College which was established by his father. He is a founding member of the UGCC.


## Edward Akufo-Addo

Akufo-Addo was born in 1906 and is from Akropong. He was not from a wealthy home as his critics touted him. His parents died in his early years so he had to struggle in life to succeed. He attended Presbyterian Schools. He attended Presbyterian Training College in Akropong-Akuapem where he was trained as a teacher. He also studied a bit of Theology.  After teaching for a while, he studied for the London Matriculation Examinations. He had the opportunity to be enrolled in Achimota where he passed the Intermediate Examination in Arts. He gained scholarship to study in Oxford due to his excellence in Mathematics. He read Mathematical Moderations and Philosophy, Politics and Economics at St. Peters Hall, Oxford. He studied Law and was called to the Bar in 1940. He returned to the Gold Coast in 1941 and worked as a lawyer. As a lawyer, he served his pupillage under Mr. Ofei Awere. Akufo Addo took over the firm when Mr. Awere became Omanhene of Akwapem.  He rose to become one of the best lawyers in Gold Coast.


## Ako-Adjei

He was born on 17 June 1916. He came from a very humble background. His parents were Ga from Labadi but they lived in Akyem Abuakwa to farm. He began school at Busoso Railway Station Presbyterian School and continued at Labadi Presbyterian Junior School and completed in 1933 at standard six. He went to Accra Academy. In 1936, he sat for the Cambridge School Certificate examination and passed it. He worked as a teacher, and also as a second Division Clerk in the Secretariat. As a student, he served under Azikiwe's paper 'The Morning Post'. His earnest service brought him into favour with Azikiwe who helped Ako Adjei to get a scholarship to study in US. He arrived at Lincoln University in January 1939. It was there he met Nkrumah. He graduated in 1942. In 1943, he gained MSc. He left for

Britain in 1944 to study Law. He was called to the Bar in January 1947 at the Inner Temple. He returned to Ghana in May 1947. He connected with Danquah in the very week he arrived in Gold Coast. Danquah briefed him about the Gold Coast political situation and the founding of the new political party UGCC which he agreed to join.

To make their defence before the commission, the UGCC hired a British lawyer by name Dingle Foot. The Big Six each had their turn to appear before the commission for evidence. The commission also engaged other Ghanaians about their worries. They travelled to a number of remote places in the Gold Coast. They went to the market especially to the *Markola* women. They asked the public to send memorandums to the commission. They also asked the Big Six to send their separate memorandum. A number of people aside the Big Six also appeared before the commission. During and after the enquiry, the women put on red gear in defiance to the Colonial Government and in support of the Big Six.

The Big Six made their defence for independence before the enquiry commission and it appears they made a good case. So on the 14th April 1948, after hearing Danquah's evidence and defence for Self-Government, the chairman of the Commission, Mr. Aikens Watson said to Danquah: **"Since you are celebrated as a constitution maker, will you produce tomorrow for the Commission a scheme for a self-governing Gold Coast?"** This Danquah happily and speedily did in 24 hours. Below is a portion of the draft constitution Danquah presented to the Commission.

## A BASIC CONSTITUTION FOR GHANALAND

15 April 1948

> IT IS NOT the policy of the United Gold Coast Convention for the actual form of the constitution for the new Gold Coast to be the work of any one, the same being a function properly performed by a Constituent Assembly. In view, however, of the request by Mr. A. Aiken Watson, Chairman of the Commission of Enquiry into recent Disturbances and their Underlying Causes, that I should provide him with the draft of a constitution, I readily submit the following outline.

2. The main characteristic of the constitution will be to blend the old with the new, chieftaincy with democracy, the inherited culture with progressive modernism.

3. I conceive that the first act of the constitution-making body will be to máke a clear break away from the memories of the days of exploitation and imperialism, and **the colonial adjective Gold Coast will give way to the substantive name of the people and country, Ghana and Ghanaland**. The Colony will become South Ghana, Ashanti will remain Ashanti, and the Northern Territories, which were made part of the Gold Coast by the enterprise of George Ekem Ferguson of Anomabu, will become either Fergusonia or North Ghana.

4. By agreement with the French in which the good offices of the United Kingdom Government will be sought in consideration for military and air bases, those parts of French Togoland and French Ivory Coast which belong ethnologically to the tribes of Ashanti, Nzima, Aowin and Eweland, will become part of Ghanaland.[11]

In addition to these points Danquah suggested a Bicameral Parliament that is a house of two chambers, a senate of Chiefs to consist of 50 members and a House of Representatives of 100 to 120 elected people. The entire country was to be governed with 12 ministers under a Governor-General and a Prime Minister. According to Danquah, Watson reply to this draft was that it would take ten years to manifest but Danquah in his joy said this was achieved in nine years. Truthfully speaking but for the political division that emerged, Ghana would have achieved that in far less years.

As I stated earlier, at the Kumasi prison, the Big Six had decided the new name to adopt for independence and Nkrumah's writing validated that. It was not surprising for Danquah to begin by stating that the name Gold Coast shall give way for the substantive name Ghana. The name Ghana was so dear to Danquah that he had publicly persuaded his compatriots to accept it as the new name for independent Gold Coast. He strongly believed that the Gold Coast was a descent of

Ancient Ghana Empire. He had explained in other presentations that the original name was Kana or Akana kingdom which was distorted by the Arabs to become Ghana. The first Clerk of Parliament at Independence, K.B Ayensu and his successor S.N Darkwa credited the name Ghana to Danquah in their publication *'The Evolution of Parliament in Ghana'* they stated **'It is not unusual for a child to be found a name before it is born. J.B Danquah had consistently espoused the name Ghana for the nation to be.**[12] In 1956, Nkrumah lastly revealed that Ghana shall be the new name for the Gold Coast at independence.

Again Danquah stated the expected geographical size by including the colonies which were not part of the Gold Coast such as Ashanti and the Northern Territories. In addition, he made it clear that they would negotiate to include the other Ghanaian ethnic groups in Cote D'Ivoire and Togo to be part of the new Ghana. That is how far sighted they were. So British Togoland (Volta Region) joining Ghana had already been envisioned as far back as 1948 by the leaders of the UGCC.

The leaders of the Convention were released. And the fame of them spread throughout the Colony, Ashanti and the Northern Protectorates. The masses were humbled by how they had stood before the trials of the white man in the defence of the nation. They had suffered or been charged for crimes committed by the others. So they could rely on them as their heroes. That is where the name Big Six emerged from. They remain the "Big Six" fathers of the independence movement of Ghana hence the founding fathers of the nation. Many people joined the movement of the Convention for the independence struggle. More branches were sooner opened in all the colonies. It is believed that the UGCC grew about 25 times after the riot. They established about 250 branches soon after the riot. Prior to that, the Convention had barely 13 branches.

After their release the governor invited Danquah and a number of people to London for an African Conference. Danquah sent a letter to the Asantehene, Otumfuor, Nana Sir Agyeman Prempeh II. Danquah wanted to kill two birds with one stone. He wrote to the Asantehene to inform him about this invitation to London. He also persuaded the King to unite with Gold Coast as one colony. Danquah had officially included

Asante in Gold Coast governance in the drafted constitution and he would need the Asantehene to stand with them on self-governance. The letter is as follows:

**SELF-GOVERNMENT IS COMING SOON**

181/UC/48                                                           7th July, 1948

Otumfuo Sir Osei Agyeman Prempeh II,

K.B.E., Asantehene, Manhyia,

Kumasi.

Dear Nana,

I have not had the honour of hearing from you since my last visit to Kumasi, but as matters are moving so swiftly it occurs to me that a letter from me will not go amiss.

First of all, I should like to intimate that Honourable B. D. Addai and myself have been invited by Government to attend the Pan-African Phytosanitary Conference in London. We leave Accra by air on July 30, and return on or about 6th August. I thought it wise to accept the invitation, not because I think there is anything new to be said at the Conference which is not already known to us from Tafo or told the Watson Commission, but because I think it timely[13] that we in the Colony should register our power (i.e. knowledge) over them in England.

In the past the Government had held such Conferences without us, in the belief that we Africans had not the men to meet their men. Now the events of the last few months have compelled them to show us much greater respect. I for that reason alone believe that we should not let the opportunity pass without registering our achievement of a new power or right - the right to be heard in all matters affecting our interests.

I believe the last cocoa Conference in London attended by any African was in 1924 when Mr. E. C. Quist, and Mr. J. C. Glover and Mr. E. K. Adisi were sent by the Chiefs of the

Colony to represent the country and the farmers. I am glad that this time Ashanti is included. Last year there was a similar Conference on Cocoa and we were neither told about it nor even consulted. This time things have changed. It is in our country's greater interest that Addai and I should attend.

As regards the United Gold Coast Convention, I was very happy to learn of your declaration in the Confederacy Council that you had no objection to the Convention as such except that you have not been made sufficiently familiar with our policy. As to that, our policy is to seek persistently for self-government: "The direction and control of Government shall as early as possible pass into the hands of the people and their Chiefs."

I hear that certain political officers are going round telling the Chiefs that the Convention plans to take power away from the Chiefs. I am not afraid of this kind of propaganda. Our own Chiefs are intelligent enough to see through it at once. If there is to be self-government, who will be the first to lose? Surely that type of political officer. So it is not surprising if he tries to get people to believe that if the Convention succeeds in its policy it will be bad for the Chiefs. The position is rather that it is, at the present time, very bad for the Chiefs and their people, and we of the Convention believe that the time has arrived for the bad things to be replaced by a good thing - self-government.

**There is one thing of which Nana must be well aware. Already the Government has accepted the position that self-government must come within our own time, within say the next five years. Only they think they should gradualise its coming for as long as they can. But everybody can see that God is against that kind of delay. Man proposes but God disposes.** I hear that attempts are being made to get the Colony Chiefs to join the Aborigines Society, so as to set up a Chiefs "Party" against a "Party" of the people. That, of course, must be recognised as suicidal. It will mean the worse kind of 'Divide and Rule'. It will mean setting the people against their Chiefs in the hope that one will conquer the other. I don't think it will be good for the country for the people to conquer the Chiefs or the Chiefs to conquer the people. They are and have always been one people and they should be left alone to pursue their own policy of unity - a united Gold Coast.

Of course, some people, especially those who are thinking only of present benefits, will not have the vision to see thus far. They think that if the Chiefs are placed in an upper segment against their people, then "it will be all right". The true statesman will see through this at once that it will be all right for a year or two, but not for long. Pakistan and India are not all right. They will be better united.

Three years ago when the Government gave us the new constitution, those without vision thought it was all right, and that it would last for some 15 to 20 years. But God had his own plans ready, and now everybody, even the Governor, is saying that a new and better constitution is required.

I personally feel that the hand of God is in all these things, and I personally feel that what the country is waiting for is for a big man to express to the people and Government that voice of God. I think in 1943 you took the country by storm and made the British Government sit up by rejecting the Ashanti Advisory Council Ordinance and asking to have a share of the Legislative Council for Ashanti at Accra. It was that your decision that has altered Gold Coast history completely, and, instead of a slow march, we are now being rushed by sequence of events - by the unity of Ashanti and the Colony - into the formative state of a nation, a real sovereign state of the Gold Coast - Ghana. The opportunity is again there now, waiting for you to declare that you are in favour of self-government. It was a sad thing for the heart of the country that in all the recent struggles the voice of the Chiefs did not resound clearly above the din and declare the will of the people to the expectant and waiting world.

But I do not consider that it is too late. It may, however, appear too late after July 31, for the Watson Report will have come out by then. I think that it must be left to Nana and not to the Watson Commission to declare the voice and desire of the people clearly. This can be done now by Otumfuo's acceptance of the declared policy of the Convention "Self-government, at the earliest possible time."

As to the particular form this self-government should take, the procedure is to call a Constituent Assembly of the Chiefs (as was done in 1852) or of their delegates, and let them think out how everything should be arranged. Neither the Convention nor the Aborigines, neither the Confederacy Council nor the Joint Council, can, by itself, initiate the future form of the constitution. It should be drawn up and debated in open assembly until everybody is satisfied that what is put forward is the best for the country and the people. I am informed that Dr. the Honourable I. B. Asafu-Adjaye has expressed a view to some of my friends at the Rodger Club, Accra, that when it comes to a new constitution, he would have nothing short of complete independence, that is to say, a real independent sovereign state and not merely a dominion.

That is how the country is thinking. I am myself for dominion status to start, with a Governor-General, and later on full independence may come. But then, that is an individual's view. What the whole country shall determine will rule the day. It must be determined in a constituent assembly. 3ho na Nananom bebo ade.'

Whatever that may be, the present situation is for the Otumfuo alone to solve. The voice of the country must be declared by Otumfuo to resound here, as well as abroad. You may explore the situation by asking the Convention to see you privately or publicly to explain themselves. If, after that, you feel completely satisfied you will then be in a strong position to let the voice of the country be heard. We are all convinced beyond every reasonable doubt that self-government is coming soon.

With my dutiful respects,

I remain, Otumfuo,

Yours sincerely & obediently,

J.B DANQUAH

In Danquah's official letter to the Otumfuo, the Asantehene, he was informing the king on rising matters concerning their quest for self-governance. Firstly, he briefed the Otumfuo about the Government invitation for him and another legislature to attend a conference. This Danquah thought was a result of the Convention's recent influence on the colonial government. But more importantly, he was informing the Otumfuo their recent success over the British government to accept their request of political independence.

There is one thing of which Nana must be well aware. Already the Government has accepted the position that self-government must come within our own time, within say the next five years. Only they think they should gradualise its coming for as long as they can. But everybody can see that God is against that kind of delay. Man proposes but God disposes.

This is a reality the Ghanaian public is not familiar with, that the UGCC won the battle of independence and what was left was convincing the sister colonies, Ashanti, British Togoland and the Northern Territories to form one nation- Ghana, drafting of a new self-governing constitution, establishing structures such as an electoral system for the new nation. This testament of Danquah is supported by David Rooney in his book, "Nkrumah: Vision and Tragedy", that in December 1949, the governor, Arden Clarke's persuading the Legislative Council against Positive Action, confirmed that Britain was determined to grant self-government as soon as practicable.[14]   In the light of that, Danquah wanted the Asantehene to add his voice for self-governance so that the leaders of the Convention would use that to facilitate the unity of the Gold Coast and Asante as one nation. That is why Danquah reminded the Asantehene:

> Pakistan and India are not all right. They will be better united…. It was that your decision that has altered Gold Coast history completely, and, instead of a slow march, we are now being rushed by sequence of events - by **the unity of Ashanti and the Colony - into the formative state of a nation, a real sovereign state of the Gold Coast - Ghana**. The opportunity is again there now, waiting for you to declare that you are in favour of self-government.

Danquah was a master artist in his choice of words. He tried to touch on the conscience of the King that it was not well with Pakistan and India which the king knew and that they would be better off when united. He reminded the king how his voice opened the door for Asante to have representatives at the Legislative Assembly. He used this to appeal to the conscience of the king to rally behind them for self-governance and to bring Ashanti and Gold Coast together as one nation.


In his appeal, even though Danquah did not want to appear to be pressing the king against his wish or setting deadlines for him, he wished the King could speak before the Watson report was released. That is why he wrote this to the king.

> But I do not consider that it is too late. It may, however, appear too late after July 31, for the Watson Report will have come out by then. I think that it must be left to Nana and not to the Watson Commission to declare the voice and desire of the people clearly. This can be done now by Otumfuo's acceptance of the declared policy of the Convention "Self-government, at the earliest possible time."

Danquah's joy for persuading the king was as he said the government had accepted the position of self-government or the political independence and that the Convention and the people must indicate their readiness to get it materialize within their own time.

The fact of the matter is that, the Asantehene, Nana Sir Osei Agyeman Prempeh II accepted Danquah's request to unite with the Gold Coast as one country. This became a reality after the 1951 election. This, as Danquah revealed, significantly contributed to Gold Coast quest for independence and he praised the King for his contribution towards self-government in 1955. This is what Danquah had to say: **"If you will refer to Martin Wight's *Gold Coast Legislative Council* you will discover that it was by a special act of the present Asantehene that Ashanti, after half-a-century under the British, joined the Colony in a legislative union and made the demand for independence possible".**[14] In 2024, during the 150 years anniversary of the 1874 (Sagranti) war against the British, the Asantehene, Otumfuo Osei Tutu II briefly narrated how Dr J.B Danquah convinced the then Asantehene Nana Sir Osei Agyeman Prempeh II to join the Gold Coast as one nation to fight for independence. He revealed that Danquah and Nana Osei Agyeman Prempe shared the same name as Kwame Kyeretwie and that Danquah was the lawyer of the then Asantehene. In addition, both were members of the Youth Conference. This I believe made the proposal of Danquah easier to sail through. This was no mean an achievement of the Asantehene and Danquah.

Danquah's position towards self-government was clear; he wanted a dominion status constitution. This means that government shall be passed on to Ghanaians but shall have limited power. The advantage of this is, it would give opportunity for all Ghanaians to write the most appropriate constitution for full independence. It would give opportunities for Ghana to train more skilled people for the civil service. At the time, Ghana had insufficient and many unskilled men and women for diplomatic and public services. For instance, there were only 57 lawyers and 47 doctors in the Gold Coast in 1948. That year, 98 Africans served in the Administration of the Gold Coast of whom many were not eligible for parliament duties.[15] The Watson Commission revealed that Gold Coast's lack of adequate educated people was a challenge that could jeopardise independence. Hence they advised the government to improve education that could empower the Africans to solve their problems. In spite of his support for dominion status constitution, Danquah rightly admitted that it was just an individual's view and that what the whole country would determine should rule the day and that should be determined in a constituent assembly. That is to say, there never was any disagreement between those who wanted full independence now or full independence within the shortest possible time.

The Watson report was released by 31 July 1948. It showed interest in the activities of the Convention. It described Danquah as an intelligent man and referred to him as the doyen of the Gold Coast politicians. Enquiring why the Convention sent their petition to international agencies besides the colonial government, the report stated, 'Dr Danquah said frankly in his evidence "we wanted the world to know".

The commission asserted that the riot had a link with the activities of the Convention. They confirmed that the secretary of the ex-Servicemen Mr. Tamakloe who led the protest was a founding member of the Gold Coast People League which amalgamated into UGCC and specifically becoming the Accra branch. They found his name was on the minutes of the working committee of the UGCC on 12 August 1947. It is true that Mr. Tamakloe was one of the people to whom invitation letters were sent for the launch of the UGCC. However, on criminal matter, it is insufficient to make the inference or conclusion that Mr. Tamakloe's future actions must have had any connection with the UGCC. But that was the Watson Commission report.

About Nkrumah, this what the report said, **'Mr. Nkrumah appears to be a mass orator among Africans of no means attainments. Nevertheless he appeared before us as 'The humble and obedient servant of the convention,' who had subordinated his private political convictions to those publicly expressed by his employers. From the internal evidence we are unable to accept this modest assessment of his position.'**[17] The report admitted he brought some fervour to the convention and Danquah and other members admired him for that. The report alluded that Danquah was aware of Nkrumah's communist orientation but had over looked because Nkrumah could help them achieve the vision of independence. The commission brought to light a secret document entitled "The Circle" where members were to swear oath of allegiance to Nkrumah and any member who broke a rule of the Circle did that at his own risk and peril. Members of the group were to fast on the 21st day of every month and meditate daily on the cause of THE CIRCLE.  This is a secret group Nkrumah was either raising or intended to form. Below are some of their rules.

I therefore accept and abide by the laws of THE CIRCLE which are as follows:-

I. I will irrevocably obey and act upon the orders, commands, instructions and directions of the Grand Council of THE CIRCLE.

2. I will always serve, sacrifice and suffer anything for the cause for which THE CIRCLE stands, and will at all times be ready to go on any mission that I may be called upon to perform.

3. I will always and in all circumstances help a member brother of THE CIRCLE in all things and in all  difficulties.

4. I will, except as a last resort, avoid the use of violence.

5. I will make it my aim and duty to foster the cause for which THE CIRCLE stands in any organisation that I may become a member.

6. I will fast on the 21st day of each month from sunrise to sunset and will meditate daily on the cause THE CIRCLE stands for.

7. I accept the Leadership of Kwame Nkrumah.

## OATH OF ALLEGIANCE

On my life, honour and fortunes, I solemnly pledge and swear that I shall always live up to the aims and aspirations of THE CIRCLE, and shall never under any circumstances divulge any secrets, plans or movements of THE CIRCLE, nor betray a member brother of the circle; and that if I dare to divulge any secrets, plans and movements of THE CIRCLE, or betray a member brother or the cause, or use the influence of THE CIRCLE for my own personal interests or advertisement, I do so at my own risk and peril.

## CIRCLE MEETINGS

The Grand Council of THE CIRCLE shall meet at least once a year and shall decide general policy and give directions to territorial and local branches of THE CIRCLE. Members of each branch of THE CIRCLE shall meet on the 21st day of each month, and at such other times as members may deem advisable.

As to why the commission took an interest in this document remains questionable. Was it to create enmity between Nkrumah and the other six? What was the intent? As a matter of fact the revelation of this document created mistrust in some members of the UGCC against Nkrumah. But when asked about THE CIRLCE before the commission, Nkrumah revealed that it was only a dream and that it was a document he had carried with throughout London. This was the commission's report: "Mr Nkrumah told us in evidence that this document was 'a dream' which he carried around with him for some years. There is no evidence that 'The Circle' ever became a live body, and we must not speculate. Suffice it to say that we are satisfied, having seen and heard Mr. Nkrumah, that given the smallest opportunity, he would quickly translate his dream into reality." The truth of the matter is that this prophecy came true.

The UGCC were not happy with Nkrumah and they did not hide their dissatisfaction about this document. They blamed Ako Adjei for recommending Nkrumah to them as if Ako Adjei knew something about the Circle and communist document, but that would be something difficult to tell.

The commission dealt with the social, economic and political causes of the unrest. They found lapses in the line of action of the then governor Greasy: his inexperience was exposed, the detention and his refusal to let the six Convention leaders hire a lawyer. They also criticized the Chief Commissioner for been autocratic and out of touch. They acquitted the police who killed the ex-servicemen of any crime committed.

The Watson commission suggested very amazing ideas that if implemented were going to solve the unrest in the nation for better development of the citizens. Among these recommendations were, consideration of constitutional and political reform, Africanisation i.e. giving Africans who qualified the first opportunities, The cutting out of cocoa trees, the Cocoa Marketing Board, The Press and Public Relations, Industrial Development, the Volta Valley Scheme, Trading Discrimination, Agricultural Development, Labour and Employment, Education, Law and Reform and Housing. They recommended the appointment of another commission to propose a new constitution. If the independence sought by the UGCC was going to be meaningful, it was going to be successive government and people of Ghana's commitment to these recommendations. It is many years since the recommendations but they are still relevant in the issues of today's Ghana. For instance this is what they had to say,

**'So far as the economic life of the country is concerned we were struck by the high cost of production ruling in the Gold Coast. Many of the commodities, both industrial and agricultural, the export of which it is hoped to develop in the future would be too costly to compete in the world markets. It is essential, therefore if the commercial aspirations of the people are to be realised that productivity be increased. This can only come in two ways: by the fuller utilization of natural resources and by more work on the part of the people.'[18]**

On education the Commission stated, 'Nothing impressed us more than the interest of the people of the Gold Coast in education. Practically every African who sent in a memorandum or who appeared in person before us sooner or later started to discuss education ... the general complaint appears to be that education provided in the schools actively discourages pupils from turning to trades and crafts. It is realised that literary education is doing great harm in the Gold Coast.' They recommended that Ghana adopt education that was practicable.

On Agriculture, the Watson Commission stated: 'the great majority of its people are dependent, directly or indirectly on agricultural production for day to day sustenance, for the payment of imports and for the revenue which has to provide such social services as they enjoy.' But they admitted that agriculture was neglected and that there was complete disregard of agriculture in education.

The Commission admitted the suffering of the cocoa farmers. The Colonial Government continued to control the sale of cocoa and the farmers were given no voice in the fixing of the selling price. Huge profits made from the sale of cocoa were still being held in Britain and not repatriated and used for the development of the country. They suggested that the Government and the Cocoa Marketing Board should establish a bank for the cocoa farmers.

The commission report suggested that the Volta River dam should be constructed to produce electricity. They requested that a smelter should be built to process the local bauxite to save the economy of Gold Coast. They further suggested that the water should be used for irrigation to boost agriculture on the Afram plains.

The British Colonial Office accepted the recommendations of the Watson Commission to grant the Gold Coast independence. As a result of this, the governor set up a constitutional committee in December 1948 to begin the independence process. And their task read as **"to examine the proposals for political and constitutional reform in paragraph 122 of the Report of the Commission of Inquiry into Disturbances on the Gold Coast, 1948, and, due regard being paid to the views expressed on them by His Majesty's Government, to consider the extent to which they can be accepted and the manner in which they should be implemented."** Mr. Justice Coussey was appointed as chairman. The committee came to be known as Coussey Commission. In spite of the fact that the governor agreed to a new constitution, he did not form a constituent assembly as the UGCC leaders demanded but rather a committee. This means that, the constitution would be subject to the final approval of the Colonial office. However, as it ended, it was this constitution that provided the Gold Coast an internal self-government which Danquah demanded should lead to full independence.

The governor appointed 40 people to form this committee. George Grant, J. B Danquah, Edward Akufo Addo were selected to the committee. The subsequent year in March 1949, Obetsebi Lamptey was invited to join. Kwame Nkrumah was not selected to this committee. This is what JH Ofusu Appiah would describe as tactical error. This error exacerbated the rivalry between Nkrumah, the UGCC and the Coussey Committee members. I have the premonition that the government deliberately excluded Nkrumah to create a possible split which did happen eventually. This is because from Nkrumah's secret document, '**The Circle**', they discerned the intent of Nkrumah and the Commission rightly predicted **'that Nkrumah had a subordinated political conviction and that given the smallest opportunity, he would quickly translate his dream into reality.'**

In spite of everything, the facts will remain that in 1948, the leadership and unity of the Big Six gave the Gold Coast its unprecedented feat over the British colonial government. It will remain the year that the Colonial Government recognized the power of the ordinary person against colonialism. It brought the colonial government to its knees to accept independence. It gave birth to the Watson Commission's recommendations which were going to shape the life of Gold Coast should they be implemented. Yet, the year also marked the beginning of a certain unending rivalry that erupted among the Convention leaders that also altered the political health of Ghana till date. Nkrumah broke away from the UGCC with his new political party, the Convention People's Party (CPP) which he formed within the UGCC to oppose the Coussey Committee and their report and to struggle for self-government for the Gold Coast.

<u>From first left to right</u>
Dr. Kwame Nkrumah, Obetsebi Lamptey, Ako-Adjei,
William Ofori Atta, J.b Danquah and Edward Akufo Addo

CHAPTER 4

# THE RIFT AND EMERGENCE OF THE CPP

At the peak of this feat over imperialism, Danquah and a few delegates left for England for Conference of African Legislative Councillors. Among the delegates that travelled with Danquah were Nana Sir Tsibu Darku, Dr. I.B Asafu-Adjaye and Nene Azu Mate Kole. Danquah was not impressed with this Conference but he thought it offered an opportunity to speak more on the self-government of the Gold Coast and also ensured that people like Nana Sir Tsibu Darku would not go and speak against the Gold Coast's request for Self-Governance. Danquah stayed in London for about two months.

According to Danquah the main reasons that moved him to accept the invitation to attend the Conference of African Legislative Councillors called by the Colonial Office in London were the following:

(1) To find out what was in the mind of the Colonial Office when they referred to the Gold Coast disturbances as the work of communists, and why they suffered the Governor to issue removal orders against some of our members;

(2) To make political and press contacts in regard to the Gold Coast for a national or self-governing constitution;

(3) To prevent the Gold Coast delegation to the Conference from doing

any acts which might jeopardise our Gold Coast case for self-government; and

(4) To expedite arrangements for a printing press for the Statesman Press and Publishing Co. Ltd.[1]

In Britain Danquah made strong defence for the UGCC on the charges of communism against them. He met the Secretary of State Creech Jones who later had confided in Danquah that the accusation of the Convention being communist was politically motivated not based on fact but on propaganda. Discussion on the new Gold Coast Self-governing constitution was made. In trying to calm Danquah, Creech Jones told Danquah the opportunity was theirs to draft the type of self-governing constitution they wanted, meaning that the Coussey Committee could have written a full dominion constitution for full independence if they so wanted. Unfortunately many of the Ghanaians selected to the committee opposed independence except the UGCC members and their sympathisers who were 8 out of the 39 members of the committee.

During the conference Danquah, a representative from the Legislative Council of Kenya and the Chairman of the African Unofficial Members, Mr. E.W. Mathu were scheduled for a filmed documentary. Danquah gave about 300 word talk. In his case, he stated that all Gold Coast wanted from Britain was a government of their own, chosen by their grandfathers, grandmothers, cousins and aunts and not a government in the hands of people who had neither cousins nor aunts nor parents in the country they governed.

Before their departure for the United Kingdom they were handed seven memoranda of the following description: -

1. African Local Government.

2. Information Services.

3. Education Policy in Africa.

4. Medical Policy

5. The Colonial Empire and the Economic Crisis.

6. The Means of Development.

7. Increased Agricultural Production.

In Britain Danquah confessed he developed a new perspective towards their political aims. Formerly, anytime, they were asked what their programme was for the Gold Coast, they would reply "to give control and direction of government to the people and their Chiefs within the shortest possible time." However true this was, he came to the consciousness that that aim did not contain any plan of what direction of Government would be in case they attained that aim. Simply, their aim lacked a political and economic theory or structure. He had become a convert to socialism in UK and therefore stated, "It seems to me socialism in the modern State, that is to say, the taking of government to the people and the authorisation of government by the people, and the carrying of government to the direct benefit of the people, should be that aim, and I humbly recommend the same for the consideration of the Working Committee and for our plans to be clarified in that regard in every field of the national life." In the light of that, Danquah affirmed that the seven memoranda given to them could only be implemented when government is passed on to Ghanaians and that government resorted to socialism. To buttress his point, he said. "On the medical policy, it will be realised at once that no colonial Government, composed as our present government is, however well intentioned, can carry out that policy. Only a government in which the people themselves are in authority, a socialist government, can apply it with any real benefit to the people, making proper and adequate use of the funds available."[2]

While Danquah was away fighting for the course of Ghana, Nkrumah and his lieutenant Komla Gbedemah rather spread propaganda to the uninformed youths that Danquah had given up on the independence struggle to the imperialist. In Britain, Danquah met Sidney Abrahams, a former Gold Coast attorney general. He founded the Gold Coast athletic Association and served as its first chairman. Danquah asked him to come to the Gold Coast again to reorganise sports in Ghana. Nkrumah and his comrades spread the propaganda that J.B had sold out the independence struggle to play golf. As uninformed as these youth were they believed in this propaganda. They felt betrayed by a man they saw as their leader to fight for their aspiration. This aroused hatred against Danquah. They had no one to turn to but the leadership of Nkrumah. Danquah spent about two months in Britain, and by the time he arrived in the Gold Coast, Nkrumah and Gbedemah had advanced with their strategies by rallying most of the youth on their side.

During the arrest of the Big Six, some students went on demonstration against the arrest. These students were sacked from their schools. The leaders of the UGCC decided to establish a school to enrol these students. In August 1948, before they realised, Nkrumah had gone ahead of them to establish the school Ghana National College without their knowledge. Nkrumah appointed Kwasi Plange who was a teacher at St Augustine and who had been sacked to be the Headmaster of the school. This young man and the students later became great activists of Nkrumah and the CPP. The formation of the school brought clash between some of the leaders of the Convention and Nkrumah.

On 3 September 1948, Nkrumah established a newspaper called the Accra Evening News also at their blind side. This did not go down well with the other leaders. He used the paper to champion his personal aspirations. He lashed out at the UGCC and also against imperialism. The tone of the message most of the time was vulgar. According to Nkrumah himself, the newspaper was charged with libel on a number of publications. With these issues building up, Nkrumah was removed from his position as secretary.

Nkrumah formed the Committee of Youth Organisation within the U.G.C.C. with Komla Gbedemah as its leader. By the time Danquah returned from Britain to the Gold Coast in October 1948, Nkrumah had gained momentum by pulling the masses to his aspirations. Many of the youth had fallen out with Danquah. They had believed that Danquah went to Britain to compromise or delay the independence. Some hooted at him when he spoke and sometimes threw stones at his car.

According to an eyewitness, Esi Grant-Aquah, daughter of Paa Grant who remained a friend to Nkrumah and all the UGCC leaders after the split, revealed that, while Nkrumah started engaging the youth against the vision of the UGCC, the leaders were signalled about it. As a result, the UGCC held a meeting at the Cape Coast Town Hall which was attended by thousands of people. According to Esi Grant-Aquah, when Paa Grant and Nkrumah spoke there was silence of approval in the hall, but as soon as Danquah got up to speak, there was an uproar – some of the young men disrupted the meeting throwing about chairs and insulting everybody. To her, this confirmed to the other leaders the rumours that Nkrumah was inciting the youth against the leaders of the UGCC. This widened the rift that had been created between Nkrumah and the UGCC.[3]

During this period, RS Blay and Dr. Ansah Koi suggested that they should promote Nkrumah as a Vice President, but Danquah and Akufo-Addo thought he should be made honorary Treasurer. I believe the reason of Blay and Ansah Koi was to relieve Nkrumah from his role to the youth. That would have been a great tactical move for their collective interest.

Mr. Sidney Abrahams visited Ghana in April 1949 and according to Dr. Danquah his presence contributed to the issuing of the first Sport Ordinance (the Gold Coast Amateur Sports Ordinance, 1952) which was able to raise funds to build the Accra Sports Stadium. Yet for political power, Nkrumah and his team spread the propaganda that Sidney Abrahams had come as an emissary of the Imperial Power to bribe Dr. Danquah and the executives of UGCC each with £25,000 and that it was only Nkrumah who refused his cheque.[4] Danquah and the rest of the leaders had become their enemies even in the same organisation. The young men began to hoot at Danquah when they saw him afterwards. Sometimes they would throw stones at his car. Danquah warned Nkrumah to stop such propaganda reminding Nkrumah of the torture they went through in prison which would make it impossible for any reasonable person to take bribe. Below is one of the excerpts of the letters Danquah wrote to Nkrumah to deny the charges of corruption against him.

> "As for the rest of your article, my dear Kwame, do please stop making those dark hints about **'bribery and corruption'** in connection with our death and life struggle, because you well know, if anyone else does not, that no offer of gold in this world could ever touch the steel of bitterness

that entered our soul as we drove that early dawn, out of the Kumasi prison into that dust-filled, dreary and long road to the Tamale African Hospital. And would anyone dare make such an offer?"[5]

The leaders of the UGCC could not fully understand the sudden attacks of Nkrumah on them until he published his autobiography and revealed his intent and his differences with the other UGCC leaders. This is what Nkrumah had to say.

**"It was during this period when we were thrown together in such close proximity that I got the first indication of disagreement between myself and the other five members. I became painfully aware that they were losing interest in me because whenever we entered into a discussion, the five of them would always make a point of supporting the opposite point of view to mine and nothing I proposed was acceptable to them. There appeared to be a general belief among them that the whole tragedy of our arrest and suffering was my fault and they began to make it plain that they regretted the day they had ever invited me to take up the secretaryship of the U.G.C.C. Not satisfied with that, they even began to blame Ako Adjei for his part in recommending me to them."** [6]

This confession of Nkrumah confirms the Watson Commission's report that Nkrumah had subordinated his political conviction from the one publicly declared by his employers and that given the slightest chance he would materialize his dream.

This perception that the other five blamed Nkrumah for their arrest has persisted from that time till now. Many of the propagators of this assertion only end up giving credit to Nkrumah. The sad part of it is that, many political historians do not read the publications of Danquah and the other leaders to at least know their view. Nkrumah's claim was refuted and reverted by Danquah who also detailed what actually transpired at the Kumasi prison. On Friday, May 10, 1957, The Daily Graphic published: **Dr. D. writes to P.M.**

**Dr. J.B Danquah, 61-year-old doyen of Ghana politics, has sent a ten-page letter to Prime Minister Kwame Nkrumah in which he alleges that there is "false and libellous" matter in Dr. Nkrumah's autobiography "Ghana," recently published by Thomas Nelson.**

**His letter ends by stating: "I hereby request you to submit a written apology to me within a fortnight. It will give me no pleasure to bring a libel action in the Supreme Court of Ghana against the first Prime Minister of Ghana.**

**"You are also requested to undertake not to repeat the said allegations in future editions of the book." [7]**

In a personal letter to Nkrumah, this is what Danquah had to say:

"I concede you one thing, At the Kumasi prison you stayed away from most of our meetings. We usually met to discuss colours of our national flag. We agreed upon the name **Ghana**. We even discussed whether our poets should speak of our country as fatherland or motherland!

"At our request the prison superintendent had supplied us with a table as well as chairs, but whenever we sat down in the spacious yard to discuss business, your chair was nearly always empty. As senior officer of the Convention, I came to your room to ask you why you looked so disconsolate and unhappy.

"What you said in reply was this: 'J.B., I left my hand bag at my residence at Cape Coast. It contains my Communist card and other things. The Police said they would search my premises after my arrest. I am afraid they have got hold of my Communist membership card.'

"**Question by me**: Communist membership card? Is your name on it?

"**Answer by you**: No.

"**Question by me**: Have you distributed similar cards to any one since your return from England? "**Answer by you**: No.

"Statement by me, cheering you up: Kwame, don't you

worry about that; the Police cannot touch you for it".[8]

Danquah went further to detail the events that transpired at the prison. The sum is this: he denied that neither he nor any of the five mistreated or accused Nkrumah of the arrest.

From a third person's perspective, I will find it very difficult and unreasonable how any of the detained executives could blame Nkrumah for their arrest. This is because Nkrumah admits in the early chapter of his autobiography that he was very new in the Gold Coast barely a month old and was out of touch with Gold Coast realities. From Nkrumah, it was Danquah who asked the masses to accept him Nkrumah at the Accra rally organized by the ex-servicemen. In those meetings with the ex-servicemen, Danquah was the one who chaired the meetings. And from the government's report, the directives that emerged were between the secretary of the ex-servicemen, Mr. Tamakloe and Danquah. There was no directive given to the ex-servicemen by Nkrumah. His name never emerged in the investigation except with his communist card. And Nkrumah being the bearer of the card was not the cause of the riot nor their arrest because before the police came into contact with Nkrumah's card, the letter of arrest had been issued and Danquah and the other four executives had been arrested.

If there was anyone to be blamed, it was Danquah because he wrote the telegram to the Colonial office demanding the removal of the governor and immediate appointment of the UGCC for interim self-government and for subsequent self-government. This was very threatening to any government. And the governor in his report detailing why he arrested the Big Six, made it very clear that Danquah had demanded that the governor be deposed for the UGCC to form interim self-government for full self-governance. How could any of the five in his right senses, knowing the reason for their arrest, blame the newcomer Nkrumah?

However, I do strongly believe that the content of Nkrumah's CIRCLE document would definitely raise suspicion against him. Exactly so, they doubted him but Nkrumah convinced them that he was innocent. To prove his innocence, Nkrumah said he asked the leaders to form a committee to investigate him which led Ofori Atta and Akufo Addo to search his office in his absence. The search in Nkrumah's absence did not go down well with him. According to Nkrumah they gathered unnecessary accusation against him that he was a communist. However, the truth of the matter is that Nkrumah's split with the UGCC had little to do with the CIRCLE or what the UGCC did to him after the enquiry of the Commission. Even before the Watson commission, he had made up his mind to move away. And his writing testifies.

> "Ever since the first indication of the divergence of views between myself and the members of the U.G.C.C. during our detention together, I knew that sooner or later a final split would have to come. I was determined, therefore, to organise things in such a way that when this break came I would have the full support of the masses behind me. By gathering together the youth of Osu, a district of Accra, I formed the Youth Study Group owing to the fact that I was too busy" [9]

So the Watson Commission was spot-on when they said Nkrumah had subordinated his private political conviction from that publicly declared by his employers - the leaders of the UGCC and that given the smallest opportunity, he would quickly translate his dream into reality.

From the quote above, Nkrumah says that there was divergence of views. This Danquah denies and says Nkrumah was quiet and when he enquired, Nkrumah revealed that he was worried about his communist card he left behind. If Danquah's words are anything to go by, they did not accuse Nkrumah nor did they lose interest in him. If it is true that Danquah told Nkrumah, 'Kwame, don't you worry about that; the Police cannot touch you for it', then there cannot be any basis for Nkrumah's reason for the split. It could only be something he was going to opt for at all cost. The other alternative reflection to consider is this: ever since Nkrumah arrived in Ghana, he had several meetings with the UGCC leaders for at least about two months. Was it fair for Nkrumah to use a mere misunderstanding that happened within three days as enough reason to move away from an organisation he had thoughtfully joined for three months? Would it not have been fair if Nkrumah had shared his grievance with the leaders of the Convention instead of keeping his thoughts to himself? Why would he think that sooner or later a final split would come? So the strategy of Nkrumah was that for a possible split, he would influence the masses to his side and then break away with his party, the CPP.

When Danquah read Nkrumah's motive in Nkrumah's autobiography, Danquah was shocked and replied, **'It is good to know from the grave disclosures you make at pages 62, 96 - 97 and 100 that you came out from England in response to our invitation, determined to break us and to capture the political initiative from the U.G.C.C. You made use of our members and branches, with a plan which resulted in a split in the country's united front, to the joy of the Imperial power'[10]**

The quote above is an indication of the reliability of Danquah's objections to Nkrumah's reasons for the split.

Nkrumah had a split on his mind before joining the Convention and therefore sought for opportunities to justify his breakaway. This is what he revealed in his book, *Dark Days in Ghana,* **"It was quite useless to associate myself with a movement backed almost entirely by reactionary middle class lawyers and merchants, for my revolutionary background and ideas would make it impossible for me to work with them."** He only accepted the invitation of the UGCC for a personal reason. He saw working with the UGCC as an opportunity to establish himself in the Gold Coast politics and later break away at the most opportune time to establish his childhood dream of the CIRCLE. He wanted to learn from them, gain acceptance from the Gold Coast politics and then stab them in the back which worked perfectly for him.

The British colonial government undoubtedly would have a sigh of breath. They were crumpling down by the collective quest of the Big Six. Whereas this split appeared to have worked for Nkrumah and the CPP as well as for the most benefit of the Imperial Power, it was to the detriment of Ghana. It was going to delay Ghana's independence.

Nkrumah's narrative clearly reveals the founding of the Ghana National College and the Accra Evening News were for his private aspiration which he eventually unravelled.

To foster his ambition, Nkrumah formed the Committee for Youth Organisation with Gbedemah as Chairman and Botsio as Secretary. They met in Gbedemah's house. To draw the youth to his side, Nkrumah would not tell them that the colonial government had already agreed to grant them independence and that this would come within the timing of the leaders of the UGCC, but rather, he instigated in them to fight for independence now. Many of these youth were academically deficit and therefore could not make critical thinking; many of them were jobless and felt the older generations had abandoned them so *Self Government Now* to get them into position was the dearest thing for them to embrace. Therefore, within a short time, the youth were chanting for Self-Government Now. The slogan of the UGCC which was "Self-Government within the shortest possible time" meant like eternity to them and it was nonsense to hold on to this. But the question again, is it fair that members of an organization could conceive their own vision to challenge the very vision that brought them to that organization? Sincerely I think this is one of the high betrayals that can ever happen.

This is what Nkrumah had to say about the UGCC concerning his decision for forming the CYO.

> **"They thought, and rightly so, that I had been responsible for this organisation of the youth and this fact strengthened their desire to remove me from office".[11]**

In the statement above, Nkrumah admits that he was responsible for this new vision of the youth in the UGCC. By this act, Nkrumah totally destroyed the Ghanaian culture of the youth having great respect for their elders and leaders and this has become a norm since then. Besides, in the spirit of nationalism and unity, was it fair for a sitting executive to break up a united front stirring division between the elders and youth? Unfortunately for them, they disclosed their intention of removing Nkrumah as secretary and this brought about open conflict between the supporters of the C.Y.O. within the U.G.C.C and the Working Committee.

**"It became obvious to all that these men who had, until that moment, complete control of the national movement, were anxious to be rid of me because I represented the radical and progressive section of the movement."[12]**

The fact is clear, the conflict that existed between the youth and the UGCC leaders was not accidental, it was not genuinely conceived by the youth themselves, neither was it a deliberate attempt of the UGCC leaders to abandon or despise the youth. It was the mastermind of one of them who wanted control on his side to inherit the government they had collectively fought for only to rebrand himself as solely fighting for that independence. Let readers also understand that Nkrumah admitted in his own writing that these UGCC leaders were in control of the national movement and not him. Yet in our time, anytime documentaries are made on the independence, Nkrumah is revealed as the sole leader of the national movement.

> With all this unpleasantness brewing up again, I decided to make a short trip to Nzima where, in the peace of my home surroundings, I hoped to be able to restore in some measure my equilibrium. I knew that the time was fast approaching when decisive action was going to be necessary, **when in all probability control would be in my hands** and I realised how important it was to plan my next steps.[13]

This statement of Nkrumah above does not really portray him as a unifier. It reveals a character who by his wits manipulates his fellows to seek control to move the masses. This was not the spirit of the UGCC. If it were so, Akufo Addo and the Gold Coast People's League would have moved separately from George Grant, Danquah and their Gold Coast National Party. Yet for the masses interest, they decided to merge to defeat the common enemy, the British Colonial government. And yet this was the case, a son of the soil they invited to join in the struggle against the imperialism was quick to find difference to go for a split before anyone's intent. Nkrumah's behaviour portrayed him as crafty for he succeeded in manipulating the masses to be on his side for a split and seized every opportunity to make himself very popular among the youth in particular.

In December 1948, the Governor formed the committee to write the new constitution which was initially called the Coussey Committee. As I revealed earlier, Nkrumah was not invited to the committee. This by all standards was strange. I strongly believe that Nkrumah should have been part of the committee. But there my question goes, did the governor intentionally omit Nkrumah's name to create a split or what was his intention? Among the Big Six, Danquah and Akufo Addo were originally selected until in March the subsequent year when Obetsebi Lamptey was invited to join the committee. In high probability, the attacks of Nkrumah against the UGCC leaders could not allow them to fight for Nkrumah to be on the committee.

Nkrumah convinced the youth that the leaders had abandoned the youth in the independence struggle that is why he has been left out of the Coussey Committee so they should rally behind him to fight against the Coussey committee and rather fight for self-government now. This made sense to the youth. So in December, Nkrumah called for youth conference in Accra at the King George V Hall. This conference was successful so they planned to hold another one in Kumasi on the 23$^{rd}$ December 1948. This conference was banned by the police so they tried to move to Lome, Togo to send telegram to the Secretary of State to the colonies. Unfortunately, when they got there, the authorities had been alerted and refused the telegram. The CYO in the Kumasi conference sent their proposals to the Coussey Committee since they were opened to the public for their views.

From Accra, Kumasi, Nkrumah went to the Northern Territories in March 1949 and annexed himself as first UGCC leader to be there. He promised them he would turn their lives into paradise in ten years when he would come to power. This made him a very popular figure above every politician in the north. In the north he wore the "fugu" which gave him a good admiration. Later this cloth would be used by him and his executives as 'Prison Graduates.'

On 11 June, 1949, the Working Committee of the U.G.C.C. issued two resolutions which were:

(1) Membership of the C.Y.O. and the U.G.C.C. were incompatible.

(2) to serve Nkrumah with charges because he had disregarded the

obligations of collective responsibility, and party discipline and had published opinions, views, and criticisms in the Evening News assailing the decisions and questioning the integrity of the Working Committee, and had undermined the Convention, abusing its leaders and stealing its ideas. The Committee recommended the appointment of a new Secretary-General and nine Assistant Secretaries.[14]

This was too little too late. Nkrumah was strategically ahead of the actions of the leaders of the Convention. He called for a CYO meeting at Tarkwa. The conference lasted for three nights. There were two main items on the agenda for discussion. The first was whether to wait for the sacking from the UGCC and second one was whether the CYO should break away to form another political party. They agreed to resist the removal of Nkrumah from the UGCC. On the second discussion, there were two schools of opinion. The first, led by Kofi Baako and Saki Scheck suggested that they should remain in the UGCC and capture the leadership of the party. I think the opinion of RS Blay and Dr. Ansah Koi to make Nkrumah vice president would have been perfectly good for Nkrumah and his CYO. The second school of thought led by Gbedemah and Botsio suggested breakaway to form their political party.

According to Nkrumah, he made no hesitation to opt for the second opinion of forming a political party. This had been his desire all this while from the time he left the Kumasi prison. The next important thing that came up was the name to adopt for this new party. According to Nkrumah, the most popular suggestion was **The Ghana People's Party**. There again Nkrumah's craftiness had to work, this is what he had to tell them,

> "This (The Ghana People's Party) would have been adopted but for one vital reason. Owing to the fact that the rank and file of the people had learnt to associate my name with that of the United Gold Coast Convention, **I felt that by omitting the word 'Convention' from the name of this new party, it would arouse doubt and suspicion in the minds of the people who would regard it as a completely new party with new ideas and new promoters. And so, in order to carry the masses with us, we all agreed that at**

**all costs 'Convention ' must appear as a part of the name. The name that we eventually agreed upon was the 'Convention People's Party'."[15]**

If the propaganda Nkrumah made against the Convention people (UGCC) were true, that the leaders were detached from the ordinary people, that they were not serious about the independence, why would he want to form a party associated with its name? Genuinely speaking, he should have used a completely different name like **Ghana People's Party** or any different name. But there again his craftiness worked on these emotional and hungry youth. Many a time people who break away from groups they have issues with do not want to have anything with its memory, let alone continue to bear its name. Yet in this case, Nkrumah at all cost wanted his new party's name to bear the name convention because that was the popular name of the UGCC. They were formally addressed as "the convention" or "the convention people" or "the people of the convention". That was how he could win the masses to his side because many people then had heard of the convention as the group fighting for independence.

This is Nkrumah confessing that he did not want to raise any doubt and suspicion in the minds of the people that he had formed a new party. Simply, Nkrumah mastered the art to sway the mass supporters of the UGCC to his side without them knowing it was actually a new party. So the masses of whom many were illiterate and ignorant believed and followed Nkrumah thinking that the CPP was the same convention they were in. They were made to hate the other leaders with the reasons that the other UGCC executives had taken bribe to delay the independence and that also the youth had been abandoned in the independence struggle. Since the CPP was still part of the old Convention, the CPP leaders passed a vote of no confidence in Danquah and the other executives. They sent a memorandum of vote of no confidence to almost all the UGCC branches and moved the masses away with them. They used force to stop as many as they could from following the old convention leaders.

Again, Nkrumah said he was not coming with new ideas and new promoters. This also suggests that he owed some of his ideas to the actual convention, the UGCC. It is no wonder Danquah told Nkrumah: **'When you formed the Convention People's Party you removed the 'gold' in the centre of our design and replaced it by 'white'. You retained the rest of our colours for the C.P.P. flag.'** The colours of the CPP are Red, White and Red with a cockerel in the white colour.

Nkrumah drew up a six-point programme for the C.P.P:

(1) To fight relentlessly by all constitutional means for the achievement of full 'Self-Government NOW' for the chiefs and people of the Gold Coast.

(2) To serve as the vigorous conscious political vanguard for removing all forms of oppression and for the establishment of a democratic government.

(3) To secure and maintain the complete unity of the chiefs and people of the Colony, Ashanti, Northern Territories and Trans-Volta.

(4) To work in the interest of the trade union movement in the country for better conditions of employment.

(5) To work for a proper reconstruction of a better Gold Coast in which the people shall have the right to live and govern themselves as free people.

(6) To assist and facilitate in any way possible the realisation of a united and self-governing West Africa[16]

The only idea Nkrumah owned differently from the UGCC was the sixth point which he brought from Britain as a result of his association with the West African Students Union. All the points stated were in the UGCCC plan. With his quest of **Self-Governance Now** which he rightly knew was nothing but a slogan or propaganda. Because before he started this agitation, the colonial government had already agreed to the independence demands of the UGCC. But independence like marriage must go through series of activities which included a constitution and the unification of the other colonies. This would take some time. But instead of telling the masses the truth, he needed to use their ignorance and impatience to form a following to win elections. So on 12 June 1949, in Accra, the CPP was formed before massive crowds while Nkrumah and those followers were still legitimate members of the UGCC without the knowledge of the UGCC leaders.

The prophetic statement made by the Watson commission was fulfilled that Nkrumah had subordinated his private political convictions to those publicly expressed by his employers. And they concluded by saying, 'Suffice it to say that we are satisfied, having seen and heard Mr. Nkrumah, that given the smallest opportunity, he would quickly translate his dream into reality.' Indeed soon after these statements, Nkrumah brought his political conviction and The CIRCLE dream to bear. He split the united front. This disunity did not only bring a sigh of relief to the colonial government, it has also jeopardised our political unity till date.

Nkrumah went on to persuade the masses that they should do everything to secure the independence now since the Labour Party was in power and that should the Conservative Party win the British election, they would not agree to the independence the subsequent year. The question we can ask is where from the sudden self-government now, independence now from Nkrumah? Because when he arrived, he put forward his plans to the UGCC and there was no 'Self Government Now'. What happened that all of a sudden he began to shout to the roof top that Self Government Now? This clearly suggests the Labour Party in power then had indeed agreed to the independence as revealed by Danquah to the Asantehene.

The formation of the CPP to become a political party to oppose the UGCC was a worry to those it mattered to. They arranged to settle the matter by inviting a barrister Mr. Gwira and Rev. Ntedu-Kyirbuwa from the Methodist Church as arbitrators. The meeting took place at Paa Grant's house. These arbitrators recommended that Nkrumah should be reinstated as the General Secretary of the UGCC and the CPP should operate as a political party serving as the vanguard within the UGCC but this matter didn't settle well with working committee. Nkrumah demanded that should the CPP be returned, the working committee should resign which included Danquah and the other detained leaders. And they did. Hereafter, Danquah wrote this article:

> "The verdict of Demos has been given. The Sekondi
> arbitrators spoke with his voice. Conscious of the noise of
> the Demos below the frontage of George Alfred Grant's

mansion where the arbitration was held, the Arbitrators said this through their spokesman, the Reverend K. N. Nredu-Kyirbuwa, even as someone from among the crowd below sounded a bugle or trumpet:

"Conscious of the adoration of the people for the C.P.P. we could not do otherwise but decide that the Working Committee should accept the C.P.P., even though it was wrongly established against the constitution and bye-laws of the Convention."

"Through noise Demos triumphed. In consequence the Working Committee resigned.

"George Alfred Grant, aged 71 in August, the Moses of our Ghana exodus from the Egypt of oppression: George Alfred Grant, inspired liberator who brought us out of the land of disunited Chiefs and people into a united convention of the Gold Coast people and their Chiefs; George Alfred Grant who leads us through the wilderness of imperialism to a new Bond or covenant of Self-government, now stands alone."[17]

Esi Acquah-Grant, daughter of George Grant who was an eye witness, during the meeting, said they could hear some agitating noise with drum beatings and singing. She narrated, "They approached and shouted in the Akan language "Danquah, Kwame Nkrumah aye wo den? Danquah, Kwame Nkrumah aye wo den? Nye wo na wo kra no ma ofiri aborakyir bei ah? Danquah –eh, Kwame aye wo den? According to her each verse they replaced Danquah with Paa Grant, Ako Adjei and the rest of the UGCC leaders".[18]

It was in this meeting that Danquah asked "Kwame who are these verandah boys?" The verandah boys carried Nkrumah away. The UGCC leaders decided to sit on the matter again. This time they brought two new arbitrators who were chiefs. According to Danquah, these chiefs reiterated the reinstatement of Nkrumah as General Secretary and also dissolve the CPP which Nkrumah agreed and took drink as native custom demanded. That was around 10 am. According to Danquah, Nkrumah was compelled by his followers to resign his appointment as General Secretary and his membership of the Convention from fear that his life was in danger. Nkrumah heeded to their call and finally resigned from the UGCC and left to continue with the CPP.

As Nkrumah himself stated categorically clear in his autobiography that he adopted the name **convention** for his new party in order not to **arouse doubt and suspicion in the minds of the people to regard his party as a completely new party with new ideas and new promoters.** Since this tactic worked and the masses did not know the difference between the UGCC which was called the Convention and the CPP which was also called Convention, Nkrumah's team had to use force and intimidation to prevent people from supporting the old or the original leaders. Violence by default became a political weapon for dominance. The CPP activists would throw stones at the old leaders and people who still wanted to remain with the UGCC. It occurred that the windscreen of Danquah and the other leaders were shattered during rallies. Nkrumah and his team had raised the propaganda that the old leaders had taken bribe from the Colonial Government to delay the independence. This ruined the reputation of Danquah and the old leaders in the eyes of the illiterate masses who were driven by emotions and believed anything they heard without thinking through. Nkrumah won the hearts of such illiterate masses while the many of the intellectuals stood with Danquah and the UGCC. The reality was that the youthful illiterates were more in number than the adult intellectuals. The nation that was supposed to have one political enemy, the colonial government, unfortunately and needlessly was divided into two opposing sides.

The departure of Nkrumah worried Danquah. He understood it was a suicide for the nation's progress. To him unity was their energy to crumple the imperial power but with division, the colonial power had regained strength or the initiative. He wrote to Nkrumah saying, **'I tell you frankly, Kwame, you blundered in breaking the country's united front - from U.G.C.C, to C.Y.O., C.P.P., and then to G.R.A., - and that blunder is costing the country a dear penalty - ,the sort of penalty which only the wise who appreciate what is meant by practical politics understand.'[19]** Danquah still pressed with his message of unity to the CPP and emphasized the reason they should be one to fight the common enemy, the Colonial master. He wrote to the

CPP again saying, **'Parties in Ghana must be formed when we begin to want different things. Today we all want the same thing, self-government, and it is criminal nonsense for anyone to suggest that we could get S.G. in the shortest possible time, or this minute, if we had several parties and several commanders-in-chief pulling themselves about in several ways. Disunited we fall.'**[20]

His persuasions fell on deaf ears. The replies of the CPP were abusive against Danquah and the UGCC leaders. The C.P.P spread more lies against Danquah that had it not been him, the Gold Coast would have gained independence long time ago. They blamed almost every problem of the nation against Danquah. In his reply to such attacks against him, Danquah wrote.

> **I love my country more than all the hatred for me put together. It seems to me Nkrumah's attacks on the U.G.C.C. is undoing us, I mean the country's united power to pull the chestnut out of the fire. Would it not have been wonderful if at this stage, with the imperial power breaking under our earlier strokes, we had stood like a Goliath of one strength to pull the whole edifice down into the valley of destruction! We, the entire united convention of the Ghana people! But now, where is our strength? Nkrumah is compelled to make up for want of solid intellectual backing with a multiplicity of organisations - C.Y.O., C.P.P. and now G.R.A., and one does not know what else, from a movement - U.G.C.C., to a Committee, then to a Party as the 'best' of all, and now back to a movement! And the country's united energy being dissipated. The Nkrumah press and platform probably think they are hurting only me and what I am known to stand for; but surely Nkrumah must know more than anyone else that this is, if ever there was, not the time for divisionism - playing the imperialists game for him so neatly.**[21]

Danquah appears to understand the essence of unity in nationalism. His points were clear. A division would always dissipate the nation's energy against the imperialist. In an earlier writing to Otumfuo he made it very clear that party against party or divide and rule would be suicidal for Ghana. Unfortunately, that is what happened and Ghana today is suffering from that disunity that occurred during its founding.

In support of Danquah's assertion, *The Time of London* in June 1949 published that, "The Formation of Dr Nkrumah's CP.P has enabled the British to capture the initiative".[22] Not only did Nkrumah's departure weaken national unity, it also gave a bit of control back to the British. This is confirmed by the horse's own mouth, Arden Clarke, the Governor who came to replace Governor Greasy. Arden Clarke narrated, **'having been briefed by Creech Jones (the Secretary of State to the colonies) with sombre warning 'I want you to go to the Gold Coast. The country is on the edge of revolution. We are in danger of losing it.'[23]** So Arden Clarke flew to Accra in August 1949. The Governor's words clearly reveal the collective impact of the independence movement. Is it not strange that a governor that was sent to ensure Britain did not lose the Gold Coast became the close ally of Nkrumah who was seen as the radical independence activist? It was Arden Clarke who led in the Gold Coast democratic process to independence. He handled matters in British interest and made independence look like the British were bequeathing a gift to Ghanaians. This is something Danquah strongly opposed. Danquah wished Ghanaians would have taken charge on matters pertaining to independence in their own way but since the national front was divided, the British served as arbitrators to the nation's independence movement.

Gone for good from the UGCC, Nkrumah began to mobilize a number of organisations, the TUC, ex-servicemen, the market women (especially from markola) and the youth to oppose the Coussey Report and push the government to call for a constituent assembly. He pressed with his message of Self-Government Now.

He introduced Positive Action campaign and was summoned by the Ga State council to explain what he meant by Positive Action. He was persuaded to stop but he rescinded. According to him the UGCC were in the meeting hoping he called it off. He later held public meetings explaining Positive Action. He explained the two ways for a colony to gain its independence either through arm struggle or through legitimate and constitutional ways. And Positive Action was of the latter. And the positive action would be in two phases. But he would not launch it until the Coussey report was published and then they would analyse it and suggest their proposals. The first phase would be to use political agitation, newspaper and educational campaigns to demand Self-Government Now. And when that one failed he would resort to the next phase which is the constitutional application of strikes, boycotts and non-cooperation based on the principle of absolute nonviolence, as used by Gandhi in India.

They Coussey Commission report was published on 26 October, 1949. The report added Asante and the Northern Territories to the Gold Coast as one Colony. It recommended a two chamber system which included a senate of Chiefs and an elected assembly, a responsible Executive Council with a majority of Africans and a new system of local government. The voting age was fixed at twenty-five years and over. Under this constitution, there was to be an Executive Council consisting of three ex-officio members and eight Ghanaian Ministers; the Executive and assembly were responsible to the Governor. There was also to be a single chamber legislature. This legislature consisted of an elected Speaker, three ex-officio ministers, six special members representing mining and commercial interests. In addition, to them were seventy-five African members[24] (thirty-seven from the Colony, nineteen from Asante and nineteen from the Northern Territories). Of the seventy-five Africans, thirty-three were to be nominated by the chiefs, five were to be elected directly by the municipals of Accra with 2 seats, Kumasi, Cape Coast and Secondi-Takoradi each with one seat. The remaining thirty-seven were to be elected through Electoral College. The voting age initially was 25 but this was later reduced to 21. With this and other roles played, the Coussey Commission laid a good foundation for the independent Ghana.

As the UGCC and Nkrumah rift persisted, Danquah pursued on his legislative responsibilities. Among the work he did was on 9 December 1949, he moved for the appointment of a Select Committee of the legislature to investigate the establishment of a National Bank and the motion was unanimously carried. He also did his best to put the

Government on its toes to implement the recommendation of the Watson Commission on Africanisation and the cocoa swollen shoot.

The greatest of all Danquah's success that year was when he vehemently pushed for the approval of the Coussey report to become a self-governing constitution. The Coussey report was written with the model of Danquah's scheme of constitution to Aiken Watson. However, about 31 out of the 39 (without the secretary who would have added up to 40) selected on the committee were not in support of independence. Only eight members of the committee pushed for independence. And Danquah was the voice of these eight. On the 12 December 1949, Danquah was the lead voice of the 8 Members of the Coussey Committee who signed the Minority Report that **"the people of the Gold Coast should be given the opportunity to make the supreme effort for a stand now as a self-governing country within the Commonwealth."** [25] Unexpectedly, the decision of the eight members was approved by the Government. The win of the minority 8 supports Danquah's message to the Otumfuo that the Government had already accepted that Self Government must come within our own time. For his exemplary statesmanship in laying the foundation of the new Ghana, the Coussey Commission also honoured J.B Danquah as the Doyen of Ghanaian politics.

The Governor amended a few portions of the Constitution. Significantly among them is that he cancelled the proposal for a bicameral legislature to make it a Single House Legislative Council. The reason given was that the proposal for a bicameral legislature was carried by a narrow majority (20 to19). For a better amendable solution, the committee put forward the alternative of a single chamber with one-third of the seats filled by persons chosen in the same way as senators (the chiefs and traditional leaders) would have been chosen in the bicameral legislature.[26] The Governor then approved the Coussey Report to be accepted as the 1950 constitution. This constitution was a semi-dominion status constitution. It would give a measure of self-government or an internal self-governance to the Gold Coast. Once the constitution was approved, the next task was to call for a national parliamentary election which was fixed on 8 February, 1951.

Nkrumah went on touring the nation and asking them to support him for 'Self-Government Now'. He called for the Gold Coast People's Representatives on the 20 November 1949 where he invited representatives of over 50 organisations. The chiefs councils, the UGCC and the Aborigines refused to attend. His intention was for them to oppose the Coussey Report. This was a way to make his campaign attractive. Nkrumah's assembly passed a resolution declaring the Coussey Report unacceptable. But in the spirit of patriotism and nationalism Nkrumah and his activists were only being self-ambitious in the sense that the Coussey report was not drafted by the British, it was drafted by fellow Ghanaians, if he had been on the committee, all his agitations would never have happened. And there again, I think it was the wit of the British at work. I believe, they used this to arouse the agitation of Nkrumah. He was fighting against the report of his fellow Ghanaians as if he was fighting the British but it was a strategy by the British to create a division among the Ghanaian nationalist movement. The Coussey report which became accepted as Coussey constitution was going to grant the Gold Coast an internal Self Governance. There was going to be a general election for the first time in the history of this country. But there again, Nkrumah had developed a very strategic and attractive slogan **Independence Now** which sold well to the ordinary people who were angry against the British, the chiefs and the intelligentsia of the society.

On 15 December, Nkrumah and the CPP sent a letter to the Governor warning him that, if the Assembly resolution was ignored, he would declare positive Action. He published an article in the Accra Evening News entitled "The Era of Positive Action Draws Nigh". They demanded a constituent assembly to decide on a full Self Government constitution which is full Dominion Status within the Commonwealth of Nations based on the statute of Westminster. They gave the governor a deadline of two weeks.

Considering the activism of the CPP, the Governor, Arden Clarke met the Legislative Council and explained clearly how Britain had already agreed to grant Gold Coast independence as soon as practically possible hence there was no need for the violent agitation of the CPP which was undermining the good relationship Britain had had with the

Gold Coast. He stressed the fact that soon there were going to be enough African ministers who would receive assistance from British staff. He strongly admonished the patriots of the land to resist politics based on greed, envy and malice which was rearing its head in the Gold Coast politics in the form of Positive Action.

Danquah felt the Positive Action of Nkrumah was impractical and wrote to him to desist from the action.

> **...I do hope, Sir Kwame, that you see the mete analogy. If therefore by positive action on the penultimate day of 1949 you mean the destructive and pernicious kind, then, I ask you, in the name of Ghana, in the name of Sergeant Adjeitey and those who died or suffered at the Crossroads for this Ghana, don't do it! ....I counsel you, Sir Kwame, that like the gallant Don Quixote, be not rash to waste your strength upon an impracticable ideal. Instead, resort to creative positive action, and abandon the destructive kind. Learn from Grant, and remember his caution and ripe experience.[27]**

Danquah felt the real challenge was the division Nkrumah had brought to the united front that had made the colonial government regain some relief but yet they had the Coussey committee which was going to grant Gold Coast a measure of self-government and that they should snatch that opportunity and seek for more. He could see clearly that there was no way Nkrumah's activism could annul the Coussey committee report.

In December 1949, there was already an industrial strife spreading in the air wave which made Nkrumah's positive action a more anticipated one. The Union of Metrological Workers called a strike but the agitating strikers were sacked. The TUC also threatened with a subsequent strike. This tension wittingly informed the governor Arden Clarke who was more experienced on the job to hold a meeting with the Security Secretary Reginald Saloway for a mutual corporation on the peace of the country. Whereas Nkrumah claimed he did not agree to the terms of the two, Arden Clarke said something contrary that Nkrumah agreed to the Coussey Constitution and that the CPP would contest on the election and that they would call off the Positive Action. However, things went the other way as it is believed the extremist in the CPP later influenced Nkrumah to call for Positive Action. It is believed men like Krobo Edusei left Kumasi for Accra to pressure Nkrumah that the Positive Action must come on. This change of mind by Nkrumah was described by Arden Clarke as "The tail wagged the dog" meaning Nkrumah allowed his followers to control him.

On 6 January 1950, the TUC called on its strike. The CPP committee met the following two days and Nkrumah revealed that Positive Action would commence on the midnight of 8th January. Right away, he left Accra to declare Positive Action in places such as Cape Coast, Sekondi and Tarkwa. In his absence, the government took to the radio to persuade the people to annul Positive Action and that they must return to work. The governor called for an emergency meeting with the Legislative Council persuading them against the Positive Action and the strike. He put forward the need to call for State of Emergency to install peace and stability in the country. His argument was that the general public was happy about the Coussey report and opposed the radicalism of the CPP. The council gave him the support to enact State of Emergency.

When Nkrumah returned to find out this, he called for a meeting at the Arena on the 11 January charging the people to support Positive Action. The paradox is that The State of Emergency was declared and a curfew imposed that evening. The Evening News, the Cape Coast Daily Mail, The Sekondi Morning Telegraph all belonging to the CPP persuaded the people to stand firm and continue with Positive Action.

The Joint Provincial Council stepped in to mend things with the TUC, CPP and the Ex-Servicemen at Dodowa. The leadership of the TUC warned them not to attend while the Ex-Servicemen also failed to attend. It was only Nkrumah and a few CPP members that attended. During this meeting Nkrumah made his views and that of the CPP clear by saying.

**'We, the people, believe that our request for the election of a constituent assembly is reasonable and just. We will not accept half measures. The report of the Coussey Committee, a committee on which the rank and file of the**

**people were not represented, is a matter that concerns us all. It is only right that we should have a chance of rejecting or accepting this report. If our request is not given consideration, then I have to tell you that Positive Action will continue.'**[28]

The Governor's failure to nominate Nkrumah on the committee for Coussey Constitution is what erupted the agitation. He was able to convince the radical youth that the government and people of the higher hierarchy had abandoned the youth in the nation's independence struggle. Hence they would do anything to support Nkrumah and his vision because they felt Nkrumah was their man.

It was a meeting with the Joint Provincial Council that Nkrumah threatened the chiefs "they will run away and leave their sandals behind them" if they failed to support his struggle for freedom.

The police on behalf of the colonial government harassed the CPP by raiding their offices, closing the newspapers of the CPP and arresting CPP leaders and charging the editors of the various newspapers of the CPP. **'The editor of the Evening News was arrested on a sedition charge for publishing an article entitled 'Pull for the Shore', the editor of the Daily Mail was similarly charged for articles appearing in that paper entitled' A Campaign of Lies' and' We speak for Freedom' and the editor of the Morning Telegraph was gaoled for contempt of court.'**[29]

According to Nkrumah, the State of Emergency declared vested power into the hands of unduly people such as Syrians, Lebanese, and British nationals who were appointed as special constables and equipped with truncheons to enforce order. These people bullied citizens unnecessarily to the extent that some lives were lost. An example of such incidents was when some ex-servicemen in solidarity to Nkrumah and the CPP held a demonstration that clashed with the police which resulted in the death of two African police.

Following this, many CPP leaders were arrested on the 21st January. The following day, Nkrumah was arrested. He had been warned by the Secretary of the Colony that he would be held accountable for any trouble caused with his Positive Action. Nkrumah was charged with three cases. The first was inciting people to take part in an illegal strike. The second was trying to coerce the government and the third charge with sedition in line with his newspaper publication in Cape Coast. Each of these charges was one year imprisonment. The good news was that he would serve them simultaneously. After the trial at Cape Coast, he was returned to James Fort with ten other CPP leaders. The CPP hired two British lawyers as their attorney.

As if by design, Nkrumah's entry to the prison marked the exit of his main armour bearer and strategist Komla Gbedemah. They had a brief communication as to how to organize the party in Nkrumah's absence. And history can tell they did the most splendid job to keep the party's hopes alive and go on to win the February 1951 elections. It is told, they would communicate matters on toilet papers.

Nkrumah and his colleagues were not treated as they would expect political prisoners but were treated as ordinary criminals. They were given one latrine bucket to share. This was to his greatest shock.

As the election season approached, Nkrumah encouraged the CPP to contest in all the seats of the coming February 1951 under the Coussey Constitution, the very constitution he opposed that had landed him in prison. On this premise, firstly Nkrumah lost his case for 'Self-Government Now.' On a principle of integrity one would wonder what persuaded him to eventually succumb to the Coussey Constitution which he said was fraudulent and bogus, a constitution he harshly described as 'Trojan gift horse'. Most obviously, he did that to win the hearts and minds of the masses. He did that to be very visible in the political light to position himself among the electorate as if he was fighting for the ordinary man more than any of his compatriot politicians. He asked his name to be on the ballot. This was possible because the Coussey Constitution provided room for people whose arrest did not exceed more than one year to be qualified for election. Nkrumah was serving his three year imprisonment simultaneously so he could contest.

During this period in 1950, the CPP won a number of by elections. The first by election was at the Cape Coast municipality where the CPP candidate Kwasi Plange won. He was about 25 years, the youngest to be in the Assembly. He pressured the Assembly to reduce the voting age or the youth would fail to pay taxes. Eventually he was able to win his case and the voting age was reduced from 25 to 21 years.  In addition, more elections were won by the CPP that strengthened their chances. Nkrumah and a number of the CPP leaders languished in prison, but Gbedemah and the party faithful were putting things on ground, for instance, the CPP established branches in all the constituencies and wrote its party manifesto.

While this was going on, the Governor with the assistance of the Legislative Assembly established the new electoral system for the upcoming elections. These people consisted of the chiefs and some of the members of UGCC like Danquah. Arden Clarke formed a committee called the Ewart Committee which was responsible for setting up the new system. While Danquah and other members of the UGCC contributed to this new system and structure, they could not foresee how this new system was going to end their political standing in the Gold Coast politics. Leaders were no longer going to be nominated with their good standing with chiefs or by their qualifications. They failed to realize that, the key to get one elected by the very system they were creating was how to acquaint with the masses, how to solicit for vote from people from different thinking and perspective. This is where their inefficiency showed but that was where the strength of the CPP lay. Nkrumah outsmarted them by learning how to win the loyalty of the illiterate masses and drive them.

But this strength of the CPP was not without violence and indiscipline. Their local men were always ready to destroy images and structures of any other political grouping who wanted to take up government. In addition, the CPP were adequately resourced in propagating their message through leaflets, loudspeaker vans, cinema vans and public meetings. The UGCC did not only lack in violence and indiscipline but they also lacked the ability to network the countryside masses with leaflets, cinema vans and loudspeaker vans. It is as if they left their fate into the hands of nature or good luck. This is because the new constitution could not get one nominated by a high standing in society or either being nominated by chiefs but the new political era was going to solely elect people by the masses through the ballot box. This they were supposed to know because they had representatives on the Coussey Committee.

CHAPTER 5

# THE ELECTIONS OF 1951 AND 1954

The year 1951 will remain as the third significant year in Ghana's quest for self-Governance. Whereas 1947 marks the year of conception of dream, and 1948 as the year of Action, 1951 marks the year of actualising the Dream. It was a milestone achievement of self-governance and as such a partial independence. The Coussey Constitution united Asante and the Northern Territories with the Colony as one Gold Coast.

Positive Action, that defiant struggle Nkrumah undertook to stop the acceptance of the Coussey Constitution failed and hence the quest for 'Self-Governance Now' was unsuccessful. This is not because the British Colonial Government was too strong to bow in to the struggle for "Independence Now" but it is because just as Danquah revealed to Asantehene, "There is one thing of which Nana must be well aware. Already the Government has accepted the position that self-government must come within our own time". In support of that request of Self Governance and Dominion Status, first, the Constitution had already been prepared for the internal Self Governance to commence. Rightly so, the Governor did not see any logic in Nkrumah's petition to suspend that Constitution for another constitution which in reality was going to delay the independence anyway. Whichever way, the elections were going to take place not at the dictate of the Colonial Government but firstly by the request of the leadership of the UGCC which Nkrumah was involved.

Suffice it to know that the 1951 election which was the first in the history of the Gold Coast was the result of the effort of the UGCC and their supporters of the youth, Ex-Servicemen and the women and as such a victory for every Ghanaian and African. It did not happen on a silver platter but rather through hard work, petitions, imprisonments and other constitutional means.

The intent of this election was to grant an internal self-governance to the people of the Gold Coast. The party that would win majority of seats would form a government to pursue the parliamentary procedures for the Gold Coast to attain her full independence. It was also an opportune moment to unite all the four colonies, the Gold Coast, Ashanti, Northern Territories and British Togoland into one nation.

The election took place on the 8 February and the CPP won 34 out of the 38 electoral areas contested. The UGCC won only 2 of these seats. Nkrumah contested in Accra in what is today Odododiodio Constituency and won. Danquah and Ofori Ata won the two seats in Akyem Abuakwa. As early as on Friday morning in prison, Nkrumah had heard of his victory and the landslide victory of the CPP. The CPP wrote to the governor to release Nkrumah but the governor hesitated and eventually released him on Monday afternoon at 1 pm. The governor did not want Nkrumah's release to appear as a demand from the CPP but by his own volition. Even though the governor Arden Clarke wanted to release Nkrumah unceremoniously, soon after his release the CPP and their sympathizers gathered in their masses to welcome their hero in their Prison Graduate ceremony. He was carried shoulder high. He was initiated through the blood of a sheep as a cleansing from the prison.

A number of things contributed to the success of the CPP. The first strategy was propaganda. Nkrumah's false accusation that Danquah and other UGCC leaders had taken bribe to delay the independence ate into the minds and hearts of many people. This is what Danquah had to say about that:

**"We sacrificed our worth and paid money to get out**

**Nkrumah to carry on the work like St. Paul, but a year later he turned against us, and his party went about saying the rest of us had been bribed by the Government, and he was the only honest man of the six who really wanted S.G! We were abused and vilified and criticised destructively".[1]**

This helped Nkrumah to carry the masses away with the promise that he could gain Self Government within one year. According to Prof. Adu Boahen, Paa Grant revealed that what caused the UGCC bitter defeat was the propaganda that they had taken a bribe to compromise the independence. The reality was that it was not true. This was something the leaders of the UGCC were going to find it difficult to forgive Nkrumah and the CPP. Another propaganda the CPP used was on cocoa. During the electioneering campaign, the CPP promised to stop the cutting down of the cocoa trees infected with the swollen shoot. This pleased a lot of cocoa farmers and their sympathisers but soon after the election, Nkrumah reneged on that promise.

Nkrumah's strategy of using the most popular name of the UGCC which was the convention as the name of his party helped to carry the masses along with him. His motto of 'Self-Government Now' was a captivating slogan that aroused the suffering masses to rally behind him.

The next reason was Nkrumah's ability of political organization. He was such a handsome charismatic leader who was skilled in persuading the masses. He had better strategies of organizing the masses than the remaining UGCC leaders. He had Komla Gbedemah who was the best political organizer of the time to put better structures and strategies down. They were skilful at raising money to help finance the CPP. For instance, Nkrumah organised seminars and football matches to raise money. He had the "markola" market women to sponsor the CPP campaign. The CPP understood the use of media, leaflets, cinema vans, action troopers and loudspeakers in their campaigns. Again another significant reason that helped the CPP to win was Mr Plange's success in the Legislative Assembly to reduce the voting age to 21. He had threatened the chiefs if they did not reduce the voting age, he would instigate the youth not to pay tax. The membership of the CPP consisted of the youth and since the youth were in the majority of the population, that gave the CPP the competitive advantage to win the national elections.

At the end of the election, the party that would win the majority of seats was to form government for the Gold Coast. When that was done, the next step to attain the full independence was for a motion of independence to be passed in the Legislative Council and be supported by a majority vote. If the majority voted for the motion of independence, the motion would be sent to the British Parliament by the Gold Coast government for an Act of Independence to be issued for the Gold Coast to attain her full independence. Simply, once the election was conducted, the next tasks were mere parliamentary procedures to attain the full independence because the British government had already agreed to the position of independence.

Nkrumah and the CPP had won a majority of seats in the election so it was expected of him to form a government. The governor called Nkrumah to his office on the 13th February 1951. At their meeting, the Governor asked Nkrumah to form a government. According to Nkrumah this news sounded like a dream. The previous day he was confined in prison like a criminal. His rights were ceased. He could not eat the meal of his choice neither could he go to the place of his choice. The poor ventilation, the clothes of a prisoner were some of the things that could demoralize him. In prison, he narrated how some of the CPP convicts would complain and regret of the incident. He was not excused from punishment. He had to endure any should he flout any rule and barely 13 months of such experience is no joke. It was baptism he endured. A price of sacrifice he paid for independence struggle of Ghana. But as human, he had become acquainted with prison conditions so when the governor told him this good news, he wondered if it was not a dream at the end of which he would find himself in the prison again. But the reality is that it was rather a dream come true. For the first time, a Ghanaian was going to form government and lead his people.

The sequence of events clearly reveals that Arden Clarke replaced Governor Greasy to supervise Ghana's transition to Self-Government.

Nkrumah's landslide victory had made his work easy and this is how he commended Nkrumah.

**'Nkrumah and his party had the mass of the people behind them and there was no other party with appreciable public support to which one could turn. Without Nkrumah, the constitution would be stillborn and if nothing came of all the hope aspiration and concrete proposals for a greater measure of self-government, there would no longer be any faith in the good intentions of the British Government. .. the Gold Coast would be plunged into disorders, violence and bloodshed.'[2]**

The governor was amused about Nkrumah's victory because in spite of the fact that the British agreed to independence and the new constitution, the next phase was for the Gold Coast to form a government, but that could only be possible through an election. In the election, it was expected that one party would win majority of the seats to qualify to form a government. Assuming the election was conducted and no party won majority of seats, it was going to be difficult for the governor to choose a party to form the government and that could lead to chaos. Nevertheless, Nkrumah was able to sway the masses to his side to give him and the CPP a convincing victory. This is why the Governor, Arden Clarke praised Nkrumah for his victory. Yet what the readers must know is that, if Nkrumah had not left the UGCC or if he had not lied against the leaders of the UGCC, those masses would have remained with the UGCC and voted for the UGCC to win majority of the seats to form government. Like Nkrumah, most of the masses that voted for the CPP were former members of the UGCC. Notwithstanding, it does not take the credit from Nkrumah that his victory made the struggle for full independence successful.

The day after Nkrumah was released from prison, Danquah wrote him a memorable letter dated 13th February, 1951. He wrote:

**My dear Kwame,**

**This is a glad occasion. You have fought the good fight**

**and triumphed for the justice of our cause. Your imprisonment and your release are symbolic of the conquest over imperialism. You may have made mistakes, as even the greatest do, but you have passed through a baptism of fire, a spiritual fire, and you have suffered bodily in the cause of our Motherland.**

**I feel certain you see the light ahead as our opportunity to make this Ghana the land of promise of our dream. May the Gods of Ghana help and guide you and may the baseless misrepresentations and misunderstandings of the past that engendered disunity in our struggle be buried with their own past.**

**We started with a United Gold Coast. Let us complete the work for a united motherland. Since October the course of events had been clear to me and your election and release had been my desire. May God bless you.[3]**

**Yours sincerely,**

**J B Danquah**

Nkrumah barely had two weeks to appoint his ministers and he worked hand in hand with Arden Clarke.  Per the constitution, the Executive Council members were to be eleven ministers, three were to be appointed by the governor and these were the Attorney General, Financial Secretary and Chief Secretary. The rest of the eight were to be appointed by Nkrumah who was the Leader of Government Business. He chose

Gbedemah for Health and Labour,

Botsio for Education and Social Welfare,

Hutton-Mills Commerce, Industry and Mines,

Casely-Hayford as the minister for Agriculture and Natural Resources

Ansah Koi as Communication and Works.

Arden Clarke persuaded Nkrumah to extend his appointments to non CPP legislators in the territorial members. These two were appointed:

Asafu Adjaye for Local Government (form Ashanti)

and Braimah for Without Portfolio (from the Northern Territories).

The New Legislative Assembly was formally opened on the February 20, 1951.  On the 26 February, the House voted on the eight members of the Executive council.  These appointees were later confirmed in the Governor's office the same day in the afternoon. Nkrumah was officially approved as the Leader of the Government Business. The official formal sitting of the house took place on the 29 March which was accompanied by decoration of colours, the governor in full ceremonial dress with police outriders, and inspection of guard of honour. Our fellow African ministers were in their "kente" and African clothes. The military, judges and all other professionals were in their respective formal clothes.

A message from the King of England was read to the house which was followed by trumpets and 17 gun salute. There was greeting from the Secretary of State. There was a delegation from the House of Commons who conveyed the Speaker's message. The Speaker was called Hon. Emmanuel Quist. The Governor finally gave his speech on the throne. This ceremony was captured by the world media.

In the following year in 1952, provision was made for the creation of the office of the Prime Minister and Nkrumah was duly approved.

About three months after his victory, in May, Nkrumah was invited by his alma mater to receive an honorary doctorate degree in Law in the US. Nkrumah travelled with Kojo Botsio. He used this moment to reconnect with his old friends in America and also make a number of political links like meeting the State Department, and the Mayor of Pennsylvania. He gave a number of speeches which brought more honour to him.

As the colony embarked on this constitutional or parliamentary process, it was expected for the incumbent government to implement developments to improve the welfare of the people. Nkrumah had a lot of success in this aspect and must be duly honoured for that.

Nkrumah inherited the Colonial Government Ten-Year Development Plan. This plan was aided by economists Seers and Ross. The budget for this plan was £31 m and additional £15 m.  Nkrumah reduced this to the 5 Years Development Plan with an increased budget of £127 million. This plan highlighted Infrastructure, Education, Health,

Agriculture etc.

On infrastructure, Nkrumah developed Tema harbour and Tema township to be an industrial city. He allocated £16 m into building this project. He allocated £2m to the Takoradi Harbour for renovation and expansion. More modern roads with bitumen were constructed all over the country. These include Accra Takoradi, Accra to Tema, Kumasi to Bolgatanga. The Akyease –Kotoku railway was built. The Accra-Kumasi railway and Kumasi to Takoradi railway which trundled poorly were improved. The Adomi Bridge was constructed to ease the ferry-poor transport on the Volta.

On education, Nkrumah did a lot of significant jobs. He introduced free Compulsory Basic Education for children from 6 to 12 years. He introduced post primary school system. He continued to support the mission schools in the country. The number of primary schools trebled from 1000 to 3000. The effect of this was that the population of pupils increased from 200,000 to 500,000. The number of government assisted secondary schools increased from 16 in 1951 to 31 in 1955. Nkrumah realised that most of the schools were non science schools so he introduced science based schools. He built the College of Technology in 1952 to offer engineering, architecture, pharmacy, agriculture and other science related courses at a cost of £1.5 m. He built about 16 teacher training colleges. This increased the number of teachers produced from 791 in 1952 to 1680 in 1955. He also built Cape Coast Education College which also became a university to train teaching professionals for the nation. He invested about £1.5 m into the Gold Coast University College.

Another area in which the Nkrumah government invested was agriculture. He built Research Institutions to develop this sector. Considering the widening gap that existed between the south and North, Nkrumah gave the North special attention on Agriculture. He established the Gonja Scheme. This was to farm on about 30,000 acres of land. His emphasis was on groundnut, maize, guinea corn, etc. He also invested in animal farming by establishing a vertinary school in Tamale for pig-breeding, chicken-raising and other livestock. These projects attracted foreign aid from Russia, the FOOD and Agriculture

Organisation of the UN and other agencies. At the south Ghana, Nkrumah focused on fisheries at the coast. He established dams and irrigation on rivers for this project. On the issue of Cocoa, the CPP government deferred from their propaganda of opposing the cutting of cocoa trees. Rather they persuaded the farmers to cut their cocoa trees at a fee of 4d and giving extra 2s for three years for planting a new cocoa tree. They were able to coerce a number of farmers to cut down their cocoa trees. He also established the Cocoa Purchasing Board to crush the monopoly that the expatriates enjoyed in the Gold Coast. He also used it to grant loans to cocoa farmers.

On housing the government invested about £2.5 m. Many houses were built in urban areas such as Accra, Kumasi, Cape Coast and Takoradi. The government also introduced housing loan of £2 m. he attempted building for the low income people but that project failed.

The government, upon recommendation, introduced a new salary and wage for civil servants. The government also increased the daily wage of unskilled by 50%.

On health, the British government had dispatched doctors and nurses to remote areas to operate with small hospitals. They were supported by the medical centres of the cocoa industry, timber industry and mines. For instance, the Obuasi mine has a big hospital that provides health care to the indigenous people. Nkrumah's government supported this by providing good drinking water, establishing Bore holes. Due to the lower percentage of doctors and nurses, health centres were established and people were given education on hygiene, first aid education, sanitation and other health education. The milestone achievement during this period was the construction of the new hospital in Kumasi at a cost of £1.5 million.

Last but not the least, Nkrumah's government began its first practical steps on the Volta River Project during this period. It was a dormant plan under the British government which was devised in the 1920s. But Nkrumah revived this project because it was his utmost expectation to use that as the engine for his industrialisation. Nkrumah's Government negotiated with the Aluminium Company Limited of Canada and the British Aluminium Company and set up the Volta River

Preparatory Commission in 1953. The chairman of this commission was R.G.A. Jackson. The total cost of the Volta scheme and its smelter to process the local bauxite issued by the Government White paper in 1952 was in the estimates of £100m for the first phase and £144 million for the full scheme. This cost was agreed to be shared by the government and the aluminium companies involved.[4] Nevertheless, the Volta project did not materialize until in the mid-sixties.

On governance, Nkrumah terminated the authorities of traditional leaders at the district and urban places by introducing Local Government system. He set up district and urban councils which consisted of elected members. The elections of these councils were swept by many CPP youngsters mainly of school leavers. Subject to whether abolishing the chiefs' role at the district and urban level was a good thing to do or not, this local governance only bred corrupt and incompetent administrators. Right from this onwards, the nation created structures to accommodate people who were not nurtured on good governance and patriotism. The quest for abolishing the old trend was what mattered to Nkrumah. But there again, this alternative proved unfruitful under his own administration.

Nkrumah's feats in government lifted his popularity more. Towns and communities were all clamouring for development. This made the CPP very attractive and a force to reckon with. However, these developments posed their own challenges. For instance, the policy of free Education and the abolishing of Standard Seven Exams compromised the quality of education given. Besides, there was a shortage of trained teachers.

The next challenge was posed by the increase of Ghanaians in the public service. This brought much corruption. It is not bad to Africanize, increase African representation in the civil or public service but where the individuals were not cultured with ethics and patriotism but just to get indigenous people to take over from the British engendered corruption which has escalated in today's Ghanaian life.

Again, the success of Nkrumah strengthened the hooliganism and violence which had characterised the youth right at the birth of the CPP. This was a premonition Arden Clarke perceived about Nkrumah, "a skilful politician, he has, I think, the making of real statesman and this he may become if he has the strength to resist the bad counsels of the scallywags by whom he is surrounded." Right from the commencement of their relationship, the governor saw this in Nkrumah and his followers, the CPP. He admitted Nkrumah was a skilful politician who was on the path of becoming a real statesman and this Nkrumah proved soon after his 1951 victory and here again, his followers did not prove Arden Clark wrong. He described them as 'scallywags.' Not only was Nkrumah's CPP violent, Nkrumah enjoyed the hero-worship and blind adulation from his followers.

The truth of the matter is, these scallywags did not choose Nkrumah, he chose them. Initially he worked with the UGCC but in order to get his vision done, he swayed the masses especially the less educated, the more agitated who fitted into his so called revolutionary training. But this revolutionary training was tearing the nation's unity both the top and bottom apart. Whereas we were supposed to see the colonial government as the only opponent for our freedom, our own Ghanaians on the train for self-governance became enemies among themselves.

The political opponents of Nkrumah saw him as a dictator and an intolerant politician. They felt he would soon get rid of any political grouping in the country so they had to reorganize themselves. Seeing the UGCC was no longer any threatening opponent to the CPP, some of these politicians mainly from the UGCC formed the Ghana Congress Party in May 1952. It was made up of Danquah, Ofori Atta, Ako Adjei, Obetsebi Lamptey, N.A Ollennu and K.A Bossman. Dr K.A Busia a sociologist professor and M. Dowuona the registrar from the Gold Coast College became active members. It had members who had defected CPP like Saki Scheck, former Nkrumah's personal secretary, Ashie Nikoi, Kwesi Lamptey, Dzenkle Dzewu, and H. Nyemitei. Busia became the chairman of this party.

Their aim was clear, to be an alternative government for independence and also to offer the highest standards of life for the Ghanaian. But soon, they revealed among themselves that, neither the CPP nor the Colonial Government was their main enemy. Their main enemy lay within them. The party was full of infighting for positions. They fought over the position of president and vice presidents. They held on to their academic and high standard in society and could not match on to the grassroots to sell their party to the ordinary man. Soon some left. Among them is Ako Adjei. Obetsebi was penalised and left to form his own party, Ghana National Party. Ansah Koi also left to form the Ghana Action Party.

On the parliamentary floor a number of debates went on. Among them were matters concerning independence. When Nkrumah assumed the position of opposing the Coussey Constitution as to Self-Government Now, Danquah and the UGCC expected Nkrumah to fight relentlessly for that vision that made him very popular among the ordinary man. But none of that happened so Danquah put it to him how he had betrayed the people of Ghana with his promise of Self Government Now and that he had sold himself to the imperialist.

Interestingly, it was Danquah who tabled a motion on April 24 1951 to speed up the full independence of Ghana in the assembly. Danquah proposed that the Legislative Assembly should appoint a Select Committee to examine all available Dominion and similar constitutions and report upon the terms of a constitution suitable for the Gold Coast as a fully self-governing Dominion within the Commonwealth, and to make the necessary recommendations for its early implementation. Strangely, Nkrumah and the CPP turned down the motion on the following thinking.

> MINISTER OF COMMUNICATION AND WORKS (Dr Ansah Koi):[5]
>
> I am afraid to say that I am not at all in favour of the motion. It seems to me that this motion is rather too premature and destructive in the working of the new constitution
>
> MINISTER OF AGRICULTURE AND NATURAL RESOURCE (Mr Casely Hayford):
>
> Mr. Speaker, I did not become Minister of Agriculture and Natural Resource to see the liquidation of my ministry in so short a time as now, not even if as the result of the constitution that is sought to be promulgated by the doyen of

Gold Coast politics. It will be unwise to try to push a second morsel into the mouth when the first one has not been swallowed.

MINISTER OF EDUCATION AND SOCIAL WELFARE (Kojo Botsio):

If such a motion is passed what would be the repercussion in the country? We know that people are very much anxious for self-government now. As soon as this committee is formed, then it must produce its report either in one year, two years, or four years but we know what would be the result if the people did not attain their wishes. Therefore we must follow the leader and the plan and policy of the Convention People's Party which have always led the people to the right place

LEADER OF GOVERNMENT BUSINESS (Kwame Nkrumah):

All that I can say is simply this: that constitutions are not made in a day, and when we come to Dominion status constitution, the matter has already been thrashed out and anybody who takes up any textbook on British Constitution History, at the back will find the exact prototype of a Dominion Status constitution. What I am driving at is this: At this critical moment it is not for an Assembly like this to appoint a Select committee to sit down and spend time and waste time to draw up a Dominion Status constitution. Everything is plain in black and white in every constitutional textbook. The statute of Westminster 1931 makes that point clear, so I am inclined to believe that this is a sheer waste of time. The motion is actually wasting our time and I think that the only way to dismiss it is to say that those who are behind me and those who are supporters within and outside this Assembly must do everything to vote against this thing because it is purely a waste of time for us to sit down to appoint a select committee for the next six months to study the form which a new constitutional for the Gold Coast should take when, if you go back to any constitutional law textbook you will find that the full text of Dominion status constitution is there. It is purely a waste of time and that was the motive behind the motion. I do not want to employ invective. I am above invective otherwise I would simply say that the mind that actually conceived this motion is a criminal mind'

DR. DANQUAH: Mr. Speaker, I object to this….

MR. SPEAKER: The Hon. Leader of Government Business, the First Member of Akim Abuakwa is complaining about those words…

LEADER OF GOVERNMENT BUSINESS: Mr. Speaker, if he takes offence, I withdraw it.

When the House voted on the motion, only 6 out of 84 legislators voted in favour of the motion; 8 abstained, and 65 voted against it. Turning against such a motion that aimed at speeding Self Government Now, had Nkrumah abandoned his slogan or it was sheer hatred against Danquah? Whichever answer it may be, Danquah and UGCC did what they could to achieve independence for Ghana. It is therefore never true that he or the leaders of the UGCC betrayed the course of independence.

Danquah and the Opposition taunted Nkrumah that he sold out to the Imperialists since Nkrumah failed to deliver on his promise of 'Independence Now.' Nkrumah responded by asking the Opposition to join him to send an ultimatum to His Majesty's Government of the United Kingdom for 'Self Government Now', and if rejected to declare Positive Action-strike. Danquah responded to this action of Nkrumah as mere tricks and advised the Opposition to dissociate from the Nkrumah's request. In a letter dated October 10, 1951 to one J.A Obdam resident in London, Danquah wrote:

**That man Nkrumah, who is now Leader of Government Business, has started his tricks again, this time, he who is the Government is inviting all the political leaders and Chiefs to join him to send an ultimatum to His Majesty's Government of the United Kingdom for 'Self-Government Now', and if rejected to declare Positive Action-strikes,**

**boycotts etc. There has been hectic activity all over the place and on Sunday we of the UGCC met at a great meeting and turned down flat his 'challenge' as being an invitation to criminal conspiracy against law and order'**

Kabral Blay-Amihere in his book *The story of Ghana's independence* page 128 puts it in a more suitable way by writing: **'Danquah was perfectly right in deeming it strange that a party in power would call for an action that could cripple its activities and shut down the government. Nkrumah's challenge could be nothing but a mere political bluff since he himself would have recognised the suicidal nature of the proposed second Positive Action. Besides, there was no compelling reason for him to abandon the constitutional route to independence.'** What was required of Nkrumah was for him to put before the Legislative Assembly, a motion of Independence for the members to vote on.

On 16 October, 1952 Nkrumah put before the house to form a fully representative Committee to recommend a new constitution for the Gold Coast. He put forward a number of concerns largely on the limitation to the Prime Minister. He wished among other things if the Prime Minister could appoint and endorse his ministers without the Governor's endorsement. Again Nkrumah suggested the three Ex-officio Ministers of Finance, Justice and Defence to be scrapped of their responsibilities while still sitting at Cabinet. On the Finance he suggested a Ghanaian could take up the role with a British expert as adviser who will sit in cabinet but without vote. Concerning justice, he asked the possibility of choosing a Ghanaian Attorney General. Again Nkrumah revealed that it was time a Representative Minister replaced the Minister of Defence and External Affairs for the Gold Coast to provide her own security. But on this sector, Nkrumah revealed the huge task that would be on the nation. For Britain would relegate its foreign security duty on the nation. Ghana would have to provide enough army and security people and resources to take such responsibility.

Nkrumah appeared like appealing to the British Government for the approval of the proposed constitution. To Danquah this model was going to be akin to that of the Coussey Constitution where the constitution was subject to the approval of the Governor. But Danquah argued that such approach would mean mortgaging the birth right of the people of Gold Coast into the hands of the imperialists. Danquah advised that the supreme power of self-government rested with the chiefs and people, so Nkrumah should form a committee that would represent all the people. He concluded that what touched all should be approved by all- "quod omnes tangit ab omnibus approbetur".[6] On this occasion Nkrumah and Danquah agreed. Nkrumah promised to form a committee that would engage the chiefs and people and Danquah suspended his motion. This had been their collective initial petition to the Secretary of Colonies for the working Committee of the UGCC to take an interim government to set up a constituent assembly for a new constitution for self-government.

Nkrumah did not form the committee or the constituent assembly as agreed but rather called upon the Chiefs and all political organisations to send their views on the modification of the Constitution to him by post. The Opposition rejected this idea of chiefs and people sending their views on the modification on the constitution by post. Rather, the Opposition demanded full Self-Government guaranteed by an irrevocable Act of Parliament. Interestingly, the CPP disagreed with Nkrumah and demanded similar action like the Opposition. At a CPP party conference on the 28th December, 1952,  the CPP rejected the call for modifications and asked for full Self-Government by an "Act of Independence".[7] Nevertheless, Dr. Nkrumah went along to do what individually suited him and also with the colonial government. One hundred and thirty organisations submitted their views to Nkrumah by the end of March 1953.

After lengthy discussions and consultations, the Government's White Paper on constitutional Reform of 1953 was issued which gave birth to the constitution for 1954 elections. In this new constitution, the seats for traditional leaders and professionals from the mines and commerce were removed and all members of the house were to be directly elected. The house was to be a single house chamber purely for elected independent candidates or partisan politicians.

Along this same period, Nkrumah established a commission under

Justice W.B Van Lare to supervise the structuring of the new constituencies. The number of constituencies drawn was 104 for the whole nation under direct election. But the demarcation of these constituencies posed a number of problems. In Ashanti, both the opposition and members of the CPP from this region strongly argued that Ashanti deserved more constituencies of about 30 and not 21 allocated. Krobo Edusei vehemently opposed the allotted figure of 21. He is noted by saying, **'we Ashantis are not preaching tribalism or anything of the sort; we are only agitating for our legitimate right.'**[8] They felt Ashanti had been undermined considering its huge impact on the nation. This is confirmed by B.F. Kusi who said, **'...All Ashantis express the sentiment that Asante is a nation...we are not a region at all; we should be considered a nation...'**[9] This outcry remained with them and later outburst in a different fashion. Again on the issue of boundaries, some communities felt they had been wrongly demarcated to mistrusted territories or territories they simply did not belong. Sometimes a local community would be split into two different constituencies or districts. This error in my experience still persists today.

Once the house agreed on the constitution for independence, the next task was for a motion of independence to be passed and approved by the majority members in the Legislative Assembly. Dr. Kwame Nkrumah filed for a motion of Independence as a parliamentary requirement, on the 10th of July 1953, a month after the government White Paper was published. This motion became popularly known as 'The Motion of Destiny'. To Danquah, it was the effort of the Opposition to propose a full dominion constitution and their demand for full self-government that pushed Nkrumah to modify the constitution and file the independence motion. Whichever way, either by the pressure from the Opposition or Nkrumah's initiative, Danquah's prediction that the **Coussey constitution will not last beyond 1953** was fulfilled.[10]

In this motion, Nkrumah asked that the Gold Coast should be declared Independent and a sovereign nation within the Commonwealth. He stated that an Act of Independence should be passed in the United Kingdom parliament. In addition he authorized The Government to ask

Her Majesty to amend the Gold Coast (Constitution) Order in Council 1950. For this amendment, Nkrumah asked for a Legislative Assembly where all members shall directly be elected by secret ballot, and that all Members of the Cabinet shall be Members of the Assembly and directly responsible to the assembly.

Nkrumah cautioned the members that their final remarks is what would be taken to Her Majesty and therefore urged the debate should be based on national and not regional, patriotic and not partisan, communicated in a spirit of co-operation and goodwill. To buttress his point, he quoted Aristotle by saying what is important is to practice virtue as with self-government.

He stated that "The right of a people to govern themselves is a fundamental principle, and to compromise on this principle is to betray it. Self-government was a fundamental right of the people of the Gold Coast and Britain should not betray the Gold Coast about that."[9] He added that the criterion for their preparedness lay in their readiness to govern themselves and that since his government assumed office he had laid sound economic and social foundations on which Ghana could raise a solid democratic society. He revealed how the people were united for that cause and how he had collaborated with the Northern Territories, Asanteman Council and the Trade Union Congress.

He quoted Arthur Creech Jones, James Griffiths and Oliver Lyttelton and how they had all revealed that the principal British Colonial policy was to guide colonies towards responsible self-government within the Commonwealth in conditions that would ensure a fair standard of living and freedom from any oppression. He buttressed his submission by referring to the British North America Act of 1867 that also led to the independence of similar white colonies such as New Zealand, Australia and Dominions.

He reiterated the heritage of the Gold Coast by lauding its healthy economy that was better than a number of sovereign states. Again he revealed how homogenous his people and how they were immune from religious and tribal conflicts and above all how they had no racial conflicts.

He continued by explaining how the self-government of the Gold

Coast would foster a new relationship of friendship between the two nations and that Britain's unwillingness to grant self-governance could jeopardise that friendship. He quoted:

> In the very early days of the Christian era, long before England had assumed any importance, long even before her people had united into a nation, our ancestors had attained a great empire, which lasted until the eleventh century, when it fell before the attacks of the Moors of the North. At its height that empire stretched from Timbuktu to Bamako, and even as far as to the Atlantic. It is said that lawyers and scholars were much respected in that empire and that the inhabitants of Ghana wore garments of wool, cotton, silk and velvet. There was trade in copper, gold and textile fabrics, and jewels and weapons of gold and silver were carried.'

Thus may we take pride in the name of Ghana, not out of romanticism, but as an inspiration for the future. It is right and proper that we should know about our past. For just as the future moves from the present so the present has emerged from the past. Nor need we be ashamed of our past. There was much in it of glory. What our ancestors achieved in the context of their contemporary society gives us confidence that we can create, out of that past, a glorious future, not in terms of war and military pomp, but in terms of social progress and of peace. For we repudiate war and violence. Our battles shall be against the old ideas that keep men trammelled in their own greed; against the crass stupidities that breed hatred, fear and inhumanity. The heroes of our future will be those who can lead our people out of the stilling fog of disintegration through serfdom, into the valley of light where purpose, endeavour and determination will create that brotherhood which Christ proclaimed two thousand years ago, and about which so much is said, but so little done.[11]

He paid tribute to the ancient forebears whom we owe our customs and tradition to like Okomfo Anokye and Osei Tutu. He acknowledged the impact of the Fante Confederation, the Aborigine Rights and Protection Society, National Congress of British West Africa, The United Gold Coast Convention, especially the six that were arrested as a result of the fear they brought to the Colonial Government and the support from the women, students, farmers and the Trade Congress which according to Nkrumah evolved one of the most epic stories in Ghana's national struggle. He commended the new wave his party the CPP brought into the national struggle. He also acknowledged the courteous assistance the Governor Arden Clarke and the three ex-officio  had given him in shaping the destiny of the nation.

Concerning his political opponents, this is what he had to say ' And so through the years, many have been laid to final rest from the stresses and dangers of the national struggle and many, like our illustrious friends of the Opposition, notwithstanding the fact that we may differ on many points, have also contributed a share to the totality of our struggle.

He therefore challenged all the political opponents to lay aside whatever differences and be united to demand the country's freedom. He further admonished them that all Africa and The New World (USA) were looking up to them with desperate hope and so they must not disappoint.

He stressed that self-government is not an end in itself. It is a means to an end, to the building of the good life of the people. He added, "Mr Speaker, we can only meet the challenge of our age as a free people. Hence our demand for our freedom, for only free men can shape the destinies of their future."

The motion was seconded by J. A. Braimah, Minister of Communications and Works.[12]

During the debate on the motion, Danquah proposed before the House for an amendment on Nkrumah's motion that the Gold Coast Government rather be authorized to inform the British Government that in pursuance of the demand of the Chiefs and people of the Gold Coast for a sovereign nation within the Commonwealth, a declaration of the Gold Coast independence would be passed by the Legislative Assembly on March 6 1954. And that the Gold Coast Government should use all practical means to get the United Kingdom Parliament to pass an Act of Independence for the Gold Coast as full Dominion Status i.e. a sovereign nation in the Commonwealth. Eventually, as we know Ghana gained her political independence on 6 March 1957.  K.B Ayensu and S.N Darkwa all former clerks of Ghana's parliament attribute Ghana's independence date to Danquah. They stated, **'The Bond of 1844 was executed on March 6, and Danquah settled on that date for independence'**[13]

To Danquah, the freedom was ours and that it was inappropriate to beg for it but rather fight for it and that it was not fitting for freedom to be bestowed upon us so the assembly should declare themselves free. Concerning the constitution, Danquah wanted the people of Gold Coast to write their own independent constitution instead of the one that would have to go through another scrutiny under the British Government. He opposed the retaining of the powers of the Governor and the retaining of the portfolio of Defence and External Affairs by colonial official. He challenged the Prime Minister to seek for Dominion status for the Gold Coast. He explained that Nkrumah's request could mean a status similar to that of Malta and Southern Rhodesia within the Commonwealth but did not have equality with Britain. Simply Danquah wanted our independence to be on equal terms as Britain. Nkrumah objected this amendment of motion with the reason that **should Danquah's motion be accepted, Ghana would lose the goodwill of the British.**[14] Danquah's motion was rejected yet the sad distortion in our independence narration is that Danquah did not want independence or slowly wanted it in later time that no one could wait for but that has never been true.

What any critical thinker should be interested in  is  why Nkrumah who wanted *Independence Now* had to wait till 1953 to file for the motion of Independence?, Why did he not demand *Independence Now* or *Self Government Now* in his motion of independence when it mattered most? Why did he not specify a date for his 'Independence Now' but sent an open request to the colonial government to decide on their own time to give the Gold Coast independence? And when Danquah suggested an earlier date, he rather turned it down on the grounds that the Gold Coast would lose the goodwill of the British if he accepted Danquah's amendment.

After the Nkrumah's motion had been debated upon for a few days it was carried unanimously. According to Nkrumah, with the new constitution replacing the Coussey Constitution, there was the need to put the new constitution into effect through a general election. So the fact remains again that Nkrumah faced the reality that independence was a process but not 'Now' as he used that catchy caption to sway the masses to his opinion. This makes the UGCC's demand for Self-Government within the shortest possible time a more reasonable thing to do.

The general election was scheduled for 15 June 1954. Among the parties that contested were the CPP, Ghana Congress Party, Northern People's Party, Muslim Association Party, Togoland Congress Party, Anlo Youth Association, the Ghana National Party (GNP), and the Ghana Action Party (GAP).

The Togoland Congress Party was established in 1951 in British Togoland and their primary aim was to reunite with the French Togoland. S.G Antor was its leader. This party contested six of thirteen seats in the Volta Region. Its rival party was the Anlo Youth Association. This party opposed the separation of British Togoland from the Ewes in Gold Coast. It contested two of the seats in south Volta Region. The Ghana Congress Party contested for 22 out of the 104 constituencies. The Northern People's Party was born at the 11th hour, about two months to the election. This party was formed because many of the chiefs and elders in the North did not trust in the leadership of Nkrumah. Besides they were not too ready for independence because they had little or no benefit from the colonial governance in terms of development. Lastly, they wanted to avoid the dominance of the southerners. So they formed this party to have representatives in government to maintain their dignity, culture and welfare. It was made of great intellectuals and noble chiefs such as S.D. Dombo, the Douri-Na or Chief, Yakubu Tali, a Dagomba Chief, J.A. Braimah, an educated Gonja Chief, Mumuni Bawumia, the State Secretary of the Mamprusi State, and educated commoners like B.K. Adama, Jato Kaleo and Adam Amandi. They contested 18 of the 26 seats in Northern Territories.

Ally to the NPP was the Muslim Association Party also formed in 1954 out of the Gold Coast Muslim Association which was established in 1932. This party's main aim of contesting the election was to seek the interest of Muslims in the Zongo communities and entire Muslims elsewhere in the country. They contested 15 out of the 26 seats in the Northern Territories.

From the brief narration one can understand that none of these parties was appealing on the national scale because firstly they failed to file candidates for all the 104 seats in the country. They were specifically regional or tribal in orientation. This is not because they wanted it so but since Nkrumah was able to win the hearts of the masses away from the UGCC, the remnants were left with no other choice than to protect their regional territories with these parties at least to keep their political aspirations alive.

That was not the case with the CPP. 1000 people showed up to contest the 104 seats. This bred so much pressure and indiscipline in the party. Originally Nkrumah and the party heads did not want new candidates to contest official existing candidates. This fell on deaf ears of many party people. Some felt the people elected to the assembly had lost the fervour with which they started and needed to be replaced. At a rally in Arena Accra, Nkrumah listed the candidates to contest on the ticket of the CPP. Nkrumah warned all members whose names were not on his list to step down. Some agreed to step down and others refused. As a result of this, about 84 people were expelled from the party.

The reality of the matter is that most of the CPP candidates were of less academic standing or lower credibility. Yet the fact remains that CPP was more strategic and serious than any of the contesting political parties. The reality is it was a parliamentary democracy and the election demanded a party to win majority of seats to form government. How were any of these parties contributing in forming a Gold Coast government for independence? The best possible way for the opposition parties was to form alliances to form government but that could be problematic. This made the CPP the most obvious party to be handed over the government of the Gold Coast.

At the end of the elections, the CPP had a landslide victory of winning 72 out of the 104 seats. The NPP won 12 seats, the MAP won 1, GCP won 1, TC won 3, AYO won 1. This victory was not a surprise because Nkrumah's government had impressed the citizens with the government rapid developments. This increased his popularity. Secondly the CPP was more politically organized and charged to win power more than any of the political parties. Consider the fact that none of the political parties could even file for half of the constituencies the electoral system demanded. Right from the outset it was evident that they were in many ways not prepared to contest the CPP. The opposition parties full of intelligentsia could not drive the ordinary illiterate masses, rather many of them were at the top rivalling for positions which resulted in unnecessary infightings. The CPP had effective strategists like Komla Gbedemah who was influential in mobilizing the masses. Again the CPP had enough money to sponsor their propaganda. Signs and sequence of events proved the Governor, Arden Clarke, and the British Government supported Nkrumah, as a result they turned deaf ears and blind sight to the violence and electoral irregularities.

This election was supposed to be the last election for the Gold Coast to be granted full independence. This is because all the parliamentary requirements had been fulfilled. There was an agreed constitution and elected members of the Legislative Assembly had voted in favour of the motion of Independence. Yet this did not happen according to expectation because there emerged a new political party which raised new concerns on the constitution. The next delay was the Togoland issue. As Britain was parting way with Ghana, there was going to be a major concern whether British Togoland would be part of Ghana or Togo.

# CHAPTER 6

## NLM AND THE 1956 ELECTIONS

Barely three months after the 1954 election, a new party, the National Liberation Movement, (NLM) emerged. Its birth was as a result of disappointment some people from the CPP and political activists from the Opposition in Ashanti felt under the Nkrumah administration.

During the 1951 election, Nkrumah and the CPP attacked the colonial government for cutting down the cocoa trees due to the swollen shoot. This cutting down of the trees did not go down well with farmers and it made the colonial government unpopular. It was this grievance of the farmers that the UGCC sympathised with to win their support in 1948. To win the farmers to his side, Nkrumah promised the electorates he would stop the cutting of the cocoa trees. This gave the CPP a large following and most of these farmers were in Ashanti. So they voted massively for the CPP in the 1951 election. However, after the CPP inherited government, Nkrumah changed his stand and persuaded the farmers to cut down the cocoa trees affected by the swollen shoot. He promised to give 3s for cutting down an affected cocoa tree and gave extra 2s for three years if they planted new cocoa trees. Many people saw this as unfair. They felt Nkrumah and the CPP had deceived them. This caused them to be sceptical about the CPP. But during the 1954 elections Nkrumah and the CPP had another bait to catch them again.

Chieftaincy is revered as the symbol of culture and democracy in Ashanti and other parts of the nation. However, in his attempt to empower the youth, Nkrumah abolished the district and urban governance and established a new structure called the Local Government with councils in local districts and urban areas for leaders to occupy through the ballot. This paved room for the youth many of whom were CPP activists to win such leadership positions. This structure was intended not only to terminate the loyalty, influence and governance of the chiefs but also deny them of their financial revenues. For in time past, many chiefs made their wealth by the sale of plots of land and settling of disputes. Many of the chiefs and their loyalists saw Nkrumah and the CPP as a threat against the chieftaincy institution and the entire Asanteman. This soon brought a number of chiefs together to fight to reclaim their position. And the best weapon to resort to was politics. It was this reason that attracted many chiefs to the NLM.

Preparing for the 1954 elections, Nkrumah established a new commission called Van Lare Commission to allocate constituencies to the various colonies. This commission allocated 44 seats to the Colony, 26 seats to the Northern Territories, 21 seats to Ashanti and 13 seats to the British Togoland. The Ashantis felt they had not been treated fairly and that they deserved more. This infuriated not only the Asantes in opposition but also the Asantes in CPP like Krobo Edusei. They felt Asante deserved 30 and not 21. With the passage of time, this grievance of Asante did not die but rather escalated in different forms. It made the Asante Anti-CPP very strong and gathered a big following. The thought of hatred or the marginalization of Asanteman by the CPP grew with each and every step Nkrumah and the CPP took.

Another reason that got the Ashantis angry and made them distance themselves from the CPP was how Nkrumah dismissed a number of CPP loyalists who had wanted to contest in the 1954 elections. Nkrumah had forewarned that CPP members were not to contest against the party's official candidates during the elections. However, all over the country, a number of CPP people stood to contest in the elections. Many of such people were in the Ashanti. In the end many of these CPP youth were dispelled, about 81 activists, from the party. Most of these disgruntled activists were from the Asante Youth Organisation who in their defiance to the chiefs had joined the CPP for self-governance. They had been the core of the masses Nkrumah gathered in Asante. But they were beginning to see things differently. They were seeing the deviation of the CPP from its core principles. They were seeing dictatorial tactics of Nkrumah. Among these infuriated activists were Yaw Kankam, B.K. Owusu Antwi, Kusi Anane, E.Y. Baffoe, Osei Asibe Mensah and Kusi Ampofo. They went to Nana Osei Yaw Baffuor Akoto Chief linguist of the Asantehene to share their grievances with him. They wanted him to do something about what was happening.

Among all the frustration, the one that broke the Carmel's back was the cocoa price in 1954. The cocoa price worldwide had been increased to £450 a ton. This naturally aroused the expectations of many cocoa farmers that their share of the price would be increased. To whet their expectation, Nkrumah and the CPP propaganda machinery promised the electorates that should CPP be elected in the 1954 elections, they would increase the cocoa price to £5 a load and that a new £5 currency note had already been issued to help payment. In spite of the cracks that were tearing on, many people believed in the CPP and voted for them. CPP won in Ashanti, but to their utmost shock, the CPP government failed to increase the cocoa price to £5, rather they passed an amendment bill called the Cocoa Duty and Development Funds in the Legislative Assembly. This amendment pegged the cocoa price at 72s (£3 12s) per a load for four years. Upon hearing this, the agitated farmers, including Baffour Akoto travelled to Accra to meet the minister of Finance, Komla Gbedemah. The farmers requested for 8s increase to add up to £4 for a load but this passionate petition fell on deaf ears. As a result of this disappointment, all Farmers Meeting was conveyed in Kumasi. This meeting was countered by the CPP who issued threats to these farmers some of whom it is believed, fled the country.

Notwithstanding these threats, Baffour Akoto and the CPP rebels founded the National Liberation Movement on Sunday 19 September, 1954. This was inaugurated with war songs maybe with the aim of reviving that ancient Asante bravery that made them conquer and resist the oppressors. Their aims and objectives were clear. They wanted to banish hooliganism, lawlessness, rebellion against authority, suppression of individual conscience and the emerging communism in the Gold Coast politics. Secondly, they wanted to restore the honour and loyalty to traditional rulers and the cultural image of the society. To recognize the diversities of economic, cultural and social strengths and contributions of the involved regions that make the country and formulate federal or any better constitution suitable for such aspiration. The fourth was to fight and protect the interest of farmers and workers. The fifth was to speed up the achievement of self-government in order to create a healthy, prosperous, tolerant and God-fearing Ghana nation. Above all the NLM wanted to build cordial relationship between Ghana and the Commonwealth and other democratic nations.

Since the grievances that led to the formation of the NLM were clear, many youth and people, especially the chiefs, joined the NLM. Among these people are the chiefs who felt the CPP was not only robbing them of their wealth in cocoa but also bringing their institution of chieftaincy into disrepute. Strong officials of CPP like Victor Owusu, RR Amponsah and Joe Appiah joined the NLM. The Asantehene also added his support to the NLM since, according to the royal majesty, this was a movement but not a party. They felt the CPP had betrayed them and when indications were clear of such defiance in Kumasi, Nkrumah kept deaf ears to such warnings. He in one way or the other underestimated the power of the chiefs when he relegated them from their traditional roles by putting the youth in the Local Government. This time the chiefs trooped in their numbers to oppose the CPP.

Barely a month after its founding in October, Baffoe, an NLM man, was murdered by Twumasi Ankrah, a CPP activist, in Kumasi. This obviously would generate violent revenge from the NLM. Though Twumasi Ankra was charged and killed by hanging, this did not appease the anger of the NLM. A gang of NLM killed Krobo Edusei's sister. This revenge did not sit well with citizens. They became offended by the NLM action and rather sympathised with the CPP. The violence between the two persisted and houses and properties were burnt largely in Kumasi. At the time the NLM was formed, Danquah was not in the country. After his loss in the 1954 election, he was invited by the United Nations. In New York, he was contacted by the British Times about his opinion about the NLM, and he described the formation of the new party as timely and strategic. In principle, the NLM was not an ideal party for Danquah since they were as radical as the CPP. However, since this new force had come to challenge the CPP, he cast his support behind them. When he returned in 1955, the NLM had no branches and following in the Colony Danquah therefore decided to organize people to establish the NLM in the Colony. However, the NLM could not grow in the Colony firstly because their message was more regionally centred.  Secondly the CPP raised the propaganda that if they voted for the NLM, Asante would rule over them as in time past. This fear made many of the people in the Colony rally behind the CPP. Elsewhere in America and Europe, there was a laudable rumour that the Asantehene had founded a political party- the NLM.

On his defence for the NLM, this is what Danquah wrote: "It is not quite accurate to say that the Asantehene has "a new political party". It is also alarming to learn that the present move for national liberation in Ashanti with the Asantehene at the head will disrupt things so much as to delay independence. If you will refer to Martin Wight's Gold Coast Legislative Council you will discover that it was by a special act of the present Asantehene that Ashanti, after half-a-century under the British, joined the Colony in a legislative union and made the demand for independence possible. This happened as far back as 1943, when some of those in power today and have delayed independence by their "step by step" policy, were either boys at School or unknown in politics. Today our country is in the throes of bribery and corruption and nepotism in politics and it might go the way of Newfoundland in 50 years unless we have people like the Asantehene to apply checks and balances. The new liberation movement is intended to liberate the country from a black dictatorship and imperial chicanery".[1]

One of the agitations of the Chiefs and the NLM was for the government to investigate the Cocoa Marketing Board. Nkrumah had established a Cocoa Purchasing Company to license them to purchase cocoa as a subsidiary of the CMB. The facts remain that, directors of these groups were pro CPP people who were allocating loans and other assistance to only the CPP members. It is believed that Nkrumah raised much fund from this area to sponsor the CPP to win their landslide victory in the 54 elections. Many of the agitators who had defected from the CPP in Ashanti came up to make such allegations. As a matter of fact, the Ashanti and NLM sent a delegation to Britain for the Queen to establish a Royal Enquiry into the matter.

According to Nkrumah cocoa accounted for the two-thirds of the revenue of the nation and the government needed more revenues to embark on more projects in the country. The difference in the pegging of the local price far below the promised price was to generate funds to facilitate developments. He spoke of the recent university college built, the new hospital built and other infrastructural developments his government had embarked on in Ashanti.

Aside the worry on cocoa, the NLM wanted a new federal constitution that would give some protection to Asante and the other colonies. They made their grievances clear to the governor and the colonial office. They asked the Queen to intercede on their behalf. They had warned that without a federal constitution, Asante would secede after independence. This is what brought the slogan: 'mate me ho'. Lennox Boyd, Secretary of State interfered and suggested that Nkrumah had convincingly won a huge democratic victory and that it would be undemocratic for the Queen to interfere in such matters.

Arden Clarke was worried the nation would tear apart and disrupt the efforts the Gold Coast had made towards self-governance. However his support was with Nkrumah, a man Arden Clarke had in recent time described as 'Local Hitler' to his wife. He described Nkrumah's followers as Scary wags. Yet soon after Nkrumah's victory in 1951, he and Nkrumah agreed on many terms. He supported Nkrumah to lead the nation to full self-government. As a result of his support for Nkrumah, the British press also supported Nkrumah. But on this agitation of the NLM, he became soft. He tried to persuade the Asantehene to give up the federal constitution in support of the unitary constitution but things could not avail. He knew the Asantes had a point, but at the same time he wanted all power for Nkrumah. And when Nkrumah also asked him to do something about the numerous attacks of the NLM since he had the police under his control, he suggested to Nkrumah that the new constitution was complicated unlike the previous. He could not tell the cabinet what to do straight away.

Once the governor had the opportunity to speak with people in

Akyem Abuakwa and spoke on the subject battling with the nation. He spoke of how he could not understand the terms federalism and regionalization.

> There is too much talk of 'federalism' and 'regionalism'. As a practical administrator, I am very suspicious of 'isms' and similar generic terms unless they are precisely defined. Frankly, I do not know what 'federalism' or 'regionalism' means in terms of practical politics, and I don't believe the ordinary voter or man in the street does either.[2]

He advised that there should be consensus among the people and the Nkrumah's government in order to make proper resolutions. Clearly, the Governor was being a hypocrite. His words at Kyebi did not go down well with the Asantes. They reverted back at him with harsh words in the Ashanti Pioneer when he visited Kumasi to speak with the Asantehene. Below is what Ashanti Pioneer published.

We demand

> Commission of Inquiry into CMB and CPC affairs.

> Nkrumah's government to resign immediately-public opinion demands this.

> Setting up of a Constituency Assembly for Federation.

Are you not aware of

> Nkrumah's Dictatorial Tendencies

> Naked Fascism in this country

> The fact that you should be neutral in LOCAL POLITICS. Why take sides with the CPP?

Sir Charles

> Are you for Democracy

> Or

> For Dictatorship?

> No Federation No Self Government.

The meeting with the Asantehene could not pacify the anger of some NLM activists who attacked the Royce Rolls of the governor with bottles, stones and mud.

In spite of the support the NLM got in Asante, there was a sizeable number of people who still remained loyal to the CPP. Some of these included the youths. Others included the various tribal communities of Ewe, Fante, and Northern communities. Again, the chiefs in the Brong area of Ashanti remained loyal to the CPP. There was a promise that Nkrumah would give them independence by giving them a new regional administration. The NLM fought such chiefs with CPP and claimed their loyalty with CPP was disloyalty to the Asanteman. A number of chiefs were destooled in Ashanti. This became alarming to Nkrumah who felt most of these chiefs destooled were supporters of the CPP. To empower such chiefs to appeal for their positions back, Nkrumah thought of introducing and passing State Council Bill. This came as adding salt to injury. The NLM felt this bill was a complete threat to bring the Asanteman tradition into disrepute. The Secretary of State, Lennox Boyd, dispatched Fredrick Bourne, a constitutional lawyer to the Gold Coast for a possible way out- to consider the possibility of federation and the separation of Brong-Ahafo. The government appointed a select committee to deliberate on the federation of government and also the second chamber of parliament that was to be made of chiefs which had been a persistent proposal by Danquah. Unimaginably, the NLM boycotted this meeting and refused to meet with Bourne.

Concerning Nkrumah on the State Council Bill, he had been advised by Collin Russel acting as Chief Regional Officer not to pass the Bill because intelligence proved more violence to ensue. Nkrumah on his defence to this bill referred to Busia's publication on *'Position of the Chief in the Modern Political in Ashanti'*. Busia revealed that the senior chiefs were dictatorial and that the ordinary man had no chance of redress against the authority. His argument was that given deposed chiefs opportunity to appeal to the governor for reinstatement would help. After many back and forth, the bill was passed.

Concerning the issue of federation, Fredick Bourne brought out his report and debunked on the issue of federation. His main reason was that the Gold Coast was a small country. He advised that the powers must reside with the central government. He opposed the regionalization of Brong from Asante. He recommended the establishment of 5 regional assemblies which were to be responsible for local matters and receive grants-in-aid from the central government but should not have the power to claim taxes.

Rejecting the Bourne's proposals, the NLM and its allies insisted on a fresh election as the only way to solve this matter on the constitution. This did not go down well with Nkrumah. He opposed the idea of a new election since he had won a clear majority that was convincing enough to lead the nation to independence. He spoke with the acting governor Sir Gordon Hadow and afterwards sent a message to Arden Clarke who was on leave but nothing emerged. Later he sent Kojo Botsio to go to London to Arden Clarke who was on leave and to the Secretary of the colony to rescind the elections that the CPP had won the 1951 and 1954 elections on 'Self Government Now'. And that an election could lead to violence, bloodshed and other misfortunes that could jeopardise Gold Coast reputation on democracy. He went as planned but Arden Clarke told him he initially opposed the idea of another election but considering the political situation in the nation, it appeared it was the only way to break the political deadlock. He affirmed to Botsio he had spoken with Lennox Boyd the Secretary of State who had agreed already. He returned to Accra with Arden Clarke and hinted Nkrumah that it appeared that the only way forward to independence would be another election.

This news was heavy for Nkrumah to inform his cabinet. Later he invited the governor to meet the cabinet and break the news to them which he did. Here after, Busia and the Asantehene called on the governor at the castle that they were ready to call off their opposition for amicable constitution consideration but the governor informed them that it was too late. The election was going to come on.

Just when Nkrumah and Arden Clarke were facing this unprecedented heat from the NLM in Ashanti, a similar pressure was going on in the British Togoland. The British Government decided on what to be done to this territory if the Gold Coast gained independence. Initially, this territory was one with French Togoland as a unit nation under the colony of the Germans. But during the First World War when the Germans were defeated, the League of Nations divided German colonies between the British and the French. And when the United Nation assumed the role of the League of Nations, the British Government put the matter before them. As a matter of fact, it was a central focus of the UGCC that the territory would be part of Ghana including the Akan territories in Ivory Coast. So in 1948 when Danquah drafted the model constitution to the Watson Commission, the Togoland issue was raised to be part of Ghana.

When the British met with the UN, a plebiscite was opted for. This is something that did not sit well with the Governor, Arden Clarke. He rightly felt it ought to have been settled between the British, the French and the Togoland people. Some of the Togoland people wanted to unite with Ghana while others wanted to unite with Togoland. The Togoland Congress wanted unification with French Togoland, in other words, they wanted the separation from Gold Coast while the Anlo Youth Organisation wanted a bigger union with all the Ewes in Dahomey with the Gold Coast. Nkrumah supported the plebiscite and wanted the British Togoland to join with the Gold Coast. So as Nkrumah and Arden Clarke were battling with the NLM back and forth, some Ewes were also agitating for union with the French Togoland. The plebiscite was scheduled for 9, May 1956. After the election, majority voted to join with the Gold Coast. In the northern part, 79 percent voted to join the Gold Coast while in the southern part full of Ewe 58 percent voted for separation from the Gold Coast. The UN approved of the decision that same year in December. The Togoland Congress and its followers opposed the decision of the United Nations. They complained the elections were rigged. And partly they had wanted their issue to be handled separately from the other tribes from the North. As a result they boycotted the independence celebration.

A couple of days after the plebiscite, Lennox Boyd in the House of Commons on 11 May 1956 announced of an upcoming elections in the Gold Coast which was going to be the last for her Majesty to issue the act of independence. This election was not intended but was necessary on the part of Britain for democracy to prevail in the independence struggle. This is what he said:

" I have been in close touch with the Prime Minister of the

> Gold Coast on these matters ... I have made my view clear to him that because of the failure to resolve the constitutional dispute we can only achieve our common aim of the early independence of that country within the Commonwealth in one way and one way alone; that is, to demonstrate to the world that the peoples of the Gold Coast have had a full and free opportunity to consider their constitution and to express their views on it in a general election .... I have told Dr Nkrumah that if a general election is held Her Majesty's Government will be ready to accept a motion calling for independence within the Commonwealth passed by a reasonable majority in a newly elected legislature and then to declare a firm date for this purpose " [3]

The fact should be made clear that had the NLM not agitated for a change of constitution or if they had not insisted on an election, 1954 was going to be the last election to independence. After the 1951 elections, what was conditional for the Gold Coast independence was the unity of the political parties to pass a motion of independence. In like manner, had the CPP not been established, had Nkrumah remained with the UGCC, Ghana would have claimed her independence far earlier.

On 15 May 1956 the governor opened a new session of the Legislative Assembly. He read the Queen's Speech from the Throne. He tackled on the constitutional proposals and the details of the elections. He revealed the dates for the election would be12 and 17 July 1956. When he took his turn, Nkrumah moved that the Assembly should adopt the Independence Proposals from the White Paper that the Gold Coast should be sovereign and independent state in the Commonwealth. As Danquah had already asserted, Nkrumah informed the Assembly that Ghana would be the new name for the independent nation. K.B Ayensu first clerk of parliament at independence and S.N Darkwa also a former clerk of Ghana's Parliament credited the name of Ghana to Danquah. They quoted in their book *The Evolution of Parliament in Ghana* that, 'it is not unusual for a child to be found a name before it is born. J.B Danquah had consistently espoused the name Ghana for the nation to be.' Surprisingly, members from the Opposition opposed the name

Ghana and preferred the name Gold Coast. This is because, some of them felt that not everyone migrated from Ancient Ghana. Let the reader understand that, the Opposition here did not include the Big Six or the UGCC people. Krobo Edusei spoke his mind about this change of stand of the Opposition. This is what Krobo said in the Assembly:

> "Then I come to the name Ghana. It is always good, as I said, to tell the truth, and nothing but the truth. The leaders who now constitute the Opposition; the Hon. Member for Anlo South (M.K.Apaloo), the Hon. Member for Kumasi North (Mr. Cobbina Kessie), the Hon. Member for Offinso (Mr. J.A Owusu Ansah) were all Executive Members but the Hon. Member for Atwima Amansie (Mr.J.E Appiah) was in London and we, together with the former Leader of Opposition (Danquah) decided on this name, Ghana. But when the name came before the JPC for consideration, the Opposition sent a delegation from within their ranks to advise the JPC to oppose the name Ghana. The name Ghana is accepted by every individual in this country with the exception of the Opposition. When they attended the Conference they said that they were not all agreed on the name. The Opposition were the people who first proposed the name, but because Kwame Nkrumah will get credit by renaming the country Ghana, they say no."[4]

Other details of the White Paper were that Ghana would become an independent sovereign State and would have full responsibility for defence and external affairs. The White Paper proposed the appointment of a Governor-General by the Queen in consultation with the Ghana government. The Legislature should have supreme powers to whose laws should be enacted as Acts of Parliament. The Parliamentary life should be five years. It proposed the following regions: Western, Eastern, Ashanti, Northern, Trans-Volta/Togoland. Tema should be separated from the district of Accra. Regional Assembly could be established by an act of Parliament fully administered by district councils,

Arden Clark revealed that the assembly would be dissolved and a general election would be held on 12, 17th July 1956 with additional day on the 18th July.

Having solved the issue of the Togoland plebiscite, Arden Clarke and Nkrumah were left with solving the possibility of secession of the Northern Protectorates. Their worry was clear; they were not ready to free themselves from a British protection. They wanted to remain under her majesty the Queen, however should the independence be granted, they were not ready to submit to the uncertain leadership of Nkrumah and his CPP. Arden -Clarke saw this as unthinkable, for the Northern Territories to remain British Colony while the rest of the colonies were independent. In any case that would not be economically and politically expedient to the British Government.

The governor decided to embark on a tour to the north and announce the date for the coming elections and also admonish the northern leaders to embrace the new change and unite. In his tour there was a grand durbar held on the 29 May 1956 at Tamale. He announced the date for the election to them that it would take place on the 17 and 18 July. He and Nkrumah went all limits to persuade the chiefs of the North to accept the new fate of the nation and to decline from the idea of seceding from the Gold Coast.

He had assumed the position of a governor to supervise Gold Coast's transition to independence. Considering the chanting of the politicians and that of the ordinary masses for independence, Arden Clarke thought he was going to guide a quick transition but that was not the case. As a result he wrote:

> **"I never realized what a prolonged battle I would have with the politicians, chiefs and people of this country in order to give them the independence for which they have been clamouring all these years. Now they are going to have it whether they like it or not!"[5]**

In all his attempt of persuading the TC, NLM and NPP to avoid the seceding idea, Arden-Clarke never admonished Nkrumah to be tolerant to his political opponent. He never made any attempt to enquire about the corrupt practices under the Nkrumah administration that had prompted the leaders of the other colonies to oppose Nkrumah's leadership. These leaders put very practical and pressing issues before the governor. They told him Nkrumah was a dictator but he appeared to be a partner in crime with Nkrumah more than been a neutral administrator. One typical example was the NLM accusation of corruption on cocoa. An enquiry committee called the Jibowso Committee was established to look into the matter and report their findings but the governor delayed the release of the report most probably to favour the CPP. The report was released after the 1956 elections when it could have been released prior to the elections. In his letter to the British Times, Danquah asserted that it was not Krobo Edusei or Nkrumah who was destroying Ghana but rather it was Arden Clarke.

The notice to the election was short so both parties had to strategise as quickly as possible. Let us have a look at the CPP bulletins.

What you are asked to vote for is perfectly clear:

ALL YOU HAVE TO DO is to ask yourself two questions:

> Do I want FREEDOM and INDEPENDENCE NOW THIS YEAR- so that I and my children can enjoy life in a free and independent sovereign state of Ghana thereafter?

> Do I want to revert to the days of imperialism, colonialism and tribal feudalism?

If you favour the first question- that is, if you want your INDEPENDENCE in 1956 – then the ONLY WAY TO GET IT, IS BY VOTING FOR KWAME NKRUMAH AND HIS CONVENTION PEOPLE'S PARTY.

If you are faint-hearted and your spirit of nationalism is so pitiably deficient that you incline your mind towards the second question, then you are no concern of ours and you are an outcast as far as the movement for Gold Coast Independence is concerned. You can vote for those whose policy and avowed aim it is to split up this country thereby delaying INDEPENDENCE.

NLM

'Why you should vote for cocoa',....

Don't vote for the red cockerel which is the CPP

> CPP are thieves, rogues, traitors, double-tongued receivers of bribes, givers of bribes and gangsters.

> CPP introduced the following taxes: Local Rate, House Rate, Industrial Taxes, Taxes on domestic animals, cows, goats, sheep, and rates on bicycles.

> CPP introduced insubordination, tribal differences, disrespect, suppression, evil doing, lying, destruction of chieftaincy, greed and other evils.

> CPP wants to divide the Ewes; give half to the Gold Coast and the other half to Dahomey. For these reasons don't vote for the red cockerel, the thief.

VOTE FOR NLM

& Allies on July 12 & 17

Reject the Commission People's Party (CPP)

A Party of Crooks and Swindlers

on July 12 and 17

It is Your They Want.[6]

Giving analysis based on the brief presented by both parties it is clear that the CPP were very strategic and could easily have a place on the minds of the electorates. In spite of everything of corruption and violence, there is one thing that attracted many to the politics of the day. It was not anti-corruption campaign neither was it anti-violent campaign rather it was the call of independence that attracted them to political activism. Many people's greatest dream was to see this reality. Of all the parties, it was Nkrumah who was straight to the point about independence. He asked if you want independence, if you want freedom then vote for the CPP. This was more selling than the message of the opposition which spent time to talk about their opponent without selling more of what they could do. Besides, the message of the CPP was universal whereas the message of the NLM was on cocoa which was more regional. Again since the election was about independence, the NLM was poorly strategic on the most essential.

Aside from the publications, the CPP had cinema vans moving to all places to campaign. This was countered by the NLM though but they had limited places to move to campaign. The CPP aroused the fear of the colony that vote for NLM was to sell their freedom to the Asante. This was something none of the other tribes would want to do. What made it worse was the 'Mate me ho' slogan which the NLM adopted. This made the propaganda of the CPP so believable.

There were 104 seats. The CPP were able to file a candidate for all the seats. This was not so with the NLM. With all their allies coming together, they could only file for 76 of the seats. There were also forty-five independent candidates. Seventeen of them declared their support for the NLM and its allies. This in my opinion communicated a sign of unpreparedness on the part of these opponents of Nkrumah. The constitution demanded a clear majority in parliament to form a government and also to vote for independence. Not filing for about 28 seats means that the CPP already had won such seats in advance; all they needed was just half of the seats the NLM were contesting. Isn't it ridiculous that a political party, unable to file for all seats, was desperately anticipating to win an election ahead of its competitor who already held majority of the said seats? It is no wonder Arden- Clarke had given his support to Nkrumah right after the 51 elections. This is because the parliamentary democracy of the day, demanded a party to win clear majority of seats to form government. The inability to get a single party to win over 52 seats was going to give a hurdle to the governor not knowing whom to appoint to form government. Regarding this, Nkrumah made his work easy because he could contest all the seats and capable of winning the majority needed to form government.

The 1956 election was going to be held without Nkrumah having the opportunity to go to Kumasi to hold a mass rally with the electorates because of the tension there. The NLM out of blind optimism were hopeful of victory. Out of this confidence, Busia wrote to the governor that should the NLM and its allies win a slim majority over 52 seats, they should be allowed to form government. This did not go down well with Nkrumah. He was shocked by the words of Busia. And this was Nkrumah's reply **'If he is sincere,' .., 'we have nothing more to worry about, it will be plain sailing from now on, for we are all talking the same language, at last.'**[7] Any way by the time Busia's publication was out, the CPP repeatedly had clinched unto a landslide victory.

The CPP won 71 seats out of the 104 seats. Out of the vote cast, CPP had 398,141 while the NLM and its allies got 299,116 votes. The election did not happen without bribery, intimidation and stuffing of ballot boxes. The CPP was relatively strong in all the colonies. In the Colony it won all the seats. Danquah who had contested on the ticket of NLM lost to his nephew, Aaron Ofori Atta in Akyem Abuakwa. In Togoland, the CPP won 8 out of the 13 seats. In Ashanti, the CPP won 8 while the NLM won 13 of the seats. In the Northern Territories, the CPP won 11 seats while the NPP won 15 seats. Nkrumah remarked after this victory by saying: **'Quite apart from our large parliamentary representation, we could claim to be the only party able to speak in a national sense.'**

The governor, Arden-Clarke asked Nkrumah to form his third government. He appointed almost the same ministers as he did in the previous elections.

A. Casdy-Hayford Minister of Communications

Kojo Botsio Minister of Trade and Labour

K. A. Gbedemah Minister of Finance

A. E. Inkumsah Minister of Housing

A. E. A. Ofori-Atta Minister of Local Government

J. H. Allassani Minister of Health

Ako Adjei Minister of the Interior

N. A. Welbeck Minister of Works

J. B. Erzuah Minister of Education

B. Yeboah-Afari Minister of Agriculture

Krobo Edusei Minister without Portfolio

L. R. Abavana Minister without Portfolio

In spite of their defeat, Busia asserted that since, the CPP failed to win majority of the seats in Ashanti and in the Northern Territories clearly supports the call for federation. The Asante Youth Organisation and Muslim Association Party pressed for the federal constitution.

On 1 August 1956, the Assembly met and the independent motion was passed. The opposition regretted that an agreed constitution had still not been made. They also queried the long delayed Jibowso report. In spite of their complaints, the government moved on with the votes and it was 72 to nil votes.

The Mamprusi State Council protested against the Government's action in passing an independence motion in the Assembly "without an agreed constitution". The chiefs issued their grievances through the Northern People's Party and revealed that they were not against the independence. The chiefs contended in the report that if the North is to form part of an independent Gold Coast, then six factors must be taken into consideration in deciding a constitution for the country. These are that the North-

1. Has a protectorate status

2. Has a system of land tenure different from other regions

3. Has a different system of chieftaincy

4. Has a different civil law

5. Has a different cultural and historical experience, and

6 Is less developed than the other regions.

The Chiefs further stated that it will be absurd and highly ridiculous for both Britain and the Gold Coast Government to continue to insist on them to accept independence without any assurance that their interests would be safeguarded in an agreed constitution. (Source, The Daily Graphic Tuesday, 21st August 1956).

In September, the Jibowu Report was released. It confirmed the allegation of the NLM that the CPP government had connived and condoned with the Cocoa Marketing Board and the Cocoa Purchasing Council of corruption and irregularities. It also found that the managing Director Mr. Djin had employed his family and friends who were not fit for such positions. When called upon, he admitted they were true and had defrauded the CPP. He resigned right away. The Jibowu report, I will say, was too little too late, because in 1954, Krobo Edusei had admitted that **"The CPC is the product of a master brain, Dr. Kwame Nkrumah, and it is the atomic bomb of the  Convention People's Party. As honourable Members are aware, the Prime**

**Minister in his statements to the CPP told his Party members that organisation decided everything and the CPC is part of the organization of the Convention People's Party."[8]** The Jibowu Commission confirmed this statement of Krobo Edusei that both Nkrumah and Gbedemah knew exactly what use the CPC was being put to. Farmers who were not members of the CPP were denied loans. It was the funds from the CPC that CPP used to win the majority of seats in the assembly. Joe Appiah led the NLM to demand for the resignation of Nkrumah and Gbedemah from government. Later Nkrumah wrote **"I was quite convinced that the affair was a calculated attempt to bring my Government into disrepute by suggesting that bribery and corruption were rife among those in power."[9]**

Some writings reveal that when the British press had access to the Jibowu report, they began to accuse Arden Clarke for condoning such level of corruption these years and preparing a yet to be independent nation with such irregularities. Initially, most British press had supported Nkrumah's government because Arden Clarke supported it but it was too little too late. Nkrumah was going to lead Ghana to the final face of independence.

Nevertheless, Busia and the NLM did not rest on their demands. They pressed on Lennox Boyd. Eventually they called for a partition for Ashanti and Northern Territories to be one nation. But this was declined by Lennox Boyd. From his personal observation with the two leaders, Arden Clarke observed that but for their followers Nkrumah and Busia would have made a great team. This is what he had to say about the two.

> **The most hopeful sign is that both Nkrumah and Busia have been very reasonable and if it were left to the two of them, there would be no difficulty in finding a workable solution. Unfortunately, neither of them is a strong man and they have unruly followers whom they cannot properly control. Each dog is all right but each has a tail that is likely to wag the dog.[10]**

The indication is that the back and forth actions by the NLM were likely to cause the Secretary of State Lennox to delay the date of independence. In the writing of Arden Clarke, he insisted on the 16

September that the Secretary of State should fix the date for independence by 18 September before the house rises on that date. In his writing, the Secretary of State replied **'I feel you have left me with no alternative'**[11].

On that same day, the Secretary of State sent an immediate dispatch to the governor. When the governor was alone in his room, he opened the dispatch and read it and it was the answer to his seven years of hard work of achieving one dream- the independence of the Gold Coast. He wondered how Nkrumah would feel when he read it. After reading it, he kept his cool and decided to invite Nkrumah to his residence the following day Monday. Early Monday morning, Arden Clarke invited Nkrumah to his residence at the Castle when he was free. At 3 pm Nkrumah went to the governor. He shook Nkrumah and gently handed the despatch to Nkrumah. And this is what Arden Clarke had to say:

> It came as a surprise to him as he had never really believed that an announcement would be made so soon, though he knew I was battling with the S of S to get it. After he had read the text of the despatch he looked up and said in rather an awed voice 'H.E. that's nice'. I reminded him of our first meeting alone together after he came out of prison, when I had said that there were two men who could break this experiment in five minutes, he and I: and there were two men who could make it a success, he and I, though I thought it would take a bit longer than five minutes. Now here was the result and it had taken us five years. 'We must have a party to celebrate this', said he, 'Not yet', I replied 'we have got to plan how this situation is to be handled'. So I called Hadow in and we made our plan, and while Hadow went off to draft a telegram to the S of S I dictated the outline of what the PM should say in the House at noon today. It was rather a solemn and subdued little man who left my office. He promised that he would not divulge the contents of the despatch to anyone- I wonder if he has managed to keep his promise. He took no copy of the despatch away with him. He comes to me again at 11 o'clock this morning to collect the copies of the two despatches for distribution to the Members of the Legislative

Assembly after he has made his statement, and to make final arrangements for a press release and wireless bulletin, and then he goes to the House for his great moment, which in his own words is going to 'come as a shock to all of us'.[12]

Arden Clarke's verdict is no different from what Nkrumah wrote in his autobiography. Let us read what Nkrumah also said how he felt when he first received the message of Ghana's independence date.

It was Monday, 17th September. I had a full morning's work ahead of me and I was going over my diary of appointments. Suddenly there was a ring from the telephone that connected me direct with the Governor. 'Good morning, P.M.,' said Sir Charles.' I just wanted to tell you that I had received some good news for you. I wondered if you could come up and see me for a few minutes when you are free.' 'Yes, certainly, Sir Charles,' I said, as I hurriedly scanned through my appointments .. ' I'm afraid this morning, is pretty hectic would 3 o'clock this afternoon be all right? I arrived at Government House promptly. If there had been any doubts in my mind as to the contents of the message that was awaiting me, the look of pleasure on Sir Charles' face as I entered his office swept it away at once. He shook me firmly and warmly by the hand and then handed me a despatch from the Secretary of State. There were, as is often the case with despatches, a number of long paragraphs. When I reached the fifth one, however, the tears of joy that I had difficulty in hiding blurred the rest of the document. After a few minutes I raised my eyes to meet those of the Governor. For some moments there was nothing either of us could say. Perhaps we were both looking back over the seven years of our association, beginning with doubts, suspicions and misunderstandings, then acknowledging the growth of trust, sincerity and friendship, and now, finally, this moment of victory for us both, a moment beyond description and a moment that could never be entirely recaptured. 'Prime Minister,' the Governor said, as he extended his hand to me. 'This is a great day for you. It is the end of what you have struggled for.' 'It is the end of what we have been struggling for, Sir Charles,' I corrected him. 'You have contributed a great deal towards this; in fact, I might not have succeeded without your help and co-operation. This is a very happy day for us both! 'I arranged with the Governor that I would return the following morning and collect the despatch from him and immediately afterwards read it to the Legislative Assembly. 'This has been a national struggle,' I said, ' and it is only right that when the date of Independence is announced, the whole nation knows it from my lips.'[13]

About 10:45 am on Tuesday 18 September, Nkrumah went to Arden Clarke for the despatch. He signalled the Speaker that he had news to inform the house hence the permission to speak when it was noon day. According to Nkrumah, that was the same time that the news would be released at the British parliament and he wanted to speak at the same time. He decided not to join in the debate on the floor as he keenly set his eyes on the clock. When it was 12:00 noon, the speaker interrupted and the Prime Minister got to the floor to unfold the content of the Lennox Boyd message to the floor. Nkrumah spoke:

> Mr Speaker, with your permission, I should like to make a statement. With effect from midday to-day, the publication of two despatches of vital importance to the future of our country has been authorised.' 'They are, the despatch from the Governor at the request of my Government to the Secretary of State asking him to declare a firm date for the attainment of Independence by the Gold Coast, and the Secretary of State's despatch in reply thereto. Copies of these two despatches will be distributed to Honourable Members as soon as the House rises to-day.'

In this despatch the Secretary of State, recalling his statement in the House of Commons on 11th May, noted that a General Election had now been held, that the Convention People's Party had been returned to power with a majority of over two-thirds and that the motion for Independence had been passed in the newly elected Assembly by 72 votes to none, the Opposition members having absented themselves from the debate.

'Since the motion calling for Independence within the Commonwealth has been passed in the newly elected Legislative Assembly by a majority which must clearly be regarded as reasonable, I now have the honour to inform you that Her Majesty's Government will at the first available opportunity introduce into the United Kingdom Parliament a Bill to accord Independence to the Gold Coast and, subject to Parliamentary approval, Her Majesty's Government intends that full Independence should come about on the 6th March, 1957.'[14]

The announcement of the day 6th March came as no surprise to the then Clerk of Parliament of the Gold Coast K.B Ayensu and S.N Darkwa who credit the date 6th March to Danquah. Ayensu was Ghana's Clerk of Parliament before and during independence and Darkwa was a subsequent clerk of parliament. They wrote, 'The Bond of 1844 was executed on March 6, and Danquah settled on that date for independence. In a message addressed to the chiefs and people on March 6 1948, following the Tragedy of the Crossroads, and published in all the local papers under the title. "The Hour of Liberation has struck", he (Danquah) said this: That Treaty was made exactly 104 years ago, on March 6th 1844. In effect we ask for a freely negotiated Bond of 1948'.[15] Prior to the 1948 riot, Danquah was celebrating the 6 March from 1944 to terminate the Bond of 1844. In 1953 when Nkrumah filed the motion of independence entitled 'the Motion of Destiny', Danquah made it clear that Nkrumah's motion should be amended for a specific date of independence on 6th March 1954 the subsequent year. His assertion on the date was very clear. It is no surprise that the clerks of Parliament saw the statement of the Secretary of State as a mere formality.

According to Nkrumah the whole assembly was for a few seconds dumb-founded. Then all of a sudden the sacred silence was broken with unprecedented cheers from all members both from the CPP and opposition. The deputy Opposition leader welcomed the idea. Nkrumah was soon carried shoulder high as fans and supporters trooped around with cheers and celebration. By evening the good news had spread to most parts of the country. In spite of their quest for a federal constitution for independence, the NLM were as cheerful as the CPP. Nkrumah was told that in Kumasi, the supporters of the N.L.M. were more wild with excitement than even the "C.P. P.- ists." Many of them, not content with a single "Freedom" salute, raised both hands in the air as they yelled "Freedom!"[16]

As Nkrumah, the CPP and the NLM were happy celebrating over the news of independence, the politicians in Britain thought differently, to them Ghana was not independent yet, the white man was only vacating his post but not necessarily freeing the people of the Gold Coast from their dependency on the West. **One of such people is James Griffiths former Labour Colonial Secretary. He said at the British Parliament after Ghana's independence was read that it would be wrong to cut off Ghana from the Colonial Development and Welfare Acts, because its economy, like that of most other colonies, had been shaped and patterned not by Ghana's needs but by British interests.**[17] And his request was accepted. James Griffiths remarks clearly vindicates Danquah that Nkrumah's split had caused the British to recapture the initiate. As a matter of fact, in 1956, the Secretary of State emphatically stated that the independence was a gift they were giving to Ghana. This is what Danquah opposed. To confirm James Griffiths, Nkrumah admitted many years after Ghana's independence that he was yet to achieve the economic independence for Ghana. But Danquah thought had there been unity at the political front, the initiative would have been in the hands of the Gold Coast. Not only the economic freedom but the whole process of independence would have proceeded with Ghana initiating the lead, the divide and rule on the part of Ghana gave pre-eminence to the British. This matter was not the concern of anyone; the ordinary person would not understand this. What mattered to the ordinary person was that Independence was coming on 6 March 1957.

CHAPTER 7

# INDEPENDENCE

If there was anything that pushed aside the opposition's repression against Nkrumah, if there was anything that brought a certain reconciliation or a common joy to the NLM and the CPP, it was the news of the Gold Coast to gain her full independence status on the 6th March, 1957. The news brought some agreement between the NLM and Nkrumah. They agreed to settle the difference on the constitution. Eventually on 24 January 1957 Lennox Boyd arrived in the Gold Coast to finalise on the constitution. Meeting the press on his arrival, he said

> 'I hope the people of the Gold Coast will do everything in their power to smooth out their differences. And I hope my help can be of some use. I am particularly anxious for things to work out smoothly.'[1]

He met with the Governor, the Cabinet and the Opposition leaders. He put before them the draft constitution Danquah presented to the British Government through the Watson Commission in 1948. The draft proposed a unitary constitution for Ghana and based upon that he was able to persuade the Opposition to accept the unitary constitution. After that he travelled to Kumasi and Tamale. From his visit, he realised the chiefs had become anxious of the fact that they had lost their position in modern government. He stated that he respected culture and custom and that the chiefs would play an important role in the nation years to come. He also stated that the Order in Council would protect the position of the chiefs.

After his departure to London, he met Gbedemah and Botsio on behalf of Nkrumah. Busia and William Ofori Atta on behalf of the opposition were also in attendance. They accepted the Colonial Office's late proposal on a compromised constitution by setting five Regional Assemblies which were to give some autonomy to the various colonies in resource allocation. In addition, they agreed on the establishment of the House of Chiefs in all the regions which were to be established three months after independence. Both parties had little or no option since a no would mean delay to the independence celebration which neither party wanted. On the 7th of February, 1957, the House of Commons passed the Ghana Independence Bill which received the Royal Assent the same day. This Act gave the authorisation to the Gold Coast as a fully responsible member within the Commonwealth of Nations. This was witnessed by Gbedemah, Botsio, Busia and Ofori Atta. The feud that existed on the agreed constitution did not sit well with Danquah. However, upon the circumstances, he admitted that it was prudent Britain intervened to work on agreeable constitution for Ghana. According to him, it was unforeseen challenges like that that motivated him to put before the Assembly to set a Constitution Committee in 1951 but was objected to by Nkrumah and the CPP.

> Today, we are reduced to the level of allowing the House of Commons to tell us that we are not even a nation, and to tell us further what they think is good for us in respect of the Constitution. Could we not have done our own thinking way back in 1951? [2]

After the Ghana Independence Act, The Ghana (Constitution) Order in Council was produced on the 22 February 1957, in the presence of 'The Queen's Most Excellent Majesty in Council'. This is to say that the Constitution Order in Council was made under the powers conferred on the Queen by (a) the British Settlements Acts, 1887 and 1945 (b), The Foreign Jurisdiction Act, 1890 (c), The Ghana Independence Act, 1957, and all other powers enabling the Queen in that behalf by and with the advice of her Privy Council[3].

With this Order, the Speaker and the members of the National Assembly of 1956 would, from 6 March 1957, be officially and duly elected as the Speaker and Members of Independence Assembly (Parliament). The ministers and their secretaries would be duly accorded as ministers and secretaries in the independence executives. The members of the assembly would now be officially known as Members of Parliament. And the Parliament would consist of the Queen and elected members of parliament.

Behind the scene was the construction of the State House, new Stadium, Prime Minister's residence, Independence Memorial Archway and other works for the preparation of independence. Nkrumah set an Independence Committee to plan for the preparation. There were other important things such as the national flag, the national anthem and the coat of arms. Theodora Oko designed the national flag. As we know it was designed with Red, Gold, Green with the Black Star embedded in the Gold. These colours were the original concept of the Big Six. The Black Star was Nkrumah's legacy from Marcus Garvey, signalling Ghana as the symbol or hope for African Freedom. Ephraim Amu gave us the national song Yen Ara Asaase ni. Philip Gbeho composed the Ghana National Anthem and the National Pledge.

There started a number of events in the country even as a number of dignitaries began to arrive in the country as early as 26 February, 1957. There was a Miss Ghana contest which was won by the contestant from the Volta Region. There were Independence race meeting, mass church services and Pontifical High Mass, the Governor's State Dinner at the new Ambassador Hotel, the opening of the National Museum, the Convocation at the University College, Legon and the Laying of wreath at the war Memorial.

Among the dignitaries who arrived for the ceremony, the most prominent of them was Marina, Duchess of Kent. What makes her visit the most prominent was because she represented the Queen. The new Parliament was supposed to be opened by the Queen. The Duchess of Kent came in her absence to open the new Independent Parliament. She arrived in the country on 2 March. She was accompanied by her personal secretary and Comptroller, Philip Hay, and Lady Rachael Davidson, sister of the Duke of Norfolk. Again there were R.A Butler, the British Home Secretary and Lord Privy Seal. They were welcomed by the Prime Minister, Nkrumah, and Governor Arden Clarke. The governor had made available about 90 new Chevrolet cars which carried the dignitaries from the airport to their lodging places. The subsequent day, the Duchess of Kent was taken through a rehearsal of the actual event to take place in Parliament on the day of event. On 5 March the Duchess of Kent unveiled the National Monument.

On 5 March at 9 pm, the Speaker, Hon. Emmanuel Quist, held a cocktail party to welcome the Duchess of Kent to Ghana. That same evening at 11, the last colonial legislative Assembly was held. The Speaker welcomed the Duchess to the house. A prayer was made. After that a motion of Adjournment was moved to enable the Prime Minister to make a statement. Nkrumah stated, **'Mr. Speaker: We have assembled on this happy occasion to honour the new status of a nation. When the day dawns we shall have left behind us the chains of imperialism and colonialism which have hitherto bound us to Britain. By twelve o'clock midnight, Ghana will have redeemed her lost freedom'.** He expressed his gratitude to Britain for their contribution so far and to the other nations that helped to bring them that far. He closed his speech by saying **'The future is bright and the country looks forward to independent status with hope and pride, but with befitting humility.'** To complement the Prime Minister statement, S.D Dombo, the Deputy Leader of the Opposition also expressed his sincere thanks to Britain for their role in helping Ghana to achieve independence. After that, the speaker read the last message of the Governor to prorogue the parliamentary session for the colony. The Clerk of Parliament, Mr. Ayensu, read the Proclamation to prorogue the Parliament of the Gold Coast. At 11:45 pm the Parliament rose.

While the parliamentary session was going on, thousands of people had gathered at the Old Polo Ground, now Nkrumah Mausoleum, which is opposite the Old Parliament House waiting for the Prime Minister. Nkrumah was carried shoulder high to the old Polo Ground. He mounted the stage in his Prison Graduate smock with Gbedemah, Botsio, Casley-Hayford, and Welbeck with the exception of Krobo Edusei who wore a typical Akan clothe. When midnight struck, the birth of the new independent nation was announced by the General Post Office Siren. The Union Jack flag was lowered down quietly as the Ghana flag was hoisted in joyous mood. Nkrumah spoke:

**At long last, the battle has ended! And thus, Ghana, your beloved country is free forever! And yet again, I want to take the opportunity to thank the chiefs and people of this country; the youth, the farmers, the women who have so nobly fought and won this battle.**

**Also, I want to thank the valiant ex-servicemen who have so cooperated with me in this mighty task of freeing our country from foreign rule and imperialism. And, as I pointed out at our conference at Saltpond, from now on, today, we must change our attitudes and our minds. We must realize that from now on we are no longer a colonial but free and independent people. But also, as I pointed out, that also entails hard work. I am depending upon the millions of country, the chiefs and people to help me to reshape the destiny of this country.**

**We are prepared to pick it up and make it a nation that will be respected by every other nation in the world. We know we're going to have difficult beginnings, but again, I am relying upon your support…. I am relying upon your hard work. Seeing you in these thousands, it doesn't matter how far my eyes go, I can see that you are here in your millions. And my last warning to you is that you are all to stand firm behind us so that we can prove to the world that when the African is given a chance, he can show to the world that he is somebody!**

**We are not waiting, we shall no more go back to sleep**

**anymore. Today, from now on, there is a new African in the world! That new African is ready to fight his own battles and show that after all the black man is capable of managing his own affairs. We are going to demonstrate to the world, to the other nations, young as we are that we are prepared to lay our own foundation. As I said to the Assembly a few minutes ago, I made a point that we are going to seriously create our own Africa personality and identity. It is the only way in which we can show the world that we are ready for our own battles. But today, may I call upon you all, that on this great day that let us all remember that nothing in the world can be done unless it has the purport support of God. We have done the battle and we again rededicate ourselves not only in the struggle to emancipate other territories in Africa, our independence is meaningless unless it is linked up with the total liberation of African continent.**

**Let us now, fellow Ghanaians, let us now ask for God's blessing for only two seconds, and in your thousands and millions.**

**I want to ask you to pause for only one minute and give thanks to Almighty God for having led us through our obstacles, difficulties, imprisonments, hardships and sufferings, to have brought us to the end of our troubles today. One minute silence! Ghana is free forever! And here I will ask the band to play the Ghana National Anthem.**

The celebration of 1951 parliamentary inauguration was one of a kind in Africa. It brought the Gold Coast into global limelight since it was the first of such internal self-government to be granted to any black African nation by the British. 6 March was an unprecedented feat of achievement. 6 March 1957 was the first time a black African nation achieved its full independence on the continent of Africa. The nation

Gold Coast as it was called was known for its rich economy in Gold and Cocoa. It had now become noted for her rise in politics and brought Britain to her knees in the 1948 riot. The success of Ghana was not only an inspiration to African nations but also blacks in America and the Diaspora. The CIA report had accurately admitted this. **'The fortunes of Ghana- the first tropical African country to gain independence – will have a huge impact on the evolution of Africa and the Western interests there...'[4]** Dignitaries from about 70 nations honoured the independence celebration. And about six hundred reporters and photographers graced the occasion. Accra became a centre to host the most powerful and greatest rivals: the USA and Russia then battling the cold war. Both of them arrived to offer help to a common nation Ghana. The US delegation was led by Vice President Nixon. British Prime Minister Macmillan was present. Sir Alan Burns, former Governor, was present. James Griffiths, Suez Nehru were all present. Ralph Bunche represented the UN. Most of these national leaders pledged their support to the newly independent nation. Dr Martin Luther King was present. He had come to draw inspiration from the freedom of Ghana.

It was on this occasion that Vice President Nixon met Martin Luther King for the first time. Not knowing King he congratulated him for their freedom and he replied 'I am not free yet. I am from Alabama. King revealed how Ghana's freedom had impacted him to send that liberation to the blacks in the US.

Early morning about 9:30 on 6 March 1957, Ghana's first independent Parliament was to be opened. And the one to do that was the Duchess of Kent on behalf of the Queen. Arden Clarke was sworn in as the Governor General. This was a position he had lobbied Nkrumah for. It is such interesting that seven years before he jailed Nkrumah he described him as a local Hitler, a year after he was calling Nkrumah to form government and guided and supported Nkrumah to lead Ghana to independence and now his position was at the mercy of the man he had had power over.

At exactly 10:00 am, the Duchess of Kent was conducted into the Chamber by the Speaker. She walked to the Speaker's Dias and bowed to the right and then to the left and then assumed the Throne. From there the Clerk of Parliament, Ayensu, read the calligraphed Letters Patent granted under the Royal Sign Manual authorising the Duchess to open the First Session of the Parliament of Ghana. After this, Nkrumah delivered the Speech from the Throne to the Duchess. The Duchess of Kent while seated on the Throne read the Speech of the Queen. In the message, the Queen apologised for her absence. She revealed the significance of the day marking one hundred and thirteen years when a number of chiefs entered into agreement to acknowledge the power and jurisdiction of her predecessor, the Late Majesty Queen Victoria and that the time had come for such a bond to be annulled. She expressed her joy with Ghanaians as they prepare to embark on a new journey of independence. After this message, the Duchess read another message by the Queen where she asked Ghanaians to take full responsibilities of independent nationhood. She revealed to Ghanaians that the hopes of many especially in Africa rested on the people of Ghana. And that it was her earnest and confident belief that Ghanaians would go forward in freedom and justice, in unity among themselves and in brotherhood with all the people of the Commonwealth.

The Speaker, in acceptance, read and presented an Address of Thanks to the Duchess which she welcomed. After the Speaker's presentation, the Duchess passed on to Nkrumah the Constitutional Instruments that contained the Ghana Independent Act, 1957 and the Ghana (Constitution) Order in Council, 1957. The Speaker then conducted the Duchess out of the Chamber. After resuming his chair, the Speaker briefed the House of goodwill messages from the House of Assembly of Northern Nigeria, the USSR, the British House of Commons and the Legislative Council of Guiana.

The Prime Minister spoke and praised the Queen for such a humble address to the house and the people of Ghana. In a similar spirit of humility Nkrumah expressed that Ghana was parting with Britain with the warmest feelings of friendship and goodwill. And that Ghana was filled with the sense of pride in becoming the first black African nation to be independent in the British Commonwealth. He espoused the preparation that had been made to assume such responsibilities by roads, harbour, buildings and rampant rise of schools. He spoke with pride that in a population of five million, half a million of her pupils are in school. He reiterated the responsibility that had been bestowed upon the people of Ghana which called for a change in perspective of life. He said:

> If we show disunited, inefficient or corrupt, then we shall have gravely harmed all those millions in Africa who put their trust in us and look to Ghana to prove that African people can build a state of their own based on democracy, tolerance and racial equality.[5]

The Prime Minister's motion was seconded by the leader of Opposition K.A Busia. In seconding the Prime Minister's motion, he expressed his heartfelt and that of many Ghanaian's joy of parting from the old colonial and imperial master to servant relationship with Britain and building a new relationship on equality in the Commonwealth. He hoped that this new journey would bring good blessings and opportunities on the people of Ghana. He thanked the Queen and Britain for their legacy of education, law, science, commerce, infrastructure which Ghana had inherited from Britain. He also thanked the chiefs, farmers, women, the youth and the ordinary people of Ghana whose contribution gave birth to the confidence to govern themselves and hence the achievement of independence. He stated: **'it is by the devoted day-to-day service of many ordinary and unnoticed citizens that a nation achieves greatness, and while today we pay tribute to those, living and dead, who were privileged to serve in the limelight of publicity, we will remember, with special gratitude, the many ordinary men and women whose lot was cast in less conspicuous places but to whom we owe much that is solid and of enduring value.'[6]**

He expressed that independence apart from its joy of freedom from colonialism and imperialism also brought its own heavier responsibilities which they could not run away from. He admitted that Ghanaians would expect better and high living standards. He revealed that many communities on the continent which were not yet politically free would also look up to Ghana. He also revealed that all over the world, well-wishers would expect a notable contribution from Ghana to enrich human life or add up to the wisdom and understanding needed for peaceful co-existence on the globe.

He therefore admonished Ghanaians in whatever work or station they would find themselves to rise to the requisite discipline, integrity and service without which they would not meet these said expectations.

To achieve this, Busia hoped that Ghanaians could cherish and foster the best in their tradition welding the old and the new experiences to build a stronger democracy. He hoped that these principles could make every one truly free and also help them to use the resources of the nation to the best of economic ability by resorting to the best of science and technology.

Concluding on his speech, he said, **'Finally, we pray that the birth of our country as an Independent Nation within the British Commonwealth may mean for us also a mental and spiritual re-birth and a fresh dedication of our talents to the honest and devoted service of our country and generation.'**

The motion was carried.

The House was adjourned after about an hour and quarter. When the housed closed, Nkrumah, the Duchess and other dignitaries made a state drive in the capital through the cheerful crowds. In the afternoon, the Governor General held a party at the Castle while in the evening Nkrumah offered a gracious reception at the State House. For some days, Nkrumah had a number of his special guests like President Bourguiba around. Some of the black Americans and Africans from Diaspora never returned after the independence ceremony.

If there was a man who had an indelible print of Ghana's success after the event, that man was Dr. Martin Luther King. This man did not hide his admiration of Nkrumah and the success of Ghana. He revealed that when Nkrumah said: "We are no longer a British colony… we are a free and sovereign people" and the old jack flag was lowered as the new flag was hoisted and with the shouts of "Freedom! Freedom! He cried for joy. Deep within his spirit, he could hear the words of the Negro crying: "Free at last, free at last, Great God Almighty, I'm free at last." For King, the freedom of Ghana was also a freedom of the blacks in America. Charged with this spirit, he went to America to deepen the course of freedom for the blacks. Exactly a month after Ghana's independence on 7 April 1957, he gave a speech entitled "The Birth of a New Nation". He elaborated more about Ghana to the fellow Americans. And he admitted Ghana's victory catapulted him to make the great impact he made in the civil rights of blacks in America.[7]

Nkrumah attempted to implement a number of the recommendations by the Watson report, but as to whether his attempt solved the problem was another matter. On Africanisation, for the first time, many Ghanaians were given ministerial and civil service offers. However the fact remains that the rising of the Africans in the civil service and politics also increased the level of corruption, political abuse, human right abuse and other selfish desires in the country suggesting that Africanisation was not all about putting Africans into leadership positions but rather it was a means of representing the best interest and values of the Ghanaians.

On education, Nkrumah boasted to the parliament on Independence Day that a nation as little as five million population had half a million pupils in school signifying the feat of his government. In 1951 alone, the government increased basic schools from 1000 to 3000 on free and compulsory education. In 1957, the number of primary schools was 3571 and by 1959, the number had increased to 3713. Government secondary schools increased from thirty-eight in 1957 to fifty-nine in 1960. Private secondary schools also rose from twenty-two to fifty-two in 1960. This increased the total enrolment of students from 12119 in 1957 to 20,000 in 1960. This was a good step yet according to Prof Adu Boahen, the mass enrolment diluted the quality of education. Besides it did not solve the actual recommendation of Watson Commission Report that students should be able to put their knowledge to practical solution. However, the effort of the government cannot be undermined for making education a priority even though it provided itself its own challenges on the national development. The government continued to expand secondary schools and teacher training schools. In 1958, the National Research Council was established to promote and coordinate science research in the country. The subsequent year, the Ghana Academy was formed to promote science and scholarship. That year, about 3000 students had been sponsored on scholarship to study in Western Europe. By September 1961, University College, Legon and

Science and Technology College in Kumasi were given full university status. The government sponsored about 400 students to study medicine.

On housing and industrial development, Nkrumah made great impact in such a sector by investing about £2.5 m between 1951 and 1954. Many houses were built in urban areas such as Accra, Kumasi, Cape Coast and Takoradi. The government also introduced housing loan of £2 m. though this project was unsuccessful. He built the Tema harbour and the Tema Township with a budget of £36 million. At the time, the housing of Tema were only government well-built estates. Today, Tema remains the industrial city of Ghana which is the creativity of Nkrumah's government though the initiative has been abused by modern generation. In addition, more roads were built. Several dual carriage roads were built. The pride of all is the Tema Motorway which still remains the nation's best of roads. The challenge with Nkrumah's infrastructure and industrial development was that many were sited in urban areas which in effect increased migration of people to the cities.

On the issue of Trade Discrimination, Nkrumah did nothing about it to empower Ghanaians or give opportunities to the Ghanaian people or help Ghanaians to own the economy. The economic figures were good. His government inherited a national reserve of £200 million and a national debt of £20 million. Ghana produced two thirds of the world's cocoa and the price per ton had increased to £247 which was very good. With a population a little over five million, the nation was in a healthy economic state. The future looked promising. Many countries such as the US, Canada, Russia, Britain pledged their support or interest to work with Ghana.

In spite of the good figures on the economy, there was a problem. Ghanaians were not the owners of the economy; the foreigners were and they could punish the government anytime they wished which they did in the 60s and still do today because the structure of our economy is colonial. After independence, the Expatriates in the country who were Lebanese, Syrians and mostly British controlled over 90 percent of the import trade and as such controlled the prices of goods and services. 90 percent of the banking businesses were in the hands of two British banks and insurance companies. Expatriates controlled about 96 percent of the timber concessions. There were about seven gold mines and all were controlled by foreigners. Similarly, half of the diamond concessions were also in the hands of foreigners. Construction and industries were managed by foreigners.

Concerning the retailing business, the Indian, British, Syrian, Lebanese and European firms dominated this sector too. The sector where Ghanaians had control was the Agriculture and cocoa. Even with this area, the firms such as UAC, CFAO, UTC and SCOA controlled the marketing of these agriculture products typical being the cocoa. This is what was emphasised by James Griffiths former Labour Colonial Secretary that 'Ghana's economy, like that of most other colonies, had been shaped and patterned not by Ghana's needs but by British interests.'

Interestingly, some friends of Nkrumah and members of the CPP like W.A Wiafe, J.R Asiedu and C.K.K Baah advised him to give some of the opportunities to Ghanaians. He was told to grant import licence to Ghanaians and also restrict foreigners on the retail business in the country but he refused yet this was the cry of Ghanaians during the Watson Commission that Paa Grant, a renowned businessman, told the commission 'we are not getting licenses for the import of goods'. Rather, the number of foreigners such as the Lebanese and Syrians operating in the retail business increased between 1957 and 1960. Nkrumah in 1959 gave a huge loan to Anastasia George Leventis, a Greek, to empower him to expand his trading business in Ghana.[8]

Again Nkrumah's government gave out grants and interest-free loans to expatriates in the mining who were struggling to make profits to support their operations. The good side of this was that it prevented possible unemployment that could have resulted from the collapse of the companies. These foreign companies could transfer their profit out of the country without any restriction.

On the government part, it established the Ghana National Construction Company in partnership with an Israeli firm in 1958. The same year, the government established National Development Company. And in 1960, it established the United Farmers' Council. There were two sectors that Ghana began to own a share of the economy and that was with the purchasing of cocoa and banking. The Ghana Farmers' Marketing Cooperative and Ghana Cooperative Marketing Association which had been licensed were buying about 50 per cent of the total cocoa and other crops through agents. This relegated firms such as UTC, UAC and CFAO which were initially buying the cocoa and the crops. The Ghana Commercial Bank started to control about 40 percent of the total deposits and 50 per cent of all credit business performed by the commercial banks.

During this time, Sir Arthur Lewis, a renowned economist from West India, and Sir Robert Jackson, an industrialist from Australia, were the main economic advisers of Nkrumah and they had convinced him that Ghana could industrialise only with foreign capital. It was this reason that influenced Nkrumah to allow the foreign companies to explore. One of the main concerns was the funding of the Volta River Project which Nkrumah expected financial assistance from the West. It could be understood that when Ghana gained the republic status, Nkrumah began to shift to socialist status which had been his primary drive prior to independence even in the 1940s. My question is could not Nkrumah allow the free trade market, the laissez faire, operate by also empowering Ghanaians to compete in such market? Could he not have granted the Ghanaian entrepreneurs and business people the license to operate? This was the cry they made during the Watson Commission and yet when their own native took over government, to their shock, he turned them down.

On politics and constitutional matters, Nkrumah did not seek the welfare or the stability of the nation but his sovereignty and that of his party alone. He devised strategies to fortify himself and the CPP. During the colonial era, there were Chief Regional Commissioners who were whites. When their tenure was over, Nkrumah replaced them with CPP politicians only. In Ashanti, Nkrumah suspended the Kumasi City Council workers and replaced them with CPP politicians to break the NLM dominance. In July 1957, the CPP government passed the Deportation Act which immediately deported Amadu Baba and Alhaji Lalemi who were anti CPP in Kumasi and other anti CPP Syrians and Lebanese in Ghana. In December 1957 Nkrumah's government established the Avoidance of Discrimination Act to ban organisations, parties and societies which were focused on tribal, racial and religious groups used for political purposes.

With regard to this Act, as far back as 1949, Gbedemah had revealed that the CPP would emerge as a national party. So after the 1951 elections, the opposition divined that Nkrumah and his CPP would wipe them off if they did not position themselves well. So to the opposition, the opportune time had only arrived for Nkrumah to implement his long awaited vision. From the government side, there were too many factions rising against national peace. One of such groups was the Ga Adangme Shefimo Kpee or Ga Standfast Association which rose against the government claiming the government was not being fair to the Ga regarding promotions. They had a grievance on shortage of housing in Accra. They described Nkrumah as Mr. Dictator. In August 1957, their grievance led to a riot in Accra. Elsewhere in Togoland, the Togoland Congress threatened violence which became known as Alavanyo Riots. Nkrumah sent police and troops to deal with the situation. It was situations like these and also the violence the NLM battled Nkrumah with that led to this Act. For some time, Nkrumah and many CPP leaders could not go to Kumasi freely. Krobo Edusei, then Interior Minister, destooled many chiefs who supported the NLM. By 1966, the CPP government had destooled about 138 chiefs. Prominent among them was the Okyehene, the paramount chief of Akyem Abuakwa. These actions in our politics caused so much fear and intimidation.

Considering the tempo, and direction of government, the opposition parties advised themselves. They realised that the earlier they united the better because the Act was not going to allow any of them to operate in politics. So on 3 November 1957, the NLM, NPP, Muslim Association Party, Togoland Congress Party, Ga Standfast Association came together under the name the United Party. Their leader was Dr. K.A Busia.

In January 1958, Nkrumah's government passed The Emergency Power Act. With this Act, they created the Brong Ahafo Region which was initially part of Ashanti. During the 1956 elections, Nkrumah used that as campaign promise to get the Brong Chiefs to support him against the NLM. He promised to grant them independence of Regional Administration with their own House of Chiefs. To show their loyalty, the CPP got 4 seats from the Brong area. With the Emergency Act, CPP chiefs in Asante, Volta and Brong were made paramount chiefs. The regional councils were abolished to consolidate power to the central government.

Probably, the worst of these Acts was the Preventive Detective Act (PDA) which was passed in July 1958 to arrest and detain anybody suspected of or found acting in a manner prejudicial to the defence of Ghana, to her relations with other states and to state security. The period of arrest or detainment was five years. The evil intent of this Act was clear. The avoidance act failed to cripple the opposition parties because they were smart to unite under one party. Their synergy became too strong for the CPP so the CPP had to quickly enact this Act to crush the opposition party and all citizens that opposed the government. In 1959 12 prominent UP in Asante were detained. R.R. Amponsah and M.K. Apaloo were members of Parliament jailed with this Act. Benjamin Awhaitey, J.B Danquah, Ako Adjei, William Ofori Atta, Obetsebi Lamptey, and Kwadwo Ampim Darko, the chief of Nkonya Ahundwo in the Volta Region were arrested. Out of the 32 opposition MPs, three were arrested, one in the person of Busia was in exile and twelve crossed carpet to the CPP leaving sixteen MPs on the bench of opposition. This move by the government crippled the opposition in the country. In the end 1200 people were arrested by this Act. Many died in detention among them are Obetsebi Lamptey and Danquah. Some came out sick and some partly blind never to recover from the torture. Danquah and some others were placed in condemned cells for torturing.

Besides the physical torturing, the PDA brought so much fear on Ghanaians. Lecturers and students who criticized the government were jailed. Even students who went abroad to study were strictly warned not to go there to criticise Nkrumah's government. At the universities in Ghana, Nkrumah made himself the Chancellor to monitor that activities in the schools did not go against his will. Spies were put in the universities and other places in the nation to report opponents of Nkrumah.

With regard to health, Nkrumah showed so much passion to see the sector grow, especially empowering Ghanaian health professionals. He built new hospitals and new health centres. The significant among them is the Komfo Anokye hospital and the medical school at Korle Bu. He was warned of such radical step that many patients would die because of the inexperience of the health officers. His answer was daring, he replied that 'if they die, they will stop dying.' What he meant was that if people doubted the professionalism of Ghanaian doctors they would soon be experienced and the death would cease. By 1960, he had given scholarship to about 400 medical students to study abroad. He supported the health professionals to fight leprosy, small pox and tuberculosis which were very prevalent in the country.

On his declaration of independence at the Polo Ground, Nkrumah asserted that the independence of Ghana is meaningless unless it is linked up to the total liberation of the African continent. Soon after 6 March 1957, Nkrumah began to put his pan African vision into action. He had George Padmore who was a strong adviser on this vision even though they disagreed on a number of issues. To commence his vision, in April 1958, Nkrumah organised Conference of Independent African States in Accra inviting the eight independent nations in Africa which were Egypt, Ethiopia, Sudan, Liberia, Tunisia, Libya, Morocco and Ghana. And the intent of the conference was to explore ways and means of consolidating and safeguarding African independence; to exchange views on matters of common interests, to strengthen the economic and cultural ties, between our countries; to decide on workable arrangements for helping fellow Africans still subject to colonial rule: and to examine the central world problem of how to secure peace'.

After the conference the members agreed to make the future of independent African states a concern. They agreed to promote economic cooperation among themselves. They also agreed to meet at least once every two years. Nkrumah was satisfied with the outcome of the conference and decided to embark on a tour to these nations in June that year to strengthen ties with them.

To champion a similar course, Nkrumah financially contributed to the black movement in the USA. As a result, Maclom X and Martin

Luther King became friends and admirers of Nkrumah.

When Guinea was almost bankrupt because France abandoned it, due to Sekou Toure's refusal to align with France in the Algerian war, Nkrumah went to Sekou Toure's aid by offering their nation £10 million. Soon, Nkrumah formed Ghana-Guinea Union. Whereas Nkrumah was seeking an opportunity to form a federation with this union to attract other African nations for the goal of African unity, Sekou Toure had something different on his mind. Behind the scene, he worked his way to reconnect with France, its colonial master, suggesting clearly that, even though Sekou did admire Nkrumah, and supported his vision, he was not ready for an outright federation but rather a mutual relationship or economic ties where both nations could have their separate sovereignties. Sekou had to use tact because he would not want to destroy his relationship with Nkrumah. In November 1958, the Ghana-Guinea Union was signed.

That same year in December, Nkrumah organised All African People's Conference in Accra. This was their invitation to the three hundred delegates:

This conference will formulate and proclaim the philosophy of Pan Africanism as the ideology of the African non-violent revolution. Henceforth our slogan shall be: peoples of Africa unite!

You have nothing to lose but your chains! You have a continent to regain!

You have freedom and human dignity to attain!

Hands off Africa!

Africa must be free!!!

As captivating as the invitation heading is so was the conference. Nkrumah was able to revolutionise a number of African leaders who increased the momentum of the independence struggle.

It was this conference that turned Patrice Lumumba into such a radical leader. Roberto Holden raised a force right after his return to Angola for their liberation. Other leaders who were equally impacted to fight for their nation were Kenneth Kaunda, Julius Nyerere, Joshua Nkomo, Tom Mboya, Kanya Chiume and other African nationalists.

These conferences and subsequent ones made Ghana the Mecca of the African freedom fighters. Accra was not only the centre but Nkrumah used Ghana's coffers to finance these revolutions.

Nkrumah continued to hold such conferences with different agenda but all aiming at African liberation. One such was the All African Trade Union Federation Conference and the conference on positive action and security in Africa.

This move of Nkrumah generated its own challenges. One, it generated conflicts with leaders whose views clashed with that of Nkrumah. One of the nations that vehemently criticised Nkrumah was Nigeria. They saw in him a selfish and an ambitious leader who wanted to rule Africa. The neighbouring countries of Ghana also dissociated from Nkrumah, especially Olympio of Togo. It is believed Nkrumah pushed for the sabotage of governments that opposed his views and as such was behind the military revolutions against such leaders. This allegation was debunked by the CPP.

The other challenge is the source of funding of the Pan Africanist Movement of Nkrumah. Firstly, Ghana was the main source of finance for this huge move whereas Ghana had not won its economic battles. This action of Nkrumah did not only earn him disagreement from the opposition parties but also his own confidants from the CPP. One of them was Komla Gbedemah, the Finance Minister of Ghana. For instance, on the loan to Guinea, Nkrumah made no plan for Guinea to pay back. When Gbedemah followed up on the matter, nothing fruitful came out. According to David Rooney in his interview with Gbedemah, he revealed that Nkrumah did not understand finance and had no interest in finance. From the same source, Gbedemah claimed he did not know this side of Nkrumah until they assumed office in government. The fact will always remain that where African nations admired Nkrumah, Ghanaians complained bitterly against him for putting the economic life of Ghana into hardship.

In 1959, Nkrumah passed the Statutory Corporations Act which enabled public corporations to be set up without any parliamentary scrutiny or approval, without any formal rules for audit or control. This is interesting; it is no wonder Gbedemah did say what he said about

Nkrumah's ignorance in finance. The foreign control of the economy created losses for the economy because every year, more money was taken away than how much was invested into the Ghanaian economy. Ghana made average loss of £7 million pounds. This and lavish spending by Nkrumah brought hardship to the economy. At this time, Nkrumah had another plan to move Ghana to become a republic state to unfold his very core aspirations.

# CHAPTER 8

## THE REPUBLIC

Ghana attained independence as a monarchy kingdom under the royal majesty the Queen. Ghana's pound had the image of the Queen until it was later changed by Nkrumah for his image. Yet practically, the Queen barely interfered in any government policy, not even the questionable PDA. Exactly three years after independence, Nkrumah issued the Government White paper of a republican constitution. The news of the republic did not come with much amusement, however some Ghanaians welcomed the idea. This is because many were not proud that an English person was still the Head of State. Having gone through the content of the new republican constitution, Danquah and the opposition thought the whole constitution was simply empowering the president with unlimited powers without having any positive impact on the ordinary Ghanaian. Though the ordinary people could not bother themselves with the details of the constitution, the constitution would provide their major expectation by removing the Queen as the Head of State. A plebiscite was held in April 1960. Firstly, the people were asked whether they wanted the republican constitution or not, and secondly whether they wanted Danquah or Nkrumah to be the president. Many Ghanaians voted for the republican constitution and for Nkrumah with over 1 million votes against 130,000 votes for Danquah. On 1 July 1960, Ghana became a republic nation. Kwame Nkrumah was sworn in as President at the National Assembly.

This constitution gave unlimited powers to the President. He was the Head of State and the Chief Executive. He was the commander in Chief of the Ghana Armed Forces. His duration and that of MPs were to be every five years. He had the power to appoint and dismiss people from the judicial service, the civil service and the armed force. He was given the power to reject or assent to bills.

Danquah and the Opposition opposed the republican constitution not because they did not want Ghana to be a republic but because they always could read between the lines that Nkrumah always wanted a means to fortify himself but not the well-being of the masses. They strongly believed and held on to the belief that Nkrumah was seeking to be a constitutional dictator. For instance it was not originally in the constitution that the President could appoint and dismiss people in the judicial service and the armed forces. They were infused later into the constitution by the CPP legislators.

The legislators of the CPP later inserted in the constitution that the President had power to appoint and dismiss the Chief Justice. The President was given the power to rule by decree or Legislative instrument. Orders began like, 'The President commands…'. Ministers and public officers had to stay by their radio by 1 pm daily to find out whether they were at post or not. This generated so much insecurity among public officers.

What should be of great importance to the reader is that this model of governance defied the true meaning of a republic state. This was because what makes a nation republic is the individual sovereignty where the constitution begins by 'We the people' but this did not happen in the first republic. In other words with all the constitutional amendments, Nkrumah did not empower or protect the ordinary Ghanaian. He rather increased the sovereignty of the president and his loyalists. This is what Danquah and his cohorts perceived and opposed. Freedom and Justice were nominal. They were not in practice.

It is said action and reaction are equal and opposite. Nkrumah's sabotage on his opponent from the pre-independence to the post-independence built strong opposition against him. There were a number of assassination attempts on him. Popular among them is the grenade attack on Nkrumah at Kulungugu. In August 1962, Nkrumah was attacked at Kulungugu when he was returning from Burkina Faso. A bomb targeted at Nkrumah was concealed in a flower held by a girl for presentation to Nkrumah. Nkrumah's bodyguard died when the bomb exploded. Nkrumah escaped but not without physical damage even though the government report at the time denied his injury.

The suspects were taken to court. They were Ako Adjei, Adamafio and Crabbe. After the court trial, the Supreme Court judges acquitted these suspects as 'Not Guilty' in December 1963. The court's decision irritated Nkrumah. Two days after the decision, he sacked the Chief Justice, Sir Arku Korsa, Justices Akufo-Addo and Van Lare. Soon after that, Nkrumah sought for a bill to be passed in parliament to enable the president to dismiss any judgement in the country's courts. Nkrumah's reason for his action was that he wanted the judges to have consulted him before passing the judgement. He reappointed new Supreme Court judges who found the suspects guilty and sentenced them to life imprisonment. This was again interfered by Nkrumah who reduced Ako Adjei, Adamafio and Cofie Crabbe sentenced years to twenty years imprisonment.   There were protests overseas against Nkrumah's decision. This action of Nkrumah destroyed his international reputation.

But in Ghana, the CPP Press and Radio clamoured for the blood of the detained suspects. Some chiefs and the T.U.C and other organisations held 'loyal marches' around the Flagstaff House to show their solidarity to Nkrumah to create the impression that the nation was behind him. The terrorists decided to halt such 'spontaneous loyalty marches' by throwing bombs into the crowd in front of the Flagstaff House. Initially, the Government thought it was the work of foreign terrorists. They even rounded up some of the 'freedom fighters' whom they were training for similar attacks in other African states. But the terrorists proved the Government wrong by sending letters to Nkrumah to inform him in advance of any projected attacks.   Eventually, the Government declared a State of Emergency after the death of many people through the bombings. They went further with house to house search for the terrorists. It was through this search that they found Obetsebi Lamptey who was very ill but still arrested him and sent him to the Nsawam prison where he died[1]

Commemorating Positive Action day on 8 January 1963, Nkrumah held a mass rally against the State of Emergency which had been passed at the time. During the event, there was an attack on him by the terrorists but he managed to escape. On the 2nd January 1964, Nkrumah suffered another attack on his life. Seth Ametewee, one of Nkrumah's guards, fired gun shots at Nkrumah but he escaped. The bullet hit Nkrumah's police guard, Salifu and he died. This prompted Nkrumah to sack a number of top police commanders. Ametewe is reported to have said that if he had succeeded, J.B Danquah could have been the President. To Nkrumah that was enough evidence of Danquah's involvement in the crime so without any trial Nkrumah jailed Danquah.[2] He was put in the condemn cell and given poor treatment by the directive of Nkrumah. Danquah pleaded with Nkrumah to release him because of his health conditions but his plea fell on deaf ears. He suffered from tuberculosis and eventually died of heart attack in detention in February, 1965.[2]

During Ghana's Golden Jubilee celebration, Professor Kofi Kumado, a renowned law lecturer, in a lecture which was published in the Daily Graphic on Wednesday, April 11, 2007 described this period of Nkrumah's administration as re-colonisation. This is what he briefly said, 'After putting our political independence beyond the pale of doubt, we allowed ourselves to be re-colonised, this time by internal forces from 1964...' And the Professor was right.

In 1964, Nkrumah organised another plebiscite to decide whether Ghana had to become a one- party state and whether the president should have powers to dismiss Judges of High court at any time for reasons which would appear to him sufficient. The proposal of the one-party state further vindicated the opposition parties that Nkrumah wanted to get rid of them. Nkrumah passed the Avoidance Discrimination Act and the opposition quickly emerged into one party escaping any sanction that would come with this Act. When Nkrumah did not succeed with that, he passed the Preventive Detective Act which empowered him to arrest and detain any person without trial. In effect, he was able to arrest many of the leaders of the opposition while some opposition MPs and other members crossed carpet to the CPP. For instance, Mumuni Bawumia was a member of the opposition who crossed carpet to the CPP. These actions were not enough with Nkrumah and the CPP. They had to achieve their long awaited dream- a one party state at all cost.

The plebiscite was carried and the votes showed that 2,773,920 voted yes and 2452 voted No. This means that unimaginably 92.8% of the registered voters cast their ballot. The mysterious fact was that no single 'No' vote was registered in the whole of Ashanti region the stronghold of the opposition party. The fact of the matter was that, the election was rigged in favour of the CPP and anyone who was found with a "NO" poster was arrested. Mr. Kofi Baako, former Minister of Defence under Nkrumah arrested one Mr. Geoffrey Kweku Tei for being in possession of a "No" poster. After the overthrow of Nkrumah in 1966, Mr. Baako appeared before the enquiry commission to apologise for his bad conduct.[3]

So all political parties ceased to exist and the CPP became the only party for the people. This is not a surprising thing because this was Gbedemah's confession in 1949 that CPP would be a nationalist party. As a matter of fact in the national Assembly, any time Nkrumah and CPP legislative referred to the people they were not referring to the people of the Gold Coast or Ghana but simply the members of the CPP. They often said, 'the party is the people and the people are the party '. It therefore came as no surprise that Nkrumah changed the original Ghana flag the red, gold and green to red, white and green which were the CPP colours. It would be interesting for us to read a portion of Danquah's feedback to Nkrumah on 30 April 1957 on the colours of the convention in 1957 when Nkrumah wrote his autobiography.

> Is it true then that you (Nkrumah) acted as an executive officer of the United Gold Coast Convention for 18 months without knowing that the colours of the Convention were "Red, Gold and Green", and that the colours were chosen by the six of us in the Kumasi prison and not at a meeting in Saltpond? When you formed the Convention People's Party you removed the 'gold' in the centre of our design and replaced it by 'white'. You retained the rest of our colours for the C.P.P. flag. Today the "Red, Gold and Green" colours

of the Convention have been adopted as national colours of Ghana! "The stone which the builders rejected is become the head of the corner".[4]

The intent of Nkrumah is exposed by the letter of Danquah to him that from the beginning, Nkrumah did not support the colours of the nation's flag because it was the choice of the Big Six. With his subtle ambition to take over and dominate the country, the right time came in 1964 for him to replace the red, gold and green with the CPP red, white and green. It appears to me that most of Nkrumah's initiatives were for his personal ambition as his critics had for a long time accused him of. The question one can ask is, 'What significant importance was the change of flag going to bring to Ghanaians?' This was nothing but domination.

As per the republican constitution, Ghana was scheduled for an election every five years. So in 1965, Ghana was supposed to go to the polls but this had been annulled and never was Ghana going to the polls. Nkrumah went on radio to announce the names of new members of parliament. The funny and embarrassing thing was that some of these members of parliament did not know the constituencies they had been tasked to represent in parliament. A typical example is a lawyer called Alhaji Alhassan who was having a drink at the then Ambassador Hotel and suddenly a news bulletin reached him that he had been nominated as a member of parliament to a place he never knew. According to him, he attended parliament meetings a few times. His major surprise was that no initial discussion had gone on with him.

At this time, Nkrumah had become the life president of Ghana. He was at the same time the chancellor to all the universities in the country to monitor affairs in the universities. Nkrumah ordered for a number of lecturers to be made professors and head of departments. He opposed any directives and policies against his will. For instance, on Monday, February 10, 1964, the Daily Graphic published:

> **Mr. N.A Welbeck, former executive secretary of the Party, at the weekend, led thousands of placard-bearing demonstrators from all over the country to Legon to protest against the way students and some lecturers at the university isolated themselves from the socialist**

**revolution in the country. The demonstrators, most of them beating Asafo drums, carried placards some of which read: "Down with arrogant students" "come down to earth," "down with ostrich students" and "no amount of rumour mongering can set back the socialist revolution." They marched through all the halls.[5]**

Nkrumah had spies to report lecturers and students who spoke against his government. Lecturers and students who opposed him were dealt with; sometimes they were taken into detention. One victim was Prof. De Graft Johnson who was taken into detention. The Daily Graphic on Monday, February 10, 1964 further published 6 Lectures who had been deported. Among lecturers who were dismissed and deported are W.B. Harvey, R.B Seid-man, G Grego, W. Jean Pierre, L.H Schuster and J.V Stewart. According to the government, these lecturers were involved in subversive activities which were prejudicial to the security of the state. The government added that their presence in Ghana was not conducive to the public good.

In February, 1965 when Danquah died in detention, a third year student Otu Cantey, lowered the Ghana flag which was the CPP flag and asked for a minute silence for Danquah.[6] This student was thrown into detention. This continued to increase fear and panic in people in the universities. As a result of his intrusion at the universities, many lecturers left the country. This affected the academic output of the universities. As a matter of fact students who went abroad to study were sternly warned not to go and criticise Nkrumah's government, if they did, they would be sent to Nsawam prison on their return to Ghana. In his book, *Dark Days in Ghana*, Nkrumah admitted that the intellectual class did not like his government. They did so because of his bad leadership.

This is what the opposition spoke against; that too much power had been invested into the hands of the president, making him a constitutional dictator. The government sought to abuse the very essence of the republican constitution. What is the essence of the republican constitution? In a republican constitution, the power rests with the people. It seeks the individual sovereignty. It seeks the liberty of the people. Yet Ghana's independence struggle misguided us to seek political power to oppress the masses and to punish to death individuals who shared different views. Individuals lost their right of liberty in Ghanaian republican constitution. They could be jailed without trial. A single person had all the power to use it to his own reasonable faculty, whether his thinking made sense or not. The Ghanaian individual's sovereignty was ceased; he or she could no longer vote for the president and legislators they wanted. An individual had become a life president against the very essence of a republican constitution. The irrefutable truth was and still is that Ghana was only a nominal republic; it was just on paper but in practical terms Ghana became an oppressive monarchy state. It was a misnomer to say Ghana was a republic state. The ensuing oppression and suppression of the people of Ghana, even including the CPP members, were not known in Africa and Nkrumah was seen as a hero of freedom.

The turning to republic also brought a new direction to the economic management of Ghana. Nkrumah began to implement his socialist views and resort to Russia and the eastern world for support. He and some of his ministers like Botsio and Adamafio started visiting Russia, China and other eastern nations. The turn to socialism did come without resistance. The academia and the political opponent opposed socialism.

Nkrumah's socialism was not only opposed by the people in opposition but it also brought a rift among the cabinet, MPs and party officials of the C.P.P. In April 1961, P. Quaidoo, an M.P from the C.P.P on the floor of parliament boldly opposed the government's shift to socialism on the grounds that it was alien to the Ghanaian culture. He revealed that Ghana had a rich heritage; a heritage that commands respect for chiefs, a heritage that gives dignity and influence and a place to the Ghanaian family in society's development. According to Mr Quaidoo, Marx and Lenin's ideas were alien to Ghana's. He then advised the government to build the economy on Ghana's own culture. The fact of the matter is Mr. Quaidoo was right. However, his stance against socialism ended him in jail.

Other CPP gallant leaders like Krobo Edusei, K.A Gbedemah,

C.K.K. Baah and W.A Wiafe also opposed socialism. Some of the CPP leaders who supported socialism were Kofi Baako and Tawiah Adamafio. The reality was that the anti-socialist group had more people than the socialist group. The socialist group members who were the minority were also divided into two groups: the scientific socialist and the African socialist. The Scientific socialists were: Kofi Batsa, S.G. Ikoku, Heyman, Tawiah Adamafio, K. Amoako-Atta and T.D. Baffoe. These were opposed to the adaptation of Marxism to African conditions. The African socialists were Kofi Baako and Kwaku Boaten who supported Marxism in the African environment.

These ideological differences led to intensifying rift and bitterness among the loyalists of Nkrumah giving him a very tough time to devise psychological strategies to hold these factions together in the party. However, with time, he manoeuvred to remove or reshuffle these CPP leaders. Komla Gbedemah, Nkrumah's chief lieutenant quit the CPP and fled for his life. This even led him to occupy positions such as chairman and secretary of the CPP. He also assumed the position of the Minister of Foreign Affairs, Finance and Education while a president. Analysts have tried to state reasons for Nkrumah's shift to socialism. For instance, Fitch and Oppenheimer explained that it was Nkrumah's failure in economic policies that led to this shift to socialism to help him solve the emerging balance of payment crisis. On the contrary, W. Scott Thompson attributed the reason to the Congo crisis and the failure of Nkrumah's policy there epitomised by Lumumba's assassination.

Whereas there may be some iota of truth in the assertions of these analysts, I think every person ought to know by the sequence of Nkrumah's events and actions that his shift to socialism was a premeditated and calculated plan. Nkrumah in his publication towards *Colonial Freedom,* revealed his inclination towards socialism in 1945. During the launching of the CPP in 1949, he revealed that he was going to build a socialist state. Why did it take him this long to embark on his socialism agenda? It can be detected from the actions and strategies of Nkrumah towards the British and for that matter the western world and his attitude towards Ghanaians that Nkrumah had a hidden agenda. His secret admiration and obedience to the Governor and the British and his unwillingness to take the businesses from the expatriates at independence was because he did not want to offend the western powers.

The next major reason was that Nkrumah deliberately did not want private Ghanaian businesses to thrive. He preferred the western business men to thrive at the expense of Ghanaian businesses. That is why he kept deaf ears to the counsel of Wiafe and others who were praying him to give import license to Ghanaian traders. A typical example is the story of a man called Ocran who was the head of a successful fishing company. In 1963, Nkrumah summoned him to take over the State Fishing Corporation which would eventually absorb Ocran's company but Ocran refused. As a result, Ocran was denied import license for a machine for his fishing processing plant. He was told by Djin that he would get as many licenses he wanted on the condition that he would join the State Fishing Corporation. Nkrumah's government deliberately chose to destroy a thriving business because it was more successful than the state corporation[7]. On this premise, Nkrumah was exposed by his laudable independence speech that when the African was given the chance, he could show that he was somebody, yet his government refused to empower Ghanaian business men. Rather he encouraged them to join the cooperatives.

He held the view that the state was the better institution to compete with the foreign multinational companies. His argument was that local business would never generate enough surplus capital to provide investment on the scale he needed yet he forgot that it was the ordinary uneducated Ghanaian peasant farmers whose sweat contributed to the production of two thirds of the world cocoa. It was this cocoa revenue that was the main backbone of the economy. Why would he in his right senses doubt what other Ghanaians could do in the other sectors? His main worry was that he did not want any strong Ghanaian business which could threaten his position. Rather he encouraged the Ghanaian business men to compete for small scale businesses that had been annexed by the Lebanese and Syrians.

Nkrumah and his government revoked a number of licenses in many fields in 1961. In the banking sector, the share of Ghana Commercial Bank controlled 40 per cent total banks' deposits and 50 per cent of total banks' credit in 1961. These percentages increased with time. Similarly the State Insurance Corporation controlled 50 per cent of the total insurance business in the country by February 1966. There was a policy that for a civil servant to secure a loan to buy a car, he or she needed to have account with the Ghana Commercial Bank. Foreign purchasers of cocoa were also tasked to do their cocoa sales with this bank.

On imports, Nkrumah's government took control of them and made Ghana National Trading Corporation the main importer and distributor of goods into the country. On mining, he established the State Mining Corporation which took over six out of the seven gold mining firms with the exception of AngloGold Ashanti. The government bought some of these mines at a gargantuan price when the machines had served their usefulness. He established the Accra Diamond Company to take over all the Diamond Companies which were owned by Africans and one Dutch. The only Diamond firms left to operate were Consolidated African Selection Trust (CAST), AYCO and Akim Concessions. On construction, the government established the State Construction Corporation in 1962 which was expanded to execute 75 per cent of all the government projects. The government took over the timber industry by establishing a State Timber Corporation. The sad thing is that it nearly collapsed the whole timber export.

In October 1961, Nkrumah set up a Planning Commission for the Seven-Year Development Plan with EN Omaboe as chairman and JH Mensah as his assistant. These two were the main architects of this programme. In 1962, Nkrumah launched the Work and Happiness programme as the first part of The Seven -Year Development Plan at the party congress in Kumasi to change the social and economic structure to provide a socialist society. On agriculture, the programme aimed at developing new cash crops, increasing exports, processing more locally produced products like cocoa to replace imported goods.

During the launching of the main the Seven Year Development Plan, Nkrumah invited experts such as Arthur Lewis, Nicholas Kaldor, Dudley Seers, Albert Hirschman, Joszef Bognar and Tony Killick. They expressed their differences on the programme by questioning the feasibility studies, and little scientific plan of action and overall they felt the programme was over-ambitious. JH Mensah also criticised in vain the financial feasibility of some of the programme. He asserted that Marxist concepts and class analysis had limited applicability to the Ghanaian situation. When JH Mensah realised Nkrumah would not accept his professional advice but rather use him to work against his professional conscience, JH Mensah resigned and left for a UN appointment.[8]

Even when Nkrumah made the right point, he always had an ostensible motive that was not healthy for the ordinary Ghanaian. For instance, Nkrumah admitted that for the agricultural programme to be successful there was the need to break away from the usage of primitive farm tools for modern mechanised system. One would have expected that he would come to the aid of the ordinary peasant cocoa farmers but no, Nkrumah saw these farmers who had been the back bone of Ghana's economy as positive obstacle to his new programme. However, for years, he milked these poor cocoa farmers to sponsor his over ambitious programme and the building of the entire Ghanaian society. This is how David Rooney in his book *"Nkrumah: Vision and Tragedy"* puts it:

**Money was poured into large-scale agricultural enterprises, and seemed deliberately to challenge the independent peasant farmer. This challenge came after a decade in which millions of pounds had been milked from the cocoa farmers not only in order to finance every aspect of development, but also to finance the whole of the wasteful, corrupt and profligate society which had grown up in Accra and most of the towns of Ghana.[9]**

In 1963 Nkrumah invested £127 million into about 40 state enterprises. This was further escalated to £155 million. When Nkrumah's had high expectation for profit, the state firms made a loss of £15 million.[10] This became the trend in all the years he embarked on his state projects. In his book, *Ghana: Evolution and Change in the 19th and 20th Centuries,* Prof. Adu Boahen states that only 2 out of the 22 state-owned factories gained some profits. The question one would ask is: What was wrong? The losses were due to bad management, lack of skilled labour, lack of raw materials and lack of value for money. On bad management, a number of Nkrumah's project lacked proper feasibility studies and effective strategic management principles. They built firms in places that were not strategic; in some cases, the cost of transporting raw materials could make the business run at a loss. Most of his people who supported the idea of socialism were of low competence. This was admitted by K.B Asante that once Nkrumah told him that he had built many industries and the people who could help him manage them were in the opposition, the very people he had described as backward and arrested over a thousand of them into prison were the people he needed. On the State Farm Corporation, the employees were 30,000, out of this number, 25,000 were from the Workers Brigade who had no skilled training. The sad thing is that, they could not feed themselves let alone feed the entire nation, yet these workers and their cronies were on pay roll earning huge salaries.

With regard to lack of raw materials, The Komenda Sugar factory could not operate because there was inadequate water supply to the plant. The Wenchi Tomato factory was set up with grandiose bungalows and a large administration block. Its capacity was to process 5000 tons of tomatoes and 7,000 tons of mangoes. After completion the factory cost 80 per cent higher than its initial cost. Yet at the time of operation, they realised there were not enough mangoes to supply the plant and it would take seven years to grow new ones. Again, constructing a plant 80 per cent higher than its cost was clear case of lack of value for money and there were a number of such projects under Nkrumah that cost much higher than their original cost.

The State Fishing Industry was also in abysmal performance. Report shows that the industry was choked with corruption and nepotism that caused the business to collapse. The same can be said about the Ghana Airways, it piled up debts because the staff travelled on the air line with their families for free; they would travel as often as possible. This caused financial loss to the company. Besides, there were huge financial misappropriations which, together with financial malpractice, crippled the company.

Nkrumah and a German businessman, Dr. Drevici, entered into a contract for the construction of a housing and industrial unit project at Tema at a cost of £70 million. Yet at the time of the coup, only £9 million had been spent to build the huge cocoa silos at Tema while the rest of the money disappeared without the completion of the project and without any financial accountability.[11] All these misappropriations and unreasonable cost of contracts were possible because Nkrumah passed the Statutory Corporation Act in 1959. This Act allowed State Corporation to be established without parliamentary approval, and without any formal rules of audit or control. It is no wonder the government could buy a gold mining firm that had run out of its usefulness at a huge cost without any formal audit. It is the reason why the government could build the Job 600 complex which was about 10 times its expected cost. It should be no wonder then that such firms ran at a loss. This is because what could give service value for money was formal audit before and during the operation of the firms. This important audit was ignored. As a result, the cronies of Nkrumah and the CPP spent the ordinary tax payer's money as they wanted.

In his attempt to cut off from the west, Nkrumah asked Ghanaian firms to buy their goods from Eastern Europe. This unfortunately led to shortage of essential goods in Ghana. In 1964, basic commodities like milk, sugar, flour, soap, drugs and spare parts for motor vehicles were completely out of the markets and shops. This obviously led to price hikes and hoarding. This sad situation extended to 1965 which made life very unbearable for the ordinary Ghanaian. For instance, the masses would have to queue to the Accra Sports Stadium not to watch a football match but to buy sugar. Nkrumah had to turn back to the West for financial assistance in exchange of raw materials. They were to supply Ghana with needed imported goods on 180 day credit at high interest rates.

In spite of these hardships, Nkrumah and his ministers were found in flamboyant lifestyles. Nkrumah ordered for nine bronze statutes of himself at a cost of NC 400,000 and American Armour car at a cost of NC500,000. In 1965, ambitious to host the African Union Summit, Nkrumah speedily sponsored for the building of the Job 600 complex which was built at 9 to 10 times its original cost in the estimates of NC10-15.6 million. Krobo Edusei's wife ordered a gold bed of £3,000 which aroused public agitation that she was asked to return it. At the said time, Nkrumah's ministers had enriched themselves with a lot of wealth they acquired overnight. Krobo Edusei owned 27 houses, Asafo-Agyei owned 14 and Ayeh Kumi owned 12 houses. They had furnished their houses with modern fashionable furniture and glamorous decorations. They rented these houses for more financial return.

Besides the Statutory Corporation Act which could influence the government and its officials to be corrupt or financially indiscipline, Nkrumah set up the National Development Corporation (NADECO) which principally was to collect commission government made on issuing contracts. Ayeh Kumi was the head of NADECO and according to Krobo Edusei, every contractor, before he or she could be issued a contract, was asked to see Ayeh Kumi. He and the applicant for a contract had to agree on the commission to be paid before the government could grant the contract. Report shows that Nkrumah did not see anything wrong for ministers to meet contractors for money to support the CPP. This is confirmed by K.B Asante, a former secretary to Nkrumah who said, 'Nkrumah believed those imbued with socialism were incorruptible and would always seek the public interest. Even if they took 10% it would be for the party's coffers'.[12] At the time of his overthrow, Nkrumah was worth £2,322,009.[13] An American scholar, Victor Le Vine, who investigated into the Nkrumah's corruption issue, stated that Nkrumah was clearly involved in a number of corrupt transactions. He continued that he used public funds to distribute largesse to his favourites. He bought cars for his mistresses and gave gifts to friends, relatives and cronies.[14]

Apart from his over ambition of spending the nation's money on financially risky and technically unscientific projects which all took a nose dive, Nkrumah had set the Contingency fund, the Bureau of African Affairs and other organisations which were not subject to civil service audit, he was able to squander the nation's limited reserve and revenue to sponsor his lonely African agenda of ruling the rest of African nations. This had cost him huge sums of money beginning from 1957 right after the nation's independence. For instance, because of this ambition, he discouraged his finance minister Gbedemah not to retrieve the £10 million given to Guinea.

On 11 February 1965, the Finance Minister, Amoako Atta  at a cabinet meeting revealed that Ghana's reserves which stood over £200 million was left with £500,000. In a deep shock, President Nkrumah remained in silence for about 15 minutes and broke down in tears.[15] Yet in his book, *the Dark Days in Ghana*, Nkrumah briefly stated that he did not squander the £200 million in the national reserve.  This is what he wrote: **'In 1957, Ghana had a sterling balance of £200 million. This has not been "squandered" as the imperialist press would have its readers believe. It has been used to pay off successive balance of payments deficits due to the rise in prices of imported consumer goods, and the drastic fall in the price of our main export crop-cocoa.'[16]** Not only was the national reserve squandered but rather, the external debt which stood at £20 million in 1957 had exponentially swelled to £280 million as published by the Daily Graphic on Friday, December 23 1966. Sadly, cocoa which used to be the main back bone of the economy had fallen in price on the world market. Fact be told, Ghana was bankrupt. Yet to Nkrumah, his projects were assets and not debt. But the truth is that by 1965, all Nkrumah's hopes on his state firms were blown away for they all virtually operated on losses. The Volta River Project could not solve the problem. The government could not use the local bauxite to run the VALCO. They had to import bauxite for VALCO; it was foreign owned. The irrigation for Afram Plains to aid agriculture was not done. Practically, the Volta River Project did benefit foreigners more than Ghanaians.

Nkrumah at this time was detached from the common people that had brought him to power. He was detached from the police and army. He had his President's Own Guard Regiment who were assisted by Russian army and well-resourced than the Ghana army. The indication was clear that he would break the Ghana army down and replace them with the President's Own Guard Regiment. The State Army had no proper boots and many officers' uniforms were worn or torn.  There had been a number of rumours of coup d'etat but none were executed.

Around this period, Nkrumah presented special medals to the Chief of Defence Staff, Major-General S.J.A Otu and his deputy, Major-General J.A Ankrah at an Armed Forces Day parade. Some sources belief Nkrumah did that to win their loyalty because of the rumours of coup. Surprisingly, not long after that, the Daily Graphic on Tuesday, July 29, 1965 published:

> OTU AND ANKRAH RETIRE. It read as follows, "Osagyefo the President, Supreme Commander of the Ghana Armed Forces, has accepted the retirement of the Chief of Defence Staff, Major-General S.J.A Otu, and his deputy, Major-General J.A Ankrah. Their retirement took effect from yesterday."

However, writing in his book, *'Dark Days in Ghana'*, Nkrumah made it frankly clear without mincing words that he dismissed Ankrah and Otu. His reasons were that, they were lazy, incompetent and unreliable. Nkrumah further revealed that, both had confided in him that they had, on several occasions, been written to anonymously and asked to join plots to overthrow the government which they objected. Nevertheless, Nkrumah revealed that even if they had refused to join the enemy, their names had become associated with treason, and they should no longer continue to serve in the Ghana army. Nkrumah emphatically stated, "I retired them, gave them six months' pay, gratuities, and positions in two of the leading Accra banks."[17] The graphic publication suggests that the Nkrumah's government was not truthful to the public with information. It appears the dismissal of the Generals added salt to injury. This is because, later in 1966, Afrifa in his book, *"The Ghana Coup"* stated that the sacking of their generals was one of the factors that inspired them to overthrow Nkrumah's government.

Dr. Kwame Nkrumah was overthrown on the 24 February 1966.

Nkrumah and his loyalists publicly blame Nkrumah's internal political opponents and international rivals for the coup. There is even a public perception that America sent Nkrumah on a peace mission and stabbed him in the back with a coup d'etat. This is unfounded. Americans did not send Nkrumah. There are also reports of the Central Intelligence Agency's (CIA) involvement in the coup but as to whether that is enough case for causation is unknown. In his allegation against the CIA, Nkrumah in his book *'Dark Days in Ghana'* revealed that the CIA contacted Kotoka and Afrifa to even assassinate him which from

Nkrumah's own account, Afrifa and Kotoka refused. Nkrumah and his loyalists have always blamed the coup on the CIA and their so called traitors that is the soldiers. Yet, the factors surrounding Nkrumah's actions towards the end of his reign calls for critical assessment if he was in a way not a culprit in his own tragedy.

Dr. Obed Asamoah, a non-conformist, is one of the people who is of the view that Nkrumah was a culprit in his own tragedy. He wrote, 'Nkrumah's own propensity, (a) to dismantle the provision of the independence constitution intended to restrain executive power as it related to the Regional Assembly, House of Chiefs, and the amendment of certain clauses of the constitution; (b) to create a one party state;(c) to build statues of himself; (d) to develop programmes to ban publication not consistent to his party ideologies; and (e) to arrogate power to reverse judicial decision, lies his personal responsibility for what happened to him on the 24 February 1966.'[18]

Nkrumah's government was overthrown in a bloody coup when he was on a trip to Hanoi. How did this mission come about? In the month of July 1965, at a Commonwealth Prime Ministers conference, it was formally proposed that some members would be selected to embark on a peace keeping mission in Hanoi. Nkrumah was one of the selected leaders and he happily welcomed the idea. However, this mission was to be sooner turned down. Hanoi rejected this visitation from the Commonwealth but agreed to welcome Nkrumah. Hanoi rejected the Commonwealth delegation because they were resentful towards the West but admired Nkrumah because of his orientation towards the Eastern political philosophy. This was not the first time such a Peace initiative to Viet-Nam was declined. Earlier in 1964, the Conference of Heads of State and Governments of Non Aligned States' attempt to visit Hanoi could not materialise. Eventually, the Commonwealth mission was also declined.

But as elated as Nkrumah was, he sent an envoy to arrange for this visit in Hanoi. The visit no longer was a peace keeping but a State visit as Meyers, Ghana's ambassador to China and Hanoi rightly put it. Nkrumah could not embark on the journey in 1965 but did that in February 1966 which marked the end of his reign.

On Tuesday, February 1, 1966, this is what the Daily Graphic published.

### Ho: Kwame, come to Hanoi

President Nkrumah will visit Hanoi, capital of North Viet Nam, shortly, the Office of the President announced in Accra yesterday.

According to the announcement, Dr. Nkrumah has accepted an invitation from President Ho Chi Minh of North Viet Nam to visit Hanoi.

This will be Ho's second invitation to Osagyefo the President to visit his country.

The first was in last July when Ho personally extended an invitation to Dr. Nkrumah to visit North Viet Nam.

President Nkrumah was elected a member of the Commonwealth Peace Mission on Viet Nam.

Following the invitation, Dr. Nkrumah despatched a mission headed by Mr. Kwesi Armah, Minister of Trade, then Ghana's High Commissioner in London, with a special message to Hanoi.

President Ho Chi Minh received the mission and expressed his thanks for the concern shown and the active support extended by Osagyefo and the people of Ghana to the Vietnamese people's struggle for their legitimate national rights.

Mr. Kwesi Armah, on his return to Accra, described his talks with President Ho Chi Minh as "very cordial and useful."

Narrating in his book, *'Dr Nkrumah's Last Journey The Sensational Viet-Nam, US War'*, Joe-Fio Meyer who was responsible for the preparation of the state visit of Nkrumah to Hanoi, wrote:

**Before the publication of the joint communique that announced Osagyefo's visit, President Ho Chi Minh had expressed regret that, owing to the intensification of the air attacks, he could not recommend a visit by Osagyefo to Hanoi at that particular time. He however hoped that**

**conditions would improve to make such a visit possible in the near future. He also indicated his desire to visit Ghana himself when conditions in Viet-Nam improved.[19]**

From the response of President Ho Chi Minh that he could not recommend a visit by Osagyefo to Hanoi due to the intensity of air attacks, one would have expected Nkrumah to have been diplomatic to cancel the journey. On the contrary, Nkrumah sent another Envoy to the US president, Johnson, asking him for the cessation of air attacks on North Viet-Nam to make his visit to Hanoi possible. President Johnson assured him that there were no air attacks from the US on Viet-Nam. Nkrumah again wrote a letter to President Johnson for negotiation with him which was declined by President Johnson and said that would only be possible after Nkrumah's visit to Hanoi. The publication of Meyer, Nkrumah's ambassador, confirms what Professor Baffour Agyeman-Duah stated in his book *'General Acheampong'* that **"The circumstances surrounding the invitation were as curious as Nkrumah's own ambition to broker peace between the titans of the Cold War, the United States and the Soviet Union, who had turned Vietnam into test grounds for their prowess".[20]**

In January 1966, before embarking on this journey of no return, Nkrumah wrote his Will and bequeathed everything to the CPP. Before leaving Ghana, leaders of the CPP at the party headquarters persuaded him to abandon the journey because of several rumours of coup d'etat but Nkrumah refused. He left Ghana on the 21st February 1966.

On the fateful day of the departure of Dr. Nkrumah for Hanoi, he addressed the nation and the programme was televised on the Ghana Television. Among the important issues he spoke to was a strict admonition to the military. At that time, the Nigerian military had taken over the government and Nkrumah seemed to have had the presentiment of a similar takeover of his government.

In his strict admonition to the military, Nkrumah categorically and emphatically stated that if there should be a military takeover in his absence, the military should realise that they were not civilian administrators and that they should not perpetuate in office. He issued the order that the military, in the event of a military takeover, should hand over power to a civilian government within a possible short time. It could be inferred from this that Nkrumah had seen the writing of some kind of danger on the wall.[21]

The country was so saturated with rumours of coup d'etat that many Ghanaians expected the coup to have taken place far earlier than it happened. Information gathered is that just at the airport, someone said, 'The coup would take place tomorrow and another retorted, 'No it will take place today.'

The important thing any discerning and objective person should be curious about is, why would Nkrumah be so eager to embark on a mission that was cancelled? Why would he want to visit Hanoi when the host, the president of Viet- Nam discouraged the trip? 'why did Nkrumah write his Will a month before he embarked on the journey ?'Considering the poor performance of his State Enterprises, the economic turmoil that Ghana faced to the extent that the nation could not pay its debts, the numerous attempts on his life and the rumours of coup d'etat, did Nkrumah have any premonition that he had come to the end of the road? Was he fleeing the country to observe the possible outcome of a coup d'etat?

Early 24th February 1966, shortly before 6:00 am, an unknown voice on Ghana Broadcasting Corporation asked listeners to stay by their radio for brief announcement. Exactly 6:00 am, another voiced spoke:

> Fellow Ghanaians, I have come to inform you that the Military, in co-operation with the Ghana Police, have taken over the government of Ghana today. The myth surrounding Nkrumah has been broken. Parliament is dissolved and Kwame Nkrumah is dismissed from office. All Ministers are also dismissed. The Convention People's Party is disbanded with effect from now. It will be illegal for any person to belong to it. We appeal to you to be calm and co-operative. All persons in detention will be released in due course. Please stay by your radios and await further details.'[22]

The first voice was the voice of Major A.A. Afrifa, and the second voice was Colonel E. K. Kotoka. These were the main architects of the coup. Soon after this news broke out, the whole nation turned into massive jubilation. Various authorities in Ghana commended and welcomed the coup. Among them was the House of Chiefs. The Asantehene, Otumfuo Sir Osei Agyeman Prempeh II welcomed the coup and called chiefs and people in the Kumasi Traditional Council to rededicate themselves and work in the interest of the new regime.[23] The Oguaa Traditional Area declared: 'we fully support the Ghana Armed Forces and the Police because they have saved us from total collapse, tyranny and dictatorship.'[24] The Chiefs and people of Gbese Traditional Area in Accra said, 'The fall of Kwame Nkrumah is more spectacular than that of Satan, a most vivid warning and an appreciable lesion to all who pursue the mirage of political kingdom and its volatile treasures.'[25] The Ghana Trades Union Congress issued an eight-point resolution to welcome the coup. They said, 'this glorious cause of redeeming the people of Ghana from oppression, poverty, want and dictatorial rule.'[26]

The report remains that people celebrated the overthrow of Nkrumah almost as they did at independence. J J Rawlings, former President of Ghana, stated that never in his life had he seen such a massive and huge celebration of Ghanaians like they did at Nkrumah's overthrow. It was even a relief to some of the CPP ministers. One notable is Krobo Edusei, a former MP and minister under the CPP government who is believed to have said, 'the coup was long overdue.' Mr. Alex Quaison-Sackey, former Minister of Foreign Affairs under the Nkrumah's administration and one of Nkrumah's entourage to Hanoi, declared on his return to Ghana that there was fresh air of freedom blowing in the country. He added that the new era had relieved Ghana from oppression.[27]

The major question is, did the overthrow of Nkrumah solve the problem? Did it relieve Ghanaians from the oppression?

CHAPTER 9

# THE UNFINISHED TASK

It is many years since independence, many governments have ruled Ghana but the fact remains that Ghana still wallows in the wilderness, crying for deliverance in its governance, education, infrastructure, economy, jobs, health care, housing and many other needs of humanity. The fact remains that we appear helpless in solving our crises. When pundits thought that military regimes were the cause of Ghana's woes, time has proved that that may not be the principal cause. Because as we speak, many Ghanaians are discontented with the 1992 democracy Ghana resorted to. It is also clear that the democracy we are practising has no solution to our plights. It is only increasing corruption, and dominion of foreign rule or interference in the nation and its assets.

The question is what then is the problem of Ghana? Personally, I think the problem of Ghana is largely because successive governments failed in breaking the yoke or legacy of colonisation. Many of us were wrongly made to believe that the absence of the Whiteman's government was freedom. In chapter one, the reason why I briefly wrote on how colonisation emerged was for readers to discern the weapons or tricks of colonisation which are still at work in Ghana and Africa. These are; the Whiteman was able to pass on his culture and laws to govern us. The white man was able to implement policies that gave foreign merchants upper hand in trade. They made Ghana and Africa producers of raw materials and consumers of the Whiteman finished products. In the end, they manipulated us to lose our self-identity and self-belief for us to feel inferior about ourselves. And they succeeded in making us believe that they are superior to us. In the end, they excelled in making us to walk in their shadow be it in education, governance, and almost in every sphere of life. They controlled the trade that occurred in Ghana and Africa. They exercised an authoritarian leadership on us. All these became possible because of our tribal disunity. People sought refuge in the Whiteman's protection that is his military power. Unfortunately this is what successive governments have failed to change but rather worsen matter with dictatorship, corruption and simply bad governance.

The reason why the first political movement was called united Gold Coast was because they wanted to unite all the people together to solve these challenges but that did not work out since the united front was broken. It was in the attempt to solve these problems of the nation that brought about the recommendations of the Watson Commission. Our inability to satisfactorily implement the recommendations of that Commission is what has also contributed to the predicaments of our current situation. Therefore to solve the Ghana problem, we must collectively break the yoke of colonisation hunting us.

This can be done by reclaiming our African identity and heritage. This can be done by setting policies to defeat the constitutional dictatorship that we have created for ourselves since independence. We must think and act to review all trade policies that do not serve the building of the economy of Ghana.

Currently, there is an agitation for a constitutional review. Many people think that a change in constitution would make life better for Ghanaians. In as much as I believe in the constitutional amendment, I want Ghanaians to understand that this is not the first time such demand has been made. Ghana has adopted so many constitutions which include the Burns Constitution in 1946, the Coussey Constitution, the Independence Constitution to the 1992 Constitution. Yet none of these changes in the constitutions solved the corruption, education and governance problems of Ghana.

The reason is very simple. The current 1992 constitution does not give us a sense of direction. It does not build in us patriotism neither does it check us on patriotism. It does not create in us an identity neither does it build in us a sense of pride. It is a constitution that allows some Ghanaians to think and act as socialist or capitalist. It is a constitution that allows some Ghanaians to think and act like Americans while others like British or whatever identity that Ghanaians may so wish. Simply, it is a constitution that has not helped us to decolonise neither has it given individual sovereignty and liberty but rather it is a constitution that enhances constitutional dictatorship.

It is in this light that I think that the best way forward for Ghana is to revive or impart into the Ghanaian a sense of patriotism and nationalism. This can be done by formally introducing the common dream or aspiration of the men who started the independence movement of Ghana. They had a dream to build a new kingdom akin to that of ancient Ghana in glory, a Ghana that would demonstrate an African personality.

The sad part of it is that many Ghanaians are not aware that the forebears had a common dream.  Practically speaking, it is not their fault because the dream of the forebears is not enshrined in the Constitution to have a binding on the people. When I wrote 'The Dream of a New Ghana Reality or Myth', I gave the script to someone to read. The person asked me, 'Has Ghana got a dream?' I said yes. But her facial expression indicated her doubt about my answer and as such my book was too good to be true to her.

I am very passionate about my country Ghana. I have loved it and believed in it irrespective of its economic or political status. It is a virtue I have grown with from my childhood. Back in the days when I was growing up, as early as at about five or six years, my friends and I would meet to talk about Ghana and its leaders. This was in the Rawlings revolution era. I lived close to a police barracks and that was where my friends and I spent ample time of our lives. We met at the barracks very often to play football and also to discuss life, ourselves, Ghana, the military, the police and especially JJ Rawlings. I was very in touch with a number of patriotic militant actions the police took in arresting the criminals in society during the time. We had friends whose parents were in the police. These friends regularly informed us with some updates of actions the police had taken. We saw many criminals who had been arrested and put in the police cells. There were mango trees around. Sometimes, these prisoners would beg us to throw mangoes to them into the cells because they were hungry and needed food to eat.

We often discussed the heroism of JJ Rawlings and some alleged mysteries about him which I now believe some were myths. We were made to believe our leader could be invisible to escape in events of danger. He was powerful (in military and spiritual might) and intelligent. For instance, we narrated stories that it was difficult to poison him through food because he would not eat the food specially prepared for him, rather, he would join somebody else eating his or her food. On that premise he felt the food was safe. We heard and narrated stories such as when under military attack, he could turn into a knife. I believe this created or awakened in me a certain consciousness for nationalism and patriotism.

As I grew up a little, our teachers exposed us to Ghana's quest for self-governance that was championed by Kwame Nkrumah and the other compatriots. This was in Wamfie, a town in the Bono Region. I relocated to live in Sunyani. My love and consciousness of the political history of Ghana became increasingly heightened. Just when Ghana was preparing to enter into constitutional rule, I had lost interest in the leadership of J.J Rawlings. I did not consider him fit to lead Ghana in a proper democratic governance. I met a friend called Shadrach in Sunyani who was equally not interested in Rawlings and was very knowledgeable in world history and politics. Through him I had access to read a number of books on Ghana by Professor Adu Boahen, W.E.F Ward and many others. I became passionately interested in Adu Boahen and J.A Kufuor's political philosophy. As early as 14 years, Shadrach and I discussed who the founder of Ghana was. That should tell you how passionate or deep I was in the affairs of my beloved country. It was this passion that inspired me to conceive the idea to write *The Dream of a New Ghana Reality or Myth* in my final year at the university.

There was something I had been blinded to. I did not know a number of people, especially the youth, were ignorant of the history of the nation. This realisation came to me after the publishing of the book *The Dream of a New Ghana Reality or Myth*. I came across people who hated to hear the concerns of Ghana largely because of the hardship created by the leaders. I came across people who for their exposure to the western culture and ideology could not reconnect to their Ghanaian root. I came across innocent religious people who had been made to believe that nationalism or patriotism is secular and it is meant for the heathen. I had experience of this back in KNUST when the Student Chaplaincy Council organised a National Intercessory prayer meeting and I put Ghana flag around my neck to go and intercede for Ghana. A student I was familiar with curiously and sceptically asked what was the matter with me to have put on Ghana flag. He laughed at me and wondered why I would put on Ghana flag when it was not 6 March or any Black Stars match going on. I felt bad about that and  asked if there was anything wrong to put on Ghana flag or must it be only 6 March that I could put on the Ghana flag?

Anyway this incident did not really sensitise me about many Ghanaians' lack of patriotism until after that. The most surprising of all the concerns was the question Bhel whom I gave the script to proofread asked: 'Has Ghana got a dream?' As far as I am concerned, I wrote the book *The Dream of the New Ghana Reality or Myth?* not with the assumption that people did not know Ghana has a dream let alone believe in it. I wrote it with the assumption that people were already aware Ghana had a dream and that the only problem was that Ghanaians had abandoned that dream. However, after sometime, when I put my ears on the ground, I found out that many people were wondering whether or not Ghana had a dream. The general question was: What's the Ghanaian dream, if any?'

Recently, I read the views of some prominent Ghanaians calling for a Ghanaian dream. I found individuals trying to imagine and propound out something as a dream for the nation. They are not bad. I believe it is a step in the right direction when people begin to yearn for a common thinking pattern for the way forward for Ghana. It is this knowledge that has inspired me to write this very book as a sequel to *The Dream of the*

*New Ghana Reality or Myth?* to conscientize Ghanaians my convictions of what the Ghanaian dream is. And I do strongly believe and assert that Ghana has a dream. It might have been abandoned but that does not mean we never had.

The question then comes, what then is the Ghanaian Dream? To answer this question, I would like to use a model many Ghanaians are quite familiar with. Many Ghanaians believe or have heard of the American dream. A popular caption of the American dream reads 'We *hold these truths to be self-evident, that all men are created equal, that they are endowed by their Creator with certain inalienable rights, that among these are Life, Liberty and the pursuit of Happiness.'* Many Ghanaians are familiar with this statement but can many tell its origin?

America used to be a British colony. It was made up of 13 states. In 1775, it began to rebel against the British imperialism. These thirteen states under the army commander, George Washington, declared war against Britain. During this moment, they passed vote on their independence: 9 voted for independence, 3 voted against independence and 1 was undecided. By democratic principle the 9 carried the vote and prepared to declare their independence. They drafted their aspirations or intent of fighting for independence by Thomas Jefferson. On 4 July 1776, they made their independence declaration. In this declaration reads 'We *hold these truths to be self-evident, that all men are created equal, that they are endowed by their Creator with certain inalienable rights, that among these are Life, Liberty and the pursuit of Happiness.'* Simply the American Dream is the declaration of American independence revealing the very reason or the aspiration of the people who fought for independence and their mental model for American's future. As wise as the founding fathers of America were, they included the declaration of Independence as a preamble in the American constitution.

Since then, laws, policies, movies, songs, individual aspirations have been made after the declaration of the American dream. And every American seeks to make his or her proposals, dreams or petitions in line with the creed in the declaration of independence. For example, Dr. King was able to convince the white Americans who oppressed the blacks then that his pursuit of civil right was rooted in the American dream and that the oppression and segregation against the people of colour was a grave indictment to the American dream. The speech *I have a dream* sold to Americans because, it was rooted in the American dream. Let us consider some of his words,

> When the architects of our republic wrote the magnificent words of the Constitution and the Declaration of Independence, they were signing a promissory note to which every American was to fall heir. This note was a promise that all men, yes black men as well as white men, would be guaranteed the inalienable rights of life, liberty, and the pursuit of happiness. It is obvious today that America has defaulted on this promissory note insofar as her citizens of color are concerned.... I say to you today, my friends, that in spite of the difficulties and frustrations of the moment, **I still have a dream. It is a dream deeply rooted in the American dream.** I have a dream that one day this nation will rise up and live out the true meaning of its creed: "We hold these truths to be self-evident: that all men are created equal."

In his 2004 Democratic National Convention keynote address that skyrocketed him to limelight politics overnight, this is what Barack Obama said, "Tonight, we gather to affirm the greatness of our Nation — not because of the height of our skyscrapers, or the power of our military, or the size of our economy. **Our pride is based on a very simple premise, summed up in a declaration made over two hundred years ago**: '*We hold these truths to be self-evident, that all men are created equal, that they are endowed by their Creator with certain inalienable rights, that among these are Life, Liberty and the pursuit of Happiness.*'"

This draft which became known as the American dream did not come by the public consensus. There were no committees or gatherings to agree on a dream or vision for the country but the dream is simply the declaration of independence and the very words or aspirations their founding fathers left behind. What made and continues to make it sacred is that these fathers were wise to draft it as a preamble to the American constitution and laws. That has made it eternal and lively throughout all generations of the American people. It has through all channels of communication been effectively disseminated to all Americans irrespective of political divide, gender, age, race, religion, social or academic status. The younger generations have also performed excellent by first keeping it as original as it was passed on to them. They have done well by putting their faith in those words to live by them. There is power and life in words if we keep them sacred in our hearts and minds. The American people have, for the past two hundred years, tried to live by the premise of the written words of their founding fathers. They have amended policies and laws based on these same words their founding fathers bequeathed to them; for instance, in the era of Lincoln, he fought for the black slaves to be freed in America. His emphasis was on the fact that American dream stated that all men are equal and were endowed by their creator with their inalienable rights among these were life, liberty and pursuit of happiness. Lincoln campaigned that the black slaves ought to be free. It was as a result of this that they founded the Republican Party. When Lincoln became president, they passed the thirteenth amendment in the American constitution to free the slaves. When the slaves were freed, some were brought to Africa to form the sovereign nation of Liberia.

Similarly, the founding leaders of Ghana also had an aspiration for their quest for self-governance. Danquah confirms this in his book, *The Ghanaian Establishment* by saying, **'We of the Six suffered martyrdom in pursuit of ideology of Ghanaism- the grand and dynamic idea that from our ancient and medieval Ghana ashes, we should create a modern State in the Guinea lands.'** It was for that reason that Danquah said on 4 August 1947, in Saltpond,

> 'We have… come to Saltpond to ponder and to deliberate upon the ways and means to bring an end to this insecurity and this frustration. British freedom is a precious thing. But British freedom is not Gold Coast freedom. British liberty is grand to have, but you cannot have and possess British liberty in a Gold Coast atmosphere. We must have, here and now, if we are to be well governed, a new kind of freedom, a Gold Coast Liberty'.

'Perhaps I strain the point I speak of a new kind of freedom. Love of freedom from foreign control has always been in our blood. 870 years ago we struck against the attempt of the Arabs to impose a religious slavery upon us in Ghana. We left our homes in Ghana and came down here to build for ourselves a new home'.

'But there is one thing we brought with us from ancient Ghana. We brought with us our ancient freedom. Today the safety of that freedom is threatened, has been continuously threatened for a 100 years, since the Bond of 1844, and the time has come for a decision'.

'And remember this: when we were attacked by the Arabs in Ghana, there was plenty of land to escape into. There was this rain-forest area and gold and diamond bearing lands in the Gold Coast, Togoland and Ivory Coast, We came here and settled here'.

Today we are cut off to the south by the sea, and to the north by the desert, and, if fearing that our ancient freedom is dangerously threatened, we decided to evacuate this land and go elsewhere, there is nowhere else for us to go. So our duty is clear. We must fight against the new domination. And we must fight with the constitutional, determined, persistent, unflinching, and unceasing until the goal of freedom is attained.

This reference officially marked the unveiling of the dream and identity of the people now called Ghanaians. The founding fathers of modern Ghana believed the people of Gold Coast were descendants of ancient Ghana and regarded the identity Gold Coast as colonial adjective. That is why in the first draft independence constitution, Danquah wrote, "I conceive that the first act of the constitution-making body will be to make a clear break away from the memories of the days of exploitation and imperialism, and **the colonial adjective Gold Coast will give way to the substantive name of the people and country, Ghana and Ghanaland.** And that they were willing to rebuild that Ghana with its ancient freedom and identity. It was in that same light that inspired

Nkrumah to say, **'Thus may we take pride in the name of Ghana, not out of romanticism, but as an inspiration for the future... What our ancestors achieved in the context of their contemporary society gives us confidence that we can create, out of that past, a glorious future '** in his motion for independence in July 1953 which was dubbed as 'motion of destiny'. This is what was termed by them as **Ghanaism.**

Danquah simply puts it, **'The Ghana of which I dreamt of... is not a hell of destruction but an earth of discontent, rational struggle and, in the end, a crown of happiness for the people.'** In his bid to contest for president, Danquah clarified this Ghanaian dream by saying, **'the liberation of Ghana carries with it the liberation of a C3 nation (third class) to an A1 nation (first class). We in Ghana must become an A1 nation not only in the cultural and scientific contributions that we can make to the general progress of the world and survival and happiness of mankind, but even in the art of self-government or politics, as also in commerce and business, in literature, in moral example, and last but not least, in athletics and sports...to show the world that we too are partakers of man's great contributions to the work of God, the civilization of mankind'**

From the words of Danquah and Nkrumah choosing the name Ghana was not for mere romanticism but rather as an inspiration or a strong desire to become as ancient Ghana in glory. Simply, Ghana is not just a mere name to bear but a dream called *Ghanaism* and this dream, is for Ghana to become a golden kingdom or a first class nation, to demonstrate our African personality and identity that will make Ghana a model nation or leading example to all black or African nations to prove that when given the opportunity the black man can show that he is as good as any race on earth. Therefore, it can be deduced that bearing a birth certificate or calling oneself a Ghanaian does not necessarily make the person a genuine Ghanaian. **To be a genuine Ghanaian, the person must first believe in the Ghanaian dream. He or she must have the aspiration to be a first class person in whatever skills or potential he or she is endowed with. He or she must be passionate to demonstrate an African personality. A Ghanaian is a custodian and model of the rich African heritage. A Ghanaian is a torchbearer to demonstrate that the African is capable of managing his or her**

**affairs. Simply put, what makes a person a Ghanaian is his or her African consciousness and the willingness to demonstrate that the African is as good as any other race. That is what makes Ghana the Black Star.** The Ghanaian environment therefore must always serve as the mecca of the African heritage and freedom.

And to achieve this dream of becoming a first class nation, our founding fathers expressed that **'British freedom is not Gold Coast freedom. British liberty is grand to have, but you cannot have and possess British liberty in a Gold Coast (Ghana) atmosphere. We must have, here and now, if we are to be well governed, a new kind of freedom, a Gold Coast (Ghana) Liberty.'** To them, they brought this liberty or freedom from Ancient Ghana. Simply, they revealed that western democracy would not succeed in a Ghanaian environment. They revealed that the values, philosophy or culture of western leadership would not be the best for Ghanaians if they are to be well governed. Ghana can be well governed if Ghana lays its foundation on the principle of African personality and identity. Ghana could be well governed if Ghanaians create their own leadership model. It is in that light that when they first wrote the first draft of our independent constitution to the Watson Commission, they clearly stated **"The main characteristics of the constitution will be to blend the old with the new, chieftaincy with democracy, the inherited culture with progressive modernism.** They admonished that Ghanaians should eschew foreign influence and culture for their own culture or African created philosophy. This is what was best described by Nkrumah by saying, **'we are going to seriously create our own African personality and identity".** To them holding on to our Ghanaian heritage to build the new nation was the only way in which we can show the world that we are ready to fight our own battles.

One striking point in the Ghanaian dream made by Nkrumah was that we were to create the enabling environment to prove that when the African was given a chance, he could show to the world that he was somebody. Prior to Ghana's independence, no black African nation had gained independence except Ethiopia and Liberia which were not colonized. Ghana wanted to prove the point that the black man was as capable as any race. Whereas this has been proven by a few Ghanaians and Africans who had opportunities, many Ghanaians have been denied the opportunities to prove their full potential. And not only has Ghana failed in building the full potential of its citizens, it has failed to resist foreign influence. Today almost every Ghanaian dresses, talks like foreigners from the west. There is a clear appetite in our politicians, professionals and other influential people in society to depend on the West and East for direction. This is so because we abandoned the aspirations of the founding fathers that brought to birth this nation Ghana.

To begin the solution to the nation's predicaments, this is what the people of Ghana must do. I sincerely believe parliament and the people of Ghana must pass the 1947 inaugural address of the UGCC by Danquah and Nkrumah's popular speech on the eve of Independence into law as a preamble to our Ghanaian Dream. I believe it is time the national anthem, and the national pledge were given a legal place in the governing of this country. When this is done, it must be given to all the institutions in the nation to govern their policies. Thus our schools, churches, corporate institutions and all bodies in Ghana must build their vision and policies on the 1947 inaugural address and Nkrumah's speech on the eve of independence.

We must, in addition, start a national campaign on these aspirations and recommend them to the ordinary Ghanaians. I believe it will be a beginning of a new birth of hope, because as we can testify, patriotism in many Ghanaians is dead and no nation can progress without patriotism and a sense of nationalism. I believe it is time we broke away the tribal barriers with the spirit of Ghana. I feel sad that people are more loyal to or proud of their tribe more than their affiliation to Ghana. Yet none of these people bear any birth certificate or passport issued by their tribe; rather it is Ghana that gives us identity of birth certificate and passport. Reviving patriotism would curb corruption in so many ways because it is difficult to rob whatever you love. It will not only curb corruption but it would increase productivity in the nation.

This will give birth to a new unity in our body politics. It will closely knit the disciples of Nkrumah and Danquah. A house divided shall not stand. Ghana is not an exception. The nation has suffered so much from the political feud that existed and still exists between Danquah and Nkrumah. They are dead and gone, but the political conflicts continue. Passing these documents of the two into law would persuade us to break that barrier that exists and unite their philosophies. Analysing from the words of Danquah and Nkrumah, it appears most probably that they regretted the rivalry and wished they were united to build the country together. For instance when Nkrumah won the 1951 election and was released from prison, Danquah wrote a letter to congratulate Nkrumah stating that he had fought the good fight and triumphed over imperialism. He asked for the misrepresentations and misunderstandings between them to be buried in their own past. He asked for divine blessings and guidance for Nkrumah's governance. Finally he reminded Nkrumah that they started with a United Gold Coast and that they should complete the task with a united motherland. The events that ensued between Nkrumah and the Opposition shows that things rather went from bad to worse. At the latter part of Nkrumah's rule in Ghana, he established a one party state and according to K.B Asante, Nkrumah's personal secretary, who went to Nkrumah to ask him, "Osagyefo why one party state?" According to K.B Asante, Dr. Nkrumah replied by saying "I have established so many industries and institutions and I don't have enough competent people to man them. Many of the people who can do this are in the opposition and that was why later I found the only way out was to have a one party State so we all belong"[1] Nkrumah from this statement lauded the role the people in opposition could contribute to Ghana's development. The statements of Nkrumah and Danquah clearly suggest Ghana would reap much more from uniting their legacies than fuelling their rivalries.

Reviving the aspirations of the founding fathers will also give individual Africans opportunities to excel. For instance, if we live and put to work the statement, "that when given the chance, the black man can show that he is somebody", it will challenge many black people to brighten and excel in all corners. It will inspire Africans to excel to defeat the racial battle of inferiority. It is a fact that the few people excelling at the top got there through opportunities, through someone extending a hand to them but this reception has been reserved for a few for many years. It is time we tore down any barrier that keeps people behind the gates of destiny and opportunities and create chances for one another to prove their full potential. This will bring the respect Nkrumah spoke about to us. Supposing Ghanaians could produce all the food they consume, that would be great because it would create job opportunities for the youth, boost up the economy and then give us a sense of pride. That same applies if we had our best players participating in the Ghana league.

In 1945, after the Second World War, Japan was devastated and suffered on performance of production. An expert Sarasohn recommended to the MacArthur administration that W. Edwards Deming be invited to Japan to teach quality control. The Japanese invited him. When he arrived, he told them for Japan to rise, they must run Japan like running a system.

> Japan must see itself as a system. All of Japan is a system. There must be trust and cooperation throughout Japan. A common commitment to quality, trust, and cooperation must sweep through Japan "like a prairie fire. All Japanese on fire! Everyone will win!"[2]

He suggested to the CEOs and leaders of Japan that things would change in five years should they adopt his plan. His solution reveals the secret of America. Americans created America as a system. It is run with systemic thinking strategies and that is why over two hundred years of independence it has kept its aspiration. A system is a set of things working together as parts of a mechanism or an interconnecting network; a complex whole. It is a set of principles or procedures according to which something is done; an organized scheme or method.

The expert told the Japanese that for Japan to run successfully, they must see it as a system, as a set of things working together as parts of a mechanism or interconnecting network. Or they must see Japan as a set of principles or procedure according to which things must be done. And for every system to be successful, there must be a shared vision, there must be a mental model, and there must be structures. That is the secret of America, and they run it like a system. So they have a common shared vision which is popularly known by everyone as the American Dream. This dream also gives birth to a common mental model on which America is built.

Similarly, to borrow the words of Deming, for a new Ghana, for a first class Ghana, for a Ghana to make our independence meaningful, all Ghanaians must see Ghana as a system. There must be trust and cooperation throughout Ghana. A common commitment to quality, trust, and cooperation must sweep through Ghana "like a prairie fire. All Ghanaians on fire! Everyone will win!"

Therefore to run Ghana as an effective system, it is time to make a new policy to revive this dream of Ghana, we must make a national policy of a common shared vision that will be adopted and applied by all institutions and individuals that make up Ghana. We must develop a national mental model that will serve as our national philosophy. We must make a policy to strengthen our good African values and create new ones that can help us build a first class nation. We must make policies that will create opportunities for organisations and individuals in Ghana to achieve their Ghanaian dream. It is time we made policies that would foster unity among Ghanaians irrespective of political divide, tribe, religion, gender, age or class. Ghana must push for a lingua franca that would be used officially as a national language. Simply it is time for Ghanaians to embark on a positive constitutional revolution that will bring the best in every individual to build a first class nation. We need constitutional reforms that can give the real independence to institutions of the nation to function effectively. Over the years what Ghana has experienced has been nothing but constitutional dictatorship where the voice and knowledge of professionals and institutions are sabotaged by the political will of the executive arm of government and their political parties. This has jeopardised the country in so many ways for so many years and it has to stop.

For this to be successful, we must enforce a common commitment to quality, trust, and cooperation among all the unit structures that make the nation. And the fact remains that if all the unit structures of Ghana are on fire everyone will win. This clearly suggests that it is mandatory for individuals to pledge to be committed to Ghana. This commitment must be inherent. It is therefore expedient that every citizen will rise to the call of building a new Ghana instead of shifting blame. Your commitment to the Ghanaian dream should be independent of government performance or any body's attitude. As far as we are part of the Ghanaian system, we are either contributing positively or negatively. Unless we are willing to sell our sovereignty as people, it is mandatory and prudent for every individual to do his or her best for Ghana. If Ghana has not succeeded it is because individually, we all have abysmally contributed in a way.

One of the yokes colonisation imposed on the Gold Coast was building an economy that impoverishes indigenous Ghanaians while it enriched the foreign economies. For instance, in 1954, Ghana made revenue of £21 million out of the £110 million of gold export. This did not change after independence. Ghana continues to earn low revenues due to bad trade policies. As James Griffiths, former Secretary of the Colonies, said that Ghana's economy was not made to meet the needs of Ghanaians but for British (now other foreigners) interest. It is an economy Ghanaians produce raw materials which are bought at the buyers' price. It is an economy controlled by multinationals whose savings are outside Ghana. Any time they make profit, they return huge sum of it to their native countries. It is an economy that Ghanaians love to feed on foreign finished goods and services to the extent that it is difficult for them to patronize their fellow Ghanaian products. It is one reason why the Ghanaian cedi continues to depreciate in value. What Ghanaians fail to realize is that culture will always remain as bedrock of every economy.

This is what Nii Kwabena Bonne educated the people of the Gold Coast about. He said, **'Strangers have come to Gold Coast not for love of its people but only to take away the riches of the Country by all possible means!'** He said, **'the white men and Syrians are tricking you out of your money'.** His words are still relevant. The economy of Ghana is still in the hands of multinational companies who milk the people's money and resources away. But the earlier we accept that Ghana can be best built by Ghanaians the better. It is in that light that Nkrumah declared that we are prepared to lay our own foundation and lift it up. It is time we eschewed the foreign dependency, foreign culture, adulation of the west and believe in ourselves that yes we can build our own economy. It is time we believe that we can produce enough food to feed on, that we can build our own infrastructure; that we can produce our own services for the nation. As rightly put by Nkrumah, it is when we take such responsibilities that we will be respected by every other nation. Let us not deceive ourselves that we can depend on foreign democracies and intelligence to make any meaningful development. We cannot.

Consider the entire major gold and mineral companies of the nation, AngloGold, Tarkwa Gold mines, Newmont, and other firms, Ghana does not have more than 10 per cent of shares. The recent multinational oil companies are also controlled by foreigners. Ghana receives not more than 10 per cent of shares. The processing and manufacturing companies are all owned by foreigners who after business transfer their profit out of the country. The increasing shopping malls all over the country belong to foreigners. They also export their profit out of the country. Infrastructure projects are awarded to foreign companies. Ghana government secures loans from foreign institutions such as the World Bank and foreign governments only to award such contracts to foreign companies who eventually transfer their profits out of the country. In the end, the government would have to squeeze taxes from the ordinary Ghanaians to settle the loans of these projects. This causes nothing but stress on our economy as a result of the payment of huge debts and their huge interests.

Ghana does not manufacture many of the simple or complex machines used in the nation. We import all these and other machines into the country. In fact to sustain all our industries, Ghana imports all spare parts into the country. All these expenses adversely affect the inflation and exchange rates of the nation. After 60 years of political independence, one would have expected that Ghana should be manufacturing some of these machines and their spare parts but that has not been the case.

What is embarrassing for the nation is that a country with such rich agricultural land cannot produce enough tomatoes to feed its industries. Ghana cannot produce enough onions to feed its people. The nation has now lost direction by importing such agricultural products which could have been produced here to strengthen the economy and also create jobs and opportunities for the people. That has not been the case. In 2021, Ghana imported rice worth of $552 million; that same year, Ghana imported $410 million worth of poultry meat. On palm oil, which Malaysians owed their success to Ghana, the nation imported $289 million; on mosquito coil Ghana imported $260 million; on sugar, Ghana imported $185 million; on processed fish, Ghana imported $128 million; on onions Ghana imported $33 million; on tea Ghana imported $128 million; on tomatoes Ghana imported about $400 million and on margarine, Ghana imported about $11 million. In all Ghana spent about $2.4 billion in 2021 on imports of goods which could have been internally produced.

I must say, the battle to reclaim the Ghanaian economy is huge to win but not impossible. It is as daring as fighting for the political independence if not stronger than that. But there is a simple but very effective weapon to use for this huge battle and that weapon is patriotism, the love of our own. It is the starting point in improving the economy. It is time we disciplined and pushed ourselves to develop local appetite. That is where the supremacy of the whites resides or begins from. Many years ago, when they came to the shores of Ghana and Africa, they first seduced our appetites through gifts. Gradually, they got all of us beginning from our chiefs to that last person to love the products of the Whiteman. For instance, our chiefs and fetish priests gave high value to foreign schnapps. It is through such appetites that they began to gain influence over our way of life and choices. They went step ahead to coax us to disdain the very clothes, food, and things we loved before they came to our shores. In doing that we threw our monies to them and they used that to build great kingdoms of theirs. Now they have the money and the atomic power and the technology to oppress or control us. So if we want our freedom, it must begin from where we fell from- the love for European appetite. That is what has caused us to import tomatoes and very basic items that could easily be generated from Ghana. We must build and protect our Ghanaian appetite. We must take pride in what is Ghana and what is made in Ghana. If we do that, we shall create huge wealth for ourselves in no time.

Another thing to consider in winning the war on the economy is to review Ghana's economic structure. It has been designed in such a way that Ghana produces and exports raw materials and imports finished products. As common knowledge on the value chain of the market, finished products have more value than the raw products. This means that for years Ghana has been exporting goods that could have been processed to increase the value before sending them to the market. However, this has not been the case. The sad part is the few factories that were in the country to help produce a few items have collapsed through the weapon of globalisation and poor strategic management. Globalisation brought an influx in goods and services at relatively lower prices because they were produced with advanced technology and skills to beat the quality and prices of the goods produced by local industries. However, this must not deter the young generation to rebuild our industries, this time with strong strategic management principles to overcome the weapons of globalisation. Simply it is time to change the economic structure of Ghana. And one sure way is to start with agriculture and Agric processing. We must also continue to change the structure in the financial and service areas of the economy to yield more revenue for the nation.

We must pressure government to stop waiving taxes on foreign international companies. According to reports, government waived taxes not less than $3billion in the past few years. This is a norm that has persisted since the first republic yet it has resulted in less financial benefit to the nation. The sad part is, many a time, our government officials agree to waive such taxes only to receive kick back behind the scene at their own benefit but to the detriment of the masses. How do you exempt multinational companies from billions of dollar tax and expect groundnut sellers to pay tax to build a nation. Where needs be, government can only reduce such taxes for the new multinationals. We must know right from independence many governments have been in bed with foreign multinationals. The time for the divorce is now.

One of the economic strengths of Ghana is minerals. Ghana was called Gold Coast because of its rich possession of gold. In addition to gold, the nation is blessed with minerals such as bauxite, manganese and other rich minerals. The nation now produces oil in commercial quantities. In spite of these numerous minerals produced, the nation makes as meagre as 10 per cent of royalties. Recently the nation discovered lithium and the Ghana government negotiated for 10 per cent royalty. The Minister, Jinapor, persuaded Ghanaians that it is the best deal for the nation. Is this not sad for the nation?

The other sad part of this is Ghana lacks the requisite machines to even quantify the exact quantity of minerals produced unless they are taken overseas. For instance, Ghana did not have any gold refinery; Nkrumah tried to build one but that could not materialise because of his overthrow and the machines were left to destroy. So any time the nation produced gold, it is taken outside for final refinery to know the exact quantity. So the foreigners tell the nation how much is made. On Thursday, August 4,2024, the Vice President of the Republic of Ghana, Dr Mahamudu Bawumia commissioned a new Gold Refinery, the Royal Ghana Refinery to refine about 400kg of gold daily. I hope this refinery changes the narration to earn Ghana some revenue.

I sincerely believe it is time we altered all these financial and negotiation policies. It is time we negotiated for higher percentages of our mineral resources. Western minded Ghanaians will say that cannot be. Yes it cannot be from their neo-colonial point of view. I do know that when the military took over governance of Ghana, they were able to alter or renegotiate some of these policies. For instance, during the Acheampong regime, Ghana was earning less per cent at AngloGold Ashanti but Acheampong was able to renegotiate to give Ghana 55 per cent while the British received 45 per cent and nothing happened. We can again replicate Acheampong's bold legacy to save Ghana. Unfortunately, after him, the successive governments sold off Ghana's 55 per cent to about 3 to 5 per cent. And today that is what is happening in all our resources. We have become tenants if not squatters in our own economy and market. We have deliberately made foreigners owners of the very life blood of our nation. How can the nation prosper under such conditions?

Calling for higher shares in our mineral production will demand responsibility from Ghanaians and their government. We will have to press our government to be responsible by providing necessary financial responsibilities. For instance, our successive governments have been unconcerned and irresponsible in investing in mineral exploration in the country. All our governments want is for expatriates to come and risk their money exploring our mineral resources. It is such and other responsibilities that empower the foreigners to have the lion's share in such negotiations. The time to sit up is now. It is time we pressed our governments to stop being stingy and invest reasonable amount of money into mineral explorations.

In the year 2008, when the world economy fell, it affected the huge companies in America especially the automobile companies. The American government gave the affected automobile companies bail out. America is a capitalist economy, yet when the government realises its private companies are in crisis, it goes to their aid. This is not so in Ghana. Governments abandon profitable companies to their own fate when crisis arises. That is what happened in 2008 to Ghana Telecom, as a result of economic issues, the government sold its shares. In 2013, Anglo Gold was in serious production crisis. The mine had enough gold in reserve but it could not mine the ore because it was located far deep underground and needed financial investment to redevelop the areas for mining. The company knocked on the door of the government of Ghana, but the government failed to offer any financial assistance to the company even when many workers were being laid off. The company would have to count on other foreign partners. Even though the Akufo Addo administration showed interest for the company to bounce back, the government did not invest any pesewa in AngloGold Ashanti. It was an opportunity for Ghana to reclaim more shares or some amount of ownership of the company and the economy at large but our government failed us.

Back in the colonial days, Ghana produced two thirds of the world's cocoa. The government had a policy to buy all the cocoa and sell it. The colonial government made huge profits from this crop. On gold, all the big gold firms were foreign-owned. As a result, the government did not make a buying policy like it did with cocoa. Aside the large scale mining of gold, there is the small scale gold mining activity in Ghana. Information gathered suggests that individuals from the small scale sector smuggle gold worth not less than $7 billion annually. This is a huge loss to the nation. It is therefore my opinion that government would make a policy to buy all such gold in the country. The nation's economy would improve significantly if the government is able to find a remedy to this. Should the government succeed in this, the government will be able to earn about $2billion of the smuggled gold into the formal economy. It will appreciate the exchange rate of the Ghanaian cedi. It will increase government revenue from taxes, because the smugglers swerve taxes. This will in return appreciate the purchasing power of the cedi. Recently, the idea for the Bank of Ghana to buy gold is something worthy of praise. The government had about 64 kg worth of gold. It is my earnest request that government must use our foreign reserves to buy gold and they must be kept in the nation Ghana. Buying enough gold as national reserve will help strengthen our economy a lot.

A significant area in the economy of Ghana where the nation loses a lot of money is on the infrastructural development. Formerly, Ghana had the Highways Authority which was responsible for the construction and maintenance of roads in the country. In going for foreign aid, our governments were told to privatise the road construction and maintenance business. The reality is that Ghana lacked Ghanaian-owned companies with advanced machinery and expertise to bid for the complex ultra-modern roads projects. Therefore in compliance with privatisation requirement for the foreign aid the government was compelled to consider foreign companies for the roads projects. So every year, the Ghana government secures loans from foreign partners for road projects and hires foreign companies to do such projects. When the ordinary citizen sees such completed projects, they applaud the governments but what they do not know or forget is that government will pay back such loans with high interest. The sad part is as the dollar rate changes, our government will have to recoup more cedis to pay back its loans. What is worse is that the foreign company which was awarded the road project contract will export their profit away from the country creating huge stress on the economy and the exchange rate. Again most of these companies pay peanuts to their Ghanaian workers who virtually do everything while they pay their fellow foreigners exorbitant salaries.

Supposing the circle, Pokuase and Kasoa interchange projects were awarded to Ghanaians, there certainly would be funds in to boost the economy of Ghana. Even if we borrowed money from the foreign donors, we know for certain that the money would be utilised in the Ghanaian economy. This would appreciate the economy of Ghana by giving opportunities to many businesses. It is therefore time to take the bold step to help create Ghanaian companies to be able to construct such complex ultra-modern roads in Ghana. We have to prove that when given the chance, the black man can show that he is somebody. If the government says the private sector is the engine of growth, then the government must be willing to provide the enabling environment to empower individuals and private companies. We must empower Ghanaian-owned companies to buy all the modern machinery in road developments. We must be prepared to hire experienced international experts to work with Ghanaians in Ghana. We have had Ghanaian experts like Thomas Mensah, Boakye Agyarko, Frimpong Boateng and many great professionals who worked in foreign economies to enrich such economies. Ghana can do likewise. This will reduce the rate at which we lose money out of the country and help us to own or control our economy.

It is strangely remarkable that every government boasts of jobs they have created yet the Ghanaian youth are always crying for job opportunities; the Ghanaian economy is not anything to write home about. In building every economy, it is prudent that the government and business leaders should learn to be strategic in investing their monies in order to create more wealth for the nation. For a stronger and more reliable economy Ghana can use the SWOT analysis in creating jobs and wealth for the people. The SWOT analysis allows the nation to discover her economic strength, weakness, opportunities and threats.

For instance Ghana's economy depends on cocoa and gold and recently oil. These form the backbone of the economy. Using the SWOT analysis Ghana's **strength** revolves around cocoa, gold and oil and a few other goods and services. In every SWOT, the nation must create more opportunities with these strengths. So to build a first class or stronger economy, to create more jobs for the youth and more revenues, the entire nation, government and the private sector should create jobs in relation to these products. However, due to the lack of strategy, we have been unable to create opportunities with these industries to grow the economy of Ghana. Rather we export these goods in their raw states which by the chain value earn the minimum on the economic ladder. So to reclaim the ownership of our economy, it is time we prioritised these areas. Ghana should expand or build oil refineries to meet the consumption demand of the nation and if possible export surplus quantities. Ghana should build more cocoa processing companies to process more cocoa for higher revenues. The need for Ghana to build more gold refineries and other mineral refineries and gold companies to increase the nation's revenues cannot be overstressed.

In addition to this strategic job creation, Ghana should build factories that can take the production of the logistic needs of the areas under discussion. This means we should build companies that would be subsidiary companies to these industries. For instance on the mining sector, Ghana creates about $6billion annually. Out of this figure, Ghana makes only about 10 per cent royalties excluding taxes. What we forget is that, for these businesses to thrive, Ghana imports almost all the equipment and services needed for operations. For instance every mining operation would need working boots, Personal Protection Equipment (PPEs), and many other items. Our companies import almost all these items. This dissipates the economic energy by stressing our foreign exchange. The same applies to the oil and cocoa sectors. Therefore to give Ghana's economy a competitive advantage, the government should establish factories to provide the logistic needs of the mining and oil industries. These factories will create job opportunities for Ghanaians. For instance if the oil and mining imports goods and services worth of $1billion into the country, this can be reduced when we establish such jobs in Ghana. This will not only ease the stress on our exchange rate, but it will create jobs for the unemployed, it will grow the size of the economy and also increase the government revenue.

This has been the strategy South Africa applied to develop its economy to build its ultramodern infrastructures. They created subsidiary jobs around the mining operations to multiply the nation's revenue. This empowered them to reinvest the huge revenues into infrastructure and other areas of developments. This strategy does not only grow the economy but it is one sure way to give security to such industries. In Ghana there have been many companies that have folded up because their demands were not reliable so in any unforeseen challenge, the companies could not weather the storm. The interesting thing is that Ghana has a high demand for subsidiary services in the oil, mining and engineering fields and so establishing jobs around them would guarantee their securities.

It is good news that the mineral commission is able to retain a large sum of the gold revenue in the country through law reforms. Recently, the Commission enacted some policies in the industry that jobs like security, food and other related ones should be given to Ghanaian-owned companies. In addition, they instructed the multinationals in the mining to transact a certain percentage of revenue through Ghanaian banks. This is incredible and we need similar law reforms in other industries to empower or create more job openings for Ghanaians.

In addition to these, I believe we must be the generation to dare to call for drastic law review and reforms on the shares of Ghana on all the multinationals in the nation. I cannot in my reasonable faculty accept that a whole nation could sell its mineral resources to foreigners only to earn royalties of less than 10 per cent. I think it is time we changed these outmoded negotiations. If Acheampong was able to reclaim shares in AngloGold Ashanti, if he was able to claim ownership of Tema Oil Refinery, it should be possible for us to do likewise.

All these can be a reality only with good governance. Since the struggle for independence, one of the greatest challenges of Ghanaians and Africans over the past six decades is failure or underperformance of governments. When it comes to human rights, economic management, science and technology, development, fairness in society, Ghana's independence has always been a mockery or questionable. To begin with, our governance or politics is characterised with malice, selfishness, cronyism, lack of patriotism, lack of proper assessment. It is therefore the task of the younger generation to raise a new institution of governance that can help us build a first class economy owned by Ghanaians. It is time we raised a new institution of governance that can help us build first class infrastructure and provide the Ghanaian first class services.

Hughes, Ginnett & Curphy (2017) define leadership as the complex set of interaction between the leader, the follower and the situation.[3] This suggests that leadership and governance do not revolve around leaders or politicians alone but it includes the citizens or the masses. And one of the requirements of good governance is fair representation.

To achieve this will revolve round the commitment and integrity of the ordinary masses. They as followers play a pivotal role in choosing representatives for good governance. The reality of the matter is that many of the processes that lead to these representations are done on rigging, vote buying, oppression which impedes good governance. Where appointments are not done purely on merits of competence and integrity but by primitive selection or cronyism, then good governance has been impeded. Interestingly, that has been the trend of electing people to represent Ghanaians. It is therefore time to rise against such bad practice. It is time Ghanaians sought for fair representation.

Sadly, this problem has not been the doing of the politicians and aspirants alone, but many times by the demands of the electorates. We have situations where the electorates demand money or gifts or services from those seeking to represent them. This also hugely corrupts good governance. The reality is that, that is the case in many places in Ghana; leaders have lost elections because they did not attend a certain number of funerals, naming ceremonies and not paying school fees of so called needy children. These expectations of the masses indicate their ignorance of good governance and patriotism. It also shows how corrupt a section of the masses are. The masses must be given quality education on patriotism, good governance and the ill effects of corruption. These enlightenments will guide them to cast their votes on their assessment of the integrity of the candidates.

It is time we educated ourselves that citizens have a vital role to play at the centre of public activities and that they must do this with integrity and with high sense of patriotism. We must inspire citizens to rather contribute their best to public life through the district assembly and other public platforms. This suggests to me that we must begin an active campaign to press our governments to empower the institute of local government. We cannot deny the fact that it is a neglected ministry. Many assembly leaders would always have to use their money to service or support the activities of the community.

Ghana's democracy has not matured to the extent where people have a voice irrespective of their background. Our system misplaces many people as voiceless on matters of governance. It is an abused winner-takes-all politics. Once you are not on the ruling leader's side, your voice is silenced or ignored. In Ghana the only people who can make meaningful suggestions are the big shots or men of titles. People are trashed down because they do not have strong social standing. It is time we demolished these barriers to give voice to the voiceless and those on the other side of the political divide.

The fabric of the Ghanaian society also contributes to this unfairness. It is a society that people like to take advantage over the vulnerable. This culture permeates into many facet of the Ghanaian society. And it undermines the principles of good governance. We should shun this unfair behaviour. It is in this light that the masses can significantly help to shape the destiny of the nation.

The essence of the representatives in government is to provide security and justice to their people. The sad reality is that it is the representatives who rather prey on the innocent people in Ghana. It is the representatives, the institutions of security and justice which undermine the fundamental human rights of the people. One example is the police. It is one of the institutions to protect and ensure the enforcement of the law for the security of life and properly. They are best described as the conscience of the nation. Yet it is the institution that undermines the very laws of Ghana. For instance, the laws of Ghana demand that, an arrested person must be granted bail after 48 hours of arrest yet the Ghana police are the very abusers of such law. As a matter of fact, many Ghanaians do not trust the police. At times where the police are right, order comes from above to stop them from doing what is right. The same applies to the judiciary and the executive arm of government. Instead of administering justice, they become culprit in injustice. We cannot continue to suffer acts of injustice in the very hands of institutions responsible for our security and justice. This is constitutional dictatorship and it must stop.

For best practice, there must be an immediate Act to halt the president and ministers from appointing board members and CEOs of State Organisations. Such organisations must be tasked to appoint their own CEOs and board members. Nominated CEOs or MDs should appear before parliament for approval or dismissal. State organisations must enact strict company laws that assess performance and behaviour of all workers from the head to the least employee. Again, number of political appointees on state organisations councils must reduce to avoid the abuse of power from the executive.

Let us look at trade. Government's responsibility is to promote and protect trade for its people. In times past, kingdoms went to war to create trade opportunities for their citizens. It is the same reason that brought the Europeans to the shores of Ghana and Africa. That has not changed. Governments elsewhere fight for economic or trade opportunities for their industries and people through good policies and globalisation. Unfortunately, the Ghanaian government and for that matter the African governments have not known this. Rather they have become killers of trade and economic opportunities for their people. Right from Ghana's first independent government to now, every government fights against Ghanaian businesses and companies. Apea Menka's company was victimised. Darko Farms was sabotaged and many countless businesses have gone into extinction because of politics or bad governance, not forgetting the recent collapse of a number of banks.

To stop this, there should be an Act of Parliament to strictly prevent the executive arm of Government from interfering with businesses and victimising people. Where any business flouts the laws of Ghana or underperform, the government or any interested party should present the matter to Parliament who should strictly and fairly seek for professional advice from the universities and aligned professional bodies what to do. Hereafter, Parliament should act on the recommendation of the university or professional bodies and advise government to execute judgement. This will help curb the constitutional dictatorship which has impeded the voice and knowledge of professionals.

We need to educate ourselves and tell our representatives that their essence in authority is to protect businesses at all cost and not to destroy them on political interest. Governments owe the people a duty of creating enabling environment for businesses to thrive. It is time we pushed government to make policies that can create trade and job opportunities for Ghanaian business.

In addition to this, there should be an Act of Parliament to legitimise the university and academic institutions to give direction to the nation; advise Government on policy implementation. There should also be a direct link of feedback between the academia and industry which will help the growth and development for our country.

Another pathetic thing happening in our society is governments' weakness in protecting employees when their employers abuse or unfairly treat them. Many are the employees in Ghana who are underpaid. Many are the employees who are overused in their work without any protection. The sad truth is that the government who has to protect these employees is culpable in the hardship of the employees because these governments take commission on contracts and also financial help from these employers. And so governments over the years, have become toothless in fighting for their people. This must stop.

To speed up development in Ghana, I sincerely believe that we must empower the Local Government to be independent and develop their own communities. This is what is popularly termed as decentralisation. I believe it is time the various regions should be able to issue their own birth certificates and passports to the people in their regions. To achieve this, we must restructure the Local Government to have Area or Town Councils, District Assemblies and Regional Assemblies. These assemblies should have their own administration that would be responsible for their entire developments.

In time past, chiefs who served as the heads of governments for their people also served as the custodian of culture to their people. This consistent education gave birth to integrity and morality to the people. It brought a certain sanctity which served as means of security. As a result, in time past, it was difficult hearing of armed robbery; murder cases and a number of social vices. Today our political governments overlook the role the chiefs and traditional leaders played in time past. This has given rise to moral decadence. The consequences are that there are so many cases of murder, armed robbery, rape and acts of injustice. This is what happens when there are no leaders legally responsible in shaping society's thinking and way of life. To help curb the corruption and act of injustices, Governments should assume this role chiefs played by instilling in Ghanaians good moral ethics. It will help curb the deviancy in society.

In years past, Ghana had kingdoms whose representatives or leaders lived for the welfare of their people. They were leaders who put the pride of their nation high above anything, either strong or fearful or wealthy. It was this sense of pride and sacrifice that caused the death of Osei Tutu. It was this sense of pride that led to the arrest of Yaa Asantewaa. It was this sense of pride that inspired Twene Boa Kodua and Antwi Boasiako to sacrifice their souls for their nation. Today Ghana is filled with cowards and selfish leaders who squander the nation's resources at the expense of the masses and the unborn children. Ghana is filled with leaders who kotow to external influence rather than serving the interest of their people. Ghana is filled with opportunist leaders who think that leadership is about learning how to milk the people. It is time we understood that the representatives and the electorate must live for the national pride. It is time they demonstrated sacrifice even to the point of death for the nation.

Another principle of good governance is that public and civil servants provide transparent and accountable services to the masses. Whereas Ghana has good public and civil servant structures, their services are not without complaints. There is complaint of lack of commitment to the public, the complaint of corruption and poor customer service. These shortcomings should be seen where there are not defined rules to guide and discipline workers in the civil service. These challenges are likely to go where promotion at the civil service is not done on competency and integrity but on long service. It is time we held our civil and public service for accountability, transparency and promotion of good performance. And where people in the sector are non performing, they should be sacked from their duty. For instance, from the Auditor and Accountant General Department, Ghana loses about Gh12 billion every year, yet nothing is done to retrieve our money or get specific people accountable for such malpractices. It is time the Auditor-General department developed best accounting practice to stop financial mismanagement and corruption.

One of the principles of every good governance is ethical conduct and in this important area Ghana has been found wanting. The very people chosen to represent the people put their individual interest above that of public interest. It is not only people in service but individual Ghanaians prefer to put their individual interest above that of the public. This is sheer lack of patriotism and for a new Ghana, we should teach ourselves to put Ghana first. The fact of the matter is the ethical conduct in governance has been weak because of lack of strong and effective rule of law. It is a country where authorities rule by their personal interests but not by law.

There are occasions when some civil servants will be doing their lawful work of disciplining a defaulting subordinate but an order from superiors will come to stop the disciplinary action making the officer taking the action look stupid and helpless. As a matter of fact, that is why corruption and malice are unceasing. The very people who commit them know there is a big man somewhere to protect them. This nonsense must stop.

To remedy this canker of lawlessness, we must rise in high spirit of activism to enthrone the law as king that we can say, in Ghana we serve our law, we worship our law not humans. If the president, a government official is respected, it is because of the empowerment of the law and therefore, if such a person flouts our laws to save bad citizens, we must let them know that the law is superior and that nobody is above it. We have feared men instead of the law for far too long in Ghana. It is time we put an end to this. In the words of Danquah, we must fight against the new domination. And we must fight with the constitutional, determined, persistent, unflinching, and unceasing until the goal of freedom is attained. Let us be the generation that accomplishes the unfinished task of our independence struggle. Let us be the generation that manifests the dream of our founding fathers- that dream of a new Ghana, a first class Ghana.

Long live Ghana

Long live the Blackstar!

## NOTES

### Chapter one

1 Kimble, D, *The History of Ghana*, 1850 to 1928, Oxford University Press, 1963,p.151

2 Boahen Adu, Ghana: Evolution and Change in the 19th and 20th Centuries, London, Longman, 1975,p.30

3 Ward, W.E.F, *History of Gold Coast,* George Allen & Unwin, 1959, p.174, and also in Boahen Adu, *Ghana: Evolution and Change in the 19th and 20th Centuries*, London, Longman, 1975,p.31,32

4 Kimble, D, *The History of Ghana*, 1850 to 1928, Oxford University Press, 1963,p.193

5 Ward, W.E.F, *History of Gold Coast*, 1958,p.183-187

6 Kimble, D, *The History of Ghana*, 1850 to 1928, Oxford University Press, 1963,p.193,194

7.J.B Danquah, *The Historical Significance of the Bond of 1844,* Address delivered on 12 January 1957

8 Boahen Adu, Ghana: Evolution and Change in the 19th and 20th Centuries, London, Longman, 1975,p.46

9 Ayensu, K.B and Darkwa, S.N, The Evolution of Parliament in Ghana (IEA), 1999,p.9

10  Kimble, D, *The History of Ghana*, 1850 to 1928, Oxford University Press, 1963,p.215

11 Martinson H.B, *Ghana The UP/NPP Tradition in the National Liberation Struggle*, HBM publications, 2010

12 Kimble, D, *The History of Ghana*, 1850 to 1928, Oxford University Press, 1963,p.323

13 Busia, K.A, *The Position of the Chief in the Modern Political System of Ashanti*, Frank Gass & Co.Ltd, 1968,p.137,138

14 ibid

15 Achebe Chinua, *Things Fall Apart*, London, Heinemann, 1958,p.141

16 Busia, K.A, *The Position of the Chief in the Modern Political System of Ashanti*, Frank Gass & Co.Ltd, 1968,p.139

17 Agbodeka, F., *Ghana in the Twentieth Century,* Ghana Universities Press, 1972,p.18

18 Boahen Adu, Ghana: Evolution and Change in the 19th and 20th Centuries, London, Longman, 1975,p.96

19 Boahen Adu, Ghana: Evolution and Change in the 19th and 20th Centuries, London, Longman, 1975,p.97,98

20 Ayensu, K.B and Darkwa, S.N, The Evolution of Parliament in Ghana (IEA), 1999,p.11

21 Boahen Adu, Ghana: Evolution and Change in the 19th and 20th Centuries, London, Longman, 1975, p.142


## Chapter 2

1 Ofusu-Appiah,L.H., *The Life and Times of J.B Danquah*, Accra, Waterville Press, 1974, p.46,47

2 Danquah, *The Ghanaian Establishment*, Ghana University Press, 1997,

3 Ofusu-Appiah,L.H., *The Life and Times of J.B Danquah*, Accra, Waterville Press, 1974, p.47,48

4 Akyeampong, H.K Journey To Independence and After, Vol. III Waterville Publishing House,1972, p.123

5 Excerpt of Paa Grant speech quoted from *1947-1957, The Story of Ghana's Independence* by Blay-Amihere, 2022, p.25-27

6 Ofusu-Appiah,L.H., *The Life and Times of J.B Danquah*, Accra, Waterville Press, 1974, p.49-52

6a ibid

7 Akyeampong, H.K *Journey To Independence and After*, Vol. I Waterville Publishing House,1972, p.63

8 Akyeampong, H.K Journey To Independence and After, Vol. III Waterville Publishing House,1972, p.113

9 Akyeampong, H.K *Journey To Independence and After* Vol. I Waterville Publishing House,1970,p.34,35

10 Akyeampong, H.K Journey To Independence and After, Vol. I Waterville Publishing House,1970, p.110

**Chapter 3**

1 Watson Report, 1948, p.95

2 Watson Report, 1948, p.94

3 Nkrumah, *Ghana: the Autobiography of Kwame Nkrumah,* 1957, p.77,78

4 Akyeampong, H.K *Journey To Independence and After (J.B Danquah's Letters) 1947-1965*, Vol. I Waterville Publishing House,1970, p.40,41

5 Nkrumah, Ghana: the Autobiography of Kwame Nkrumah,1957, p.80,81

6 Watson Report, 1948, p.89

 7 Akyeampong, H.K, *Journey, To Independence and After (J.B Danquah's Letters) 1947-1965*, Vol. I Waterville Publishing House,1970, p.64

8 Akyeampong, H.K, *Journey, To Independence and After (J.B Danquah's Letters) 1947-1965*, Vol.I Waterville Publishing House,1970, p.65

9 Nkrumah, *Ghana: the Autobiography of Kwame Nkrumah,* 1957, p.82

10 Nkrumah, *Ghana: the Autobiography of Kwame Nkrumah,*1957,p.79

11 Akyeampong, H.K *Journey To Independence and After1947-1965*, Vol. I Waterville Publishing House,1970, p.123-126

12 Ayensu, K.B and Darkwa, S.N, *The Evolution of Parliament in Ghana* (IEA), 1999, p.22

13 Akyeampong, H.K *Journey To Independence and After* 1947-1965, Vol. I Waterville Publishing House,1970, p.67-70

14 Akyeampong, H.K *Journey To Independence and After* 1947-1965, Vol. III Waterville Publishing House,1972, p.123

15 Ofusu-Appiah, L.H., *The Life and Times of J.B Danquah*, Accra, Waterville Press, 1974, p.82

16 Watson Report, 1948, p.17

17 Watson Report, 1948, p.17

18 Watson Report, 1948, p.9


**Chapter 4**

1 Akyeampong, *Letters of Danquah*, Vol.1,p.75,76

2 Akyeampong, *Letters of Danquah*, Vol.1,p.78,79,85

3 Daily Graphic, 14 February, 2007

4 Danquah, *The Ghanaian Establishment*,p.77,78

5 Akyeampong, *Letters of Danquah*, Vol.2,p.90

6 Nkrumah, *Ghana: Autobiography of Kwame Nkrumah* p.82

7 Jubilee Ghana: A 50-year news journey thro' Graphic, p.13

8 Akyeampong, *Letters of Danquah*, Vol.3,p.122

9 Nkrumah, *Ghana: Autobiography of Kwame Nkrumah* p.96

10  Akyeampong, *Letters of Danquah*, Vol.3,p.123

11 Nkrumah, *Ghana: Autobiography of Kwame Nkrumah* p.97

12 Nkrumah, *Ghana: Autobiography of Kwame Nkrumah* p.97

13 Nkrumah, *Ghana: Autobiography of Kwame Nkrumah* p.97

14 Ofusu-Appiah, *The Life and Times of J.B Danquah*,p.80

15 Nkrumah, *Ghana: Autobiography of Kwame Nkrumah* p.100,101

16 Nkrumah, *Ghana: Autobiography of Kwame Nkrumah* p.101

17 Ofusu-Appiah, *The Life and Times of J.B Danquah*,p.77

18 Daily Graphic, 14 May 2007

19 Akyeampong, *Letters of J.B, Danquah,* Vol.2, 1971, p.80

20  Akyeampong, *Letters of J.B, Danquah,*Vol.2,1971p.123

21 Akyeampong, *Letters of J.B, Danquah,Vol.2,1971,*p.85

22 Akyeampong, *Letters of J.B, Danquah,* Vol.3,1972,p.124

23 Rooney, *Sir Charles Arden Clarke,* 1988, p.88

24 Rubin, Leslies & Murray, Pauli *Constitution and government of Ghana,* p.4,5

25  Ofusu-Appiah, L.H., The Life and Times of J.B Danquah, 1974,p.106/107

26 Rubin, Leslies & Murray, Pauli *Constitution and Government of Ghana,* p.4,5

27 Akyeampong, *Letters of J.B, Danquah,* 1971, p.93

28 Nkrumah, *Ghana: Autobiography of Kwame Nkrumah* p.119,120

29 Nkrumah, *Ghana: Autobiography of Kwame Nkrumah* p.119

**Chapter 5**

1 Akyeampong, H.K *Journey To Independence and After* Vol. II Waterville Publishing House, 1971, p.134

2 Rooney, *Kwame Nkrumah: Vision and Tragedy*, 1988, p

3 Akyeampong, H.K *Journey To Independence and After* Vol. II Waterville Publishing House, 1971, p.133

4 Birmingham W, Neustadt, I. & Omaboe, E.N., *The Economy of Ghana Vol one*, George Allen & Unwin Ltd, 1966, p.391

5 Legislative Assembly on 24 April 1951meeting also available in Akyeampong, H.K *Journey To Independence and After* Vol. III Waterville Publishing House, 1972,

6 Ofusu-Appiah, L.H., *The Life and Times of J.B Danquah,*1974 p.117

7 Akyeampong, H.K *Journey To Independence and After* Vol. III Waterville Publishing House, 1972, p.134

8 Awoonor, *Ghana: A Political History from- European To Modern Time,* p.154

9 Awoonor, *Ghana: A Political History from- European To Modern Time,* p.154

10 Akyeampong, H.K *Journey To Independence and After* Vol. II Waterville Publishing House, 1971, p 85

11 Nkrumah, Ghana: *Autobiography of Kwame Nkrumah*, 1957, p.197,198

12 Nkrumah, Ghana: *Autobiography of Kwame Nkrumah,*1957, p.207

13 Ayensu & Darkwa, *The Evolution of Parliament in Ghana*, IEA, 1999, p.22

14 Baffour Agyeman-Duah, *General Achemapong,*2021 p.26. Also available in Danquah, *Ghanaian Establishment,* p.60


**Chapter 6**

1 Akyeampong, H.K *Journey To Independence and After* Vol. III Waterville Publishing House, 1972, p.101

2 Rooney, *Kwame Nkrumah: Vision and Tragedy*, 1988, p.142

3 Nkrumah, *Ghana: Autobiography of Kwame Nkrumah* p.252,253

4 Blay-Amihere,*1947-1957 The Story of Ghana's Independence,* 2021, p.252

5 Rooney, *Kwame Nkrumah: Vision and Tragedy*, 1988, p.159,160

6 Rooney, *Kwame Nkrumah: Vision and Tragedy*, 1988, p.164,165

7 Nkrumah, *Ghana: Autobiography of Kwame Nkrumah,*1957,p.272

8 Ofusu-Appiah, L.H., *The Life and Times of J.B Danquah,* 1974,p.124

9 Nkrumah, *Ghana: Autobiography of Kwame Nkrumah,*1957,p.258

10 Rooney, *Kwame Nkrumah: Vision and Tragedy*, 1988, p.183

11 Rooney, *Kwame Nkrumah: Vision and Tragedy*, 1988, p.175

12 Rooney, *Kwame Nkrumah: Vision and Tragedy*, 1988, p.176

13 Nkrumah, *Ghana: Autobiography of Kwame Nkrumah,*1957, p.281,282

14 Nkrumah, *Ghana: Autobiography of Kwame Nkrumah,*1957, p.284,285

15 Ayensu & Darkwa, *The Evolution of Parliament in Ghana*, IEA, 1999, p.22

16 Nkrumah, *Ghana: Autobiography of Kwame Nkrumah,*1957, p.286,287

17 Rooney, *Kwame Nkrumah: Vision and Tragedy*, 1988, p.173


**Chapter 7**

1 Ayensu & Darkwa, *The Evolution of Parliament in Ghana*, IEA, 1999, p.22

2 Akyeampong, *Letters of J.B, Danquah*, vol.3,1972, p.106

3 Ayensu & Darkwa, *The Evolution of Parliament in Ghana*, IEA, 1999, p.22

4 Extracted from NewAfrican Magazine, March 2007

5 Rooney,1982, *Kwame Nkrumah: Vision and Tragedy* p.188

6 Daily Graphic, February 21, 2007

7 Dr. Martin Luther King, *The Birth of a New Nation*, April 1957

8 Boahen Adu, Ghana: Evolution and Change in the 19th and 20th Centuries, London, Longman, 1975,p.197


**Chapter 8**

1 Ofusu-Appiah, L.H., *The Life and Times of J.B Danquah,* p.234

2 Ofusu-Appiah, L.H., *The Life and Times of J.B Danquah,* p.125

3Daily Graphic May 10, 1966

4 Akyeampong, *Letters of J.B, Danquah*,vol.3,1972, p.117

5 Daily Graphic February 10, 1964

6 Ofusu-Appiah, L.H., *The Life and Times of J.B Danquah,* p.165

7 Rooney, *Kwame Nkrumah: Vision and Tragedy* 1988,p.263,264

8 Rooney, *Kwame Nkrumah: Vision and Tragedy* 1988,p.256-7, 266

9 Rooney, Kwame Nkrumah: Vision and Tragedy,1988, p.257

10 Rooney, Kwame Nkrumah: Vision and Tragedy,1988, p.258

11 Rooney, Kwame Nkrumah: Vision and Tragedy,1988, p.260

12 K.B Asante, 'Nkrumah and State Enterprises', Paper presented at Legon Symposium on Life and Work of Kwame Nkrumah. May-June 1985 Extracted from Rooney,1988, p.259

13 Daily Graphic January 16, 1967

14 See V.T Le Vine, *Political Corruption. The Ghana Case*, Stanford, Hoover Institution, 1975 also in Rooney, 1988, p.257

15 Cabinet Minutes, 11 February 1965. Also found in Rooney,1988, p.333

16 Nkrumah, *Dark Days in Ghana*, 1968, p.91

17 Nkrumah, *Dark Days in Ghana*,1968, p.34

18 Asamoah, O.Y, *The Political history of Ghana* (1950-2013), 2014. Extracted from Good Evening Ghana Show, Metro TV.

19 Meyer Joe-Fio N., *Dr Nkrumah's Last Journey The Sensational Viet-Nam, US War,*1984 p.36-38

20 Agyeman-Duah, B, *General Acheampong:The Life and Times of Ghana's Head of State*, 2021,p.43

21 Interview with Kwasi Okyere-Darko  former registrar of Valley University and a former member of   Young Pioneer

22 Boahen Adu, Ghana: Evolution and Change in the 19th and 20th Centuries, 1975, p.222

23 Daily Graphic 12 March 1966

24 Daily Graphic 28 February 1966

25 Daily Graphic 7 March 1966

26 Daily Graphic 2 March 1966

27 Daily Graphic 3 March 1966

**Chapter 9**

1 Faces of Africa, a documentary on Kwame Nkrumah, available on youtube.

2 Scholtes, Leaders Handbook,1998, p.7

3 Hughes & Ginnett & Curphy, *Leadership enhancing the lessons of experience*,2012,p.15

## Bibliography


Aboagye, F.B, *The Ghana Army: A Concise Contemporary Guide to its Centennial Regiment History*,1897-1999, Sedco,1999

Achebe Chinua, *Things Fall Apart, London,* Heinemann, 1958

Addae, S., *A short History of Ghana Armed Forces,* Ministry of Defence Armed Forces, 2005

Afrifa, A., *The Ghana Coup*, London, Frank Cass,1966

Agbodeka, F., *Ghana in the Twentieth Century,* Ghana Universities Press, 1972

Agyeman-Duah, B, *General Acheampong: The Life and Times of Ghana's Head of State*, Digibooks Publishers, Tema, 2021

Akyeampong, H.K *Journey To Independence and After (J.B Danquah's Letters)* 1947-1965, Vol. I Waterville Publishing House,1970

Akyeampong, H.K *Journey To Independence and After (J.B Danquah's Letters)* Vol. II 1949-1951 Waterville Publishing House, 1971

Akyeampong, H.K *Journey To Independence and After (J.B Danquah's Letters)* Vol. III 1952-1957 Waterville Publishing House, 1972

Amamoo, J.G, *Ghana:50 Years of Independence*, Jafint, 2007

Austin, D., *Politics in Ghana, 1946 - 1960*, Oxford University Press, 1964

Awoonor Nyidevu Kofi, *Ghana: A Political History from- European To Modern Times*, Sedco Publishing Ltd & Woeli Publishing Services, 1990

Ayensu, K.B and Darkwa, S.N, *The Evolution of Parliament in Ghana* (IEA), 1999

Birmingham W, Neustadt, I. & Omaboe, E.N., *The Economy of Ghana Vol one*, George Allen & Unwin Ltd,1966

Blay-Amihere K, *1947-1957 The Story of Ghana's Independence,* Digibooks Ghana ltd, 2022

Boahen Adu, *Ghana: Evolution and Change in the 19th and 20th Centuries*, London, Longman, 1975

Boahen Adu, *Topics in West African History*, London, Longman, 1966

Busia, K.A, *The Position of the Chief in the Modern Political System of Ashanti*, Frank Gass & Co.Ltd, 1968

Danquah, J.B, *The Ghanaian Establishment*, Accra, Ghana Universities Press, 1997

Davidson, B., *The Black Star: A view of the Life and Times of Kwame Nkrumah*, Allen Lane, 1973

Meyer Joe-Tio N., *Dr Nkrumah's Last Journey The Sensational Viet-Nam, US War,* Nyaniba Press, 1984

Killick, Tony, *Development Economics in Action*:  A Study of Economic Policies in Ghana, Heinemann, Lusaka 1978

Kimble, D, *The History of Ghana*, 1850 to 1928, Oxford University Press, 1963

Kugbey, R & Nguah, F., *Shackles in Darkness, A Handbook on the Trans-Atlantic Slave Trade,*NYAKOD Publishing,2015

Jones, T., *Ghana's First Republic 1960 - 1966* : The pusuit of the Political Kingdom, Methuen & Co. Ltd., London 1976

Martinson H.B, *Ghana: The UP/NPP Tradition in the National Liberation Struggle,* HBM publications, 2010

Nkrumah K., *Ghana: The Autobiography of Kwame  Nkrumah*, London, Nelson, 1957

Nkrumah,K., *Dark Days in Ghana*, Accra, Wrenco ltd, 2001

Nkrumah,K.,  *I have freedom*, London,Panaf,1961

Ofusu-Appiah,L.H., *The Life and Times of J.B Danquah*, Accra, Waterville Press, 1974

Okyere-Darko, P, *The Dream of a New Ghana Reality or Myth?* Nab Printers, 2018

Opoku-Agyeman, M., *Constitutional Law and History of Ghana*, 2009

Owusu M., *USES AND ABUSES OF POLITICAL POWER, A Case Study of Continuity and Change in the Politics of Ghana*, The University of Chicago Press, 1970

Osei K, *An Outline of Asante History*, O.Kwadwo Enterprise, 1994

Hughes & Ginnett & Curphy, *Leadership enhancing the lessons of experience,*McGraw-Hill,2012

Reindorf, CC, *History of the Gold Coast & Ashanti*, Ghana University Press, 1895

Rodney, W., *How Europe underdeveloped Africa*, Panaf Publishing, 2009

Rooney David, *Sir Charles Arden Clarke*, London, Rex Collings,1982

Rooney, D, *Kwame Nkrumah: Vision and Tragedy*, Sub-Saharan Publishers, 1988

Rubin, Leslies & Murray, Pauli, *The Constitution and Government of Ghana*, Great Britain

Ward, W.E.F, *History of Gold Coast,* George Allen & Unwin, 1959

Watson, A.A., *Report of the Commission of Enquiry into Disturbances in the Gold Coast,* H.M Stationery Off, London, 1948

Senge, P, *The fifth Discipline*, Doubleday,1994

Scholtes, R. P, *The Leaders Handbook*, McGraw-Hills Company Inc,1998

Thompson, W. Scott., *Ghana's Foreign Policy 1957-1966,* Princeton University Press, Princeton, New Jersey, 1969


**Other Sources**

Jubilee Ghana: A 50-year news journey thro' Graphic, Graphic Communications Group ltd, 2006

NewAfrican Magazine, March 2007

Citi news interview, *foot print* with Brigadier Gen Arthur. Host, Samuel Atta Mensah

Asantehene's message during the 150 years anniversary of Sagranti war, 2024

Martin Luther King, I have a Dream

Martin Luther King, The Birth of a New Nation, April 1957

Independence declaration of the United States of America

Daily Graphic, February 14, 2007

Daily Graphic, February 21, 2007

Daily Graphic, April 11, 2007

# ABOUT THE AUTHOR

The author is a nationalist preacher whose message is focused on patriotism, leadership and governance for a new Ghana and Africa. He is the author of a number of books. Some the books are The Oil in You, Africa in Prophecy, The Dream of a new Ghana reality or myth?, The Princes from Eden and some other books.  He is the leader of Awake Africa Ghana Mission.

www.ingramcontent.com/pod-product-compliance
Lightning Source LLC
Chambersburg PA
CBHW061334250726
48657CB00004B/1165

9 798345 480014